The Case Against *The Case for Christ*

The Case against *The Case for Christ*: A New Testament Scholar Refutes Lee Strobel

Robert M. Price

2010
American Atheist Press
Cranford, New Jersey

ISBN10: 1-57884-005-8
ISBN13: 978-1-57884-005-2

American Atheist Press
P. O. Box 158
Cranford, NJ 07016
Voice: (908) 276-7300
FAX: (908) 276-7402

www.atheists.org

Published February 2010
Printed in the United States of America

Library of Congress Cataloging-in-Publication Data

Price, Robert M., 1954-
The case against the case for Christ : a New Testament scholar refutes Lee Strobel / Robert M. Price.
p. cm.
Includes bibliographical references and index.
ISBN-13: 978-1-57884-005-2 (alk. paper)
ISBN-10: 1-57884-005-8 (alk. paper)
1. Strobel, Lee, 1952- Case for Christ. 2. Christianity--Controversial literature. 3. Jesus Christ--Person and offices. 4. Jesus Christ--Historicity. I. Title.
BT203.S7737 2010
232.9'08--dc22

2009054035

Dedicated To

My Generous Friend

David F. Parks

CONTENTS

INTRODUCTION
My Own Investigation

You might want to know this. It might help you to evaluate what follows. You see, though it is obvious I disagree drastically with the Reverend Lee Strobel since I am attempting to refute him, I did not start my journey where he did, as a skeptic and an Atheist. In fact, I began where he ended up and arrived at his abandoned starting point. I prayed to receive Jesus Christ into my heart as my personal savior, as my Sunday School teacher told me I should, at eleven years old. Surpassing my young contemporaries, I waxed bold to witness to my faith to all who would listen: schoolmates, people sitting next to me on the bus, people to whom I handed out evangelistic tracts in public places, *etc.*, *etc.* I had my daily devotions and confessed any unkind or risqué thought as soon as it popped onto my mental monitor. I pored over scripture every day, seeking edification in the straightforward teachings of the New Testament and allegorizing the Old. I loved church and attended three services a week. It consumed me, but I don't want to make it sound bad. I was an adolescent zealot, but it kept me out of trouble and instilled within me a long-lasting love for the Christian tradition, a sense of duty to the Christian ethic, and an endless fascination with the Bible. I still study it avidly in the hopes of understanding it ever better.

I remember when I first learned, with a sense of surprise and relief, of Christian apologetics: the defense of the faith by appealing to its historical credentials. I was satisfied with faith (which these days I would call "supposition"), but if there were good data, good reasons, for believing that it all happened, well, so much the better! And I saw immediately the advantage of apologetics for evangelism. I could appeal, not to mere subjectivism, but to the *facts*. And it frustrated the daylights out of me when friends to whom I explained "the evidence for the resurrection" did not accept the case I made. How could they be so blind?

Ironically, my doubts and questions were a direct outgrowth of this interest in apologetics. I knew it was a matter of basic honesty that I had to place myself, for the moment, in the shoes of the unbeliever if I were to evaluate each argument for the historical Jesus, or for Bible accuracy. I knew it would be phony for me to try to convince others by using arguments that I did not actually think were cogent. I didn't want to use any tactic, say anything that might work, as if I were a used car dealer or a mere propagandist. Obviously, at first I thought the arguments

I was picking up from reading John Warwick Montgomery,[1] F.F. Bruce,[2] Josh McDowell,[3] and others[4] were pretty darn good! But once it became a matter of evaluating probabilistic arguments, weighing evidence, much of it impossible to verify, much of it ambiguous, I found it impossible to fall back on faith as I once had. And this tormented me. I knew I was slipping back from preaching "good news" to entertaining "good views." I was the leader of my campus InterVarsity Christian Fellowship group. I was their chief planner of evangelistic events. And I was increasingly depressed about the nagging question: "What if I'm wrong? As good as it looks, I *might be wrong*!" And faith was eluding me, slipping away.

Again ironically, all this was happening at the very time my wider acquaintance with Christian literature was showing me that evangelical Christianity was an interesting and comprehensive worldview. I was excited to be associated with it—if it were true! For a few years in the mid-seventies, I made it my business to visit and interview evangelical writers and leaders whenever I could. I sought their wisdom, not least to buttress my uneasy faith.

---

1 John Warwick Montgomery, *History & Christianity* (Downers Grove: Inter-Varsity Press, 1974).

2 F.F. Bruce, *The New Testament Documents: Are They Reliable?* (Grand Rapids: Eerdmans, 5th ed., 1960, 1972); Bruce, *Tradition: Old and New*. Contemporary Evangelical Perspectives (Grand Rapids: Zondervan, 1970).

3 Josh McDowell, ed., *More Evidence that Demands a Verdict: Historical Evidences for the Christian Scriptures* (Arrowhead Springs: Campus Crusade for Christ, 1975).

4 J.N.D. Anderson, *Christianity: The Witness of History. A Lawyer's Approach* (London: Tyndale Press, 1969); Anderson, *The Evidence for the Resurrection* (Downers Grove: InterVarsity Press, 1966); Anderson, *A Lawyer among the Theologians* (Grand Rapids: Eerdmans, 1974); Michael Green, *Man Alive!* (Downers Grove: Inter-Varsity Press, 1971); Edwin M. Yamauchi, *The Stones and the Scriptures*. Evangelical Perspectives (NY: J.B. Lippincott/Holman, 1972); Yamauchi, *Jesus, Zoroaster, Buddha, Socrates, Muhammad* (Downers Grove: InterVarsity Press, rev. ed., 1972); I. Howard Marshall, *Luke: Historian and Theologian*. Contemporary Evangelical Perspectives (Grand Rapids: Zondervan, 1974); Marshall, *I Believe in the Historical Jesus*. I Believe Series # 5 (Grand Rapids: Eerdmans, 1977); Ralph P. Martin, *Mark: Evangelist and Theologian*. Contemporary Evangelical Perspectives (Grand Rapids: Zondervan, 1973); George Eldon Ladd, *I Believe in the Resurrection of Jesus*. I Believe Series # 2 (Grand Rapids: Eerdmans, 1975); Kenneth G. Howkins, *The Challenge of Religious Studies* (Downers Grove: InterVarsity Press, 1973); Herbert Butterfield, *Christianity and History* (London: Fontana, 1958).

So you see, I embarked on a series of "meetings with remarkable men" not dissimilar to Lee Strobel's. During these years I gratefully received the wisdom of luminaries including Carl F.H. Henry and Harold John Ockenga, great pioneers of the "neo-evangelical" movement, Billy G. Melvin, then president of the National Association of Evangelicals, spiritual writer Peter H. Gilquist (*Love Is Now* and *Farewell to the Fake I.D.*), Pentecostal New Testament scholar Larry W. Hurtado, theological historian Donald W. Dayton, Pentecostal Old Testament scholar Gerry Shepperd, Jim Wallis, editor of *The Post-American*, then *Sojourners*; Reformed theologian David F. Wells, apologist and theological critic Clark H. Pinnock, theologian J.I. Packer, evangelical New Testament scholar Merrill C. Tenney, "young evangelical" pundit Richard Quebedeaux, fundamentalist-turned Episcopalian-turned Roman Catholic philosopher Thomas Howard, Christian World Liberation Front founder Jack Sparks, and renowned New Testament specialist James D.G. Dunn. I even got most of them to autograph my New Testament!

A few years later, I had the privilege of taking graduate courses with evangelical savants Bruce M. Metzger and Gordon D. Fee, not to mention more liberal scholars like Helmut Koester, Howard Clark Kee, Harvey Cox, and Monika Helwig. (Most of the people Lee Strobel would later interview were not writing yet, but recently I have debated Greg Boyd, William Lane Craig, Craig Blomberg, and Michael Green.)

Ultimately I reached a different set of conclusions than Lee Strobel did. It puzzles and exasperates me, I will admit, as I read his accounts of his discussions with apologists, as the accumulating arguments he says won him to evangelical Christian faith were the very same ones that I found so unreliable, such weak links, limp reeds upon which to rest either faith or opinion. I have now arrived at the point where I hold no religious beliefs at all, even while cherishing the various religions as beautiful and profound products of human cultural creativity. They start creating dangerous mischief, however, when they entertain delusions of grandeur: namely, that their doctrines and symbols are literally true and that those of other religions are false. That is the literalistic fundamentalism to which I believe Lee Strobel has allowed himself to be converted, and to which he seeks mightily to win others. It is a mistaken conclusion based on a grossly slanted reading of the relevant evidence, as I hope to show in this book.

I was quite disappointed when I saw how first this apologetical argument, then that one, then pretty much all of them, turned out not to hold water, not to make sense. But the predicted despair did not follow.

Instead, I found myself gazing in wonder at a world around me in which there was no curtain sealing off the saved from the damned, in which intellectual freedom knew no prescribed limits of 'orthodoxy,' and in which there was no party-line I felt I had to defend. People were just people; opinions were just opinions, and the whole patchwork was dazzling! I never expected that when I teetered on the brink of what I once called "unbelief" I would be very much afraid Christian faith would turn out to be false or insupportable. But when I concluded just that, I was no longer scared. I hope my Christian readers will cast out their fear in favor of love—the love of the truth, whichever way it leads. We must follow it wherever it seems to go. We must not, like Lee Strobel, ride it like a horse, flogging it to go in the direction we desire.

The Reverend Mr. Strobel's whole effort is predicated on the fallacy of the *Appeal to Authority*. That is, being admittedly no expert himself, he lists the supposedly impeccable credentials of those whom he interviews, as if that should lend weight to their arguments, on top of what they actually say. And Reverend Strobel, I dare say, is being disingenuous with us when he says he embarked on his series of interviews as a way of testing out the "claims of Christ." How dare I say so? His true intention becomes clear by the choice of people he interviewed: every one of them a conservative apologist! I cannot believe he did not purposely avoid seeking the opinions of Burton L. Mack, Gerd Theissen, John Dominic Crossan, Theodore J. Weeden, James M. Robinson, Gerd Lüdemann, and countless others who would certainly have been available. No, Strobel was seeking out spin doctors for the party line. He tossed them softball questions with the faux-skeptical demeanor of the 'interviewer' on a late-night infomercial.

And then there is the manipulative use of a 'reportorial' style to make it look like Reverend Strobel is uncovering facts rather than merely soliciting opinions he already wants to promote. The irony is that, if anyone in Jesus' day had actually done what Strobel claims to be doing, seeking out informed authorities to interview, there would be no need for such exercises in apologetical futility. But the gospel writers were in no sense reporters—but then again, *neither is Strobel!* He is engaging not in journalism but in propaganda. He speaks as one trained in the law; however, he sounds not like a lawyer but like a sophist. He is the equivalent of Johnny Cochran, F. Lee Bailey, and Robert Shapiro. His Jesus is like O.J. Simpson. Strobel has signed on to make the best case he can for a client whose defense requires the obfuscation of the evidence and the confusion of the jury. The balance of Simpson's jurists were African Americans who felt they had a score to settle with Whitey, evidence be damned. Even so, it is clear that (as with all apologetics books) Strobel's *The Case for Christ* is aimed at buttressing the faith of his coreligionists, who buy almost all the copies sold. They want to be convinced of what they already believe, and Strobel's fraudulent arguments give them an illusory permission to do so.

PART ONE

EXAMINING THE WRECKAGE

Chapter One
The Utter Lack of Eyewitness Evidence
The Gospels Are Not Biographies

Before debating Craig Blomberg, naturally I read his book *The Historical Reliability of the Gospels*.[5] Since then I've also read his *Contagious Holiness: Jesus' Meals with Sinners*.[6] Reading these books and debating him taught me one thing: with only minor modifications, namely the partisan, opportunistic appropriation of some more recent scholarly theories, today's new generation of apologists are using the same old arguments InterVarsity sophomores are trained to use. Little has changed since the eighteenth century. In fact, every debate I have had with evangelicals has reinforced the same conclusion. What has happened, I think, is that the traditional apologetics have now become as fully a part of the evangelical creed as the doctrines they are meant to defend! The apologetics have themselves become doctrines. The official belief, then, is so-and-so, and the official defense is this-and–that. That is why their books all sound the same and why the new ones sound just like the old ones. That is why Lee Strobel's panel of experts are really interchangeable: any one of them could have written any of the chapters (or informed them, I guess, since Strobel maintains a dialogical format). Each and all would have said virtually the same thing when asked the same raft of questions. That would not have been the case had Reverend Strobel compiled a set of interviews with a diverse spectrum of opinion. But he didn't. He stacked the deck. Nobody else's opinion counts for him. He is an apologist, albeit, like Josh McDowell, at second hand, so he is interested only in the opinions of apologists.

Enter Craig L. Blomberg

I shall, if you don't mind, omit all of Reverend Strobel's fascinating descriptions of Dr. Blomberg pouring himself a cup of coffee, sipping it, pausing to contemplate the question, *etc.*, though I will admit that if one replaced various words with blanks, they might make for some pretty good mad-libs.

---

5 Craig L. Blomberg, *The Historical Reliability of the Gospels* (Downers Grove: InterVarsity Press, 1987).

6 Craig L. Blomberg, *Contagious Holiness: Jesus' Meals with Sinners*. New Studies in Biblical Theology 19 (Downers Grove: InterVarsity Press, 2005).

Blomberg starts in on the question of gospel authorship:

> It's important to acknowledge that strictly speaking, the gospels are anonymous. But the uniform testimony of the early church was that Matthew, also known as Levi, the tax-collector and one of the twelve disciples, was the author of the first gospel in the New Testament; that John Mark, a companion of Peter, was the author of the gospel we call Mark; and that Luke, known as Paul's 'beloved physician,' wrote both the gospel of Luke and the Acts of the Apostles... There are no known competitors for [authorship of] these three gospels... Apparently, it was just not in dispute.[7]

Blomberg imagines that the whole delegation was polled, and that no one had any other guesses as to who wrote these gospels. But we don't have everyone's opinions. We are lucky to have what fragments we do that survived the efforts of Orthodox censors and heresiologists to stamp out all 'heretical' opinions. However, we do know of a few differing opinions because Tertullian, Justin Martyr, and others had to take the trouble to (try to) refute them. Marcion knew our Gospel of Luke in a shorter form, which he considered to be the original, and he did not identify it as the work of Luke. He may have imagined that Paul wrote that version. Also, though Blomberg does not see fit to mention it, Papias sought to account for apparent Marcionite elements in the Gospel of John by suggesting Marcion had worked as John's secretary and scribe and added his own ideas to the text, which it was somehow too late for John to root out.[8] Similarly, some understood the gospel to be Gnostic (rightly, I think) and credited it to Cerinthus.

Blomberg reasons that, had the gospel authorship ascriptions been artificial, better names would have been chosen.

> [T]hese were unlikely characters... Mark and Luke weren't even among the twelve disciples. Matthew was, but as a former hated tax collector, he would have been among the most infamous character next to Judas Iscariot, who betrayed Jesus! Contrast this with what happened when the fanciful apocryphal gospels were written much later. People chose the names of well-known and exemplary figures to be their fictitious authors – Philip, Peter, Mary, James. Those names carried a lot more

---

7 Blomberg in Lee Strobel, *The Case for Christ: A Journalist's Personal Investigation of the Evidence for Jesus*. Billy Graham Evangelistic Association special edition (Grand Rapids: Zondervan, 1998), pp. 22–23.

8 Robert Eisler, *The Enigma of the Fourth Gospel: Its Author and Its Writer* (London: Methuen, 1938), pp. 145–156.

> weight than the names of Matthew, Mark, and Luke. So to answer your question, there would not have been any reason to attribute authorship to these three less respected people if it weren't true.[9]

In fact, *apocryphal* (which only means 'not on the official list' for whatever reason) *gospels* are attributed to such luminaries as Bartholomew, Judas Iscariot, the prostitute Mary Magdalene, doubting Thomas, the heretical Basilides, the even more heretical Valentinus, Nicodemus, and the replacement Matthias. They didn't always go for the star names.

As for the names to whom the canonical gospels were ascribed, it is quite easy to provide an alternate and more natural explanation as to why we have two apostolic names and two sub-apostolic names, though we can bet neither Blomberg nor Strobel will like it very much. First, the initially anonymous gospel we call Matthew was clearly the early church's favorite, and sometimes it circulated without any individual's name, as in its redacted Hebrew and Aramaic versions known to the Church Fathers as the Gospel according to the Hebrews, the Gospel according to the Nazoreans, and the Gospel according to the Ebionites. There are more copies of Matthew that survive in manuscript than any of the other gospels, which means it was used more, much more. The reason for its popularity was its utility: it is framed as a new Christian Pentateuch, organizing Jesus' teaching into five great blocks of teaching, more or less topically. It had been written for the Jewish Christian missionaries of Antioch (in view under the characters of the eleven in Matthew 28, receiving the Great Commission) to use as a church manual. And it served that purpose very well. If your goal was to "disciple the nations," this was the book to use. My guess is that some editor tagged the gospel 'Matthew' based on a pun on the Greek word for 'disciple,' especially prominent in this gospel (*e.g.*, 13:51–52; 28:19): *mathetes*.

Mark and Luke are not organized so conveniently. If you have chosen Matthew as your standard, then Luke and Mark are going to suffer by comparison (though no one could deny their great value). And in the early days, before they were considered inspired scriptures, people felt they could make value judgments and rank the gospels. Matthew was the first tier, all by itself. Mark and Luke were placed on the second tier — 'deuterocanonical gospels' so to speak. And that is why these sub-apostolic names were chosen for them (likely by Polycarp).[10] It is a way of

---

9 Blomberg in Strobel, p. 23

10 David Trobisch, *The First Edition of the New Testament* (NY: Oxford

damning them with only faint praise, but not damning them too severely at that. Insofar as they vary from Matthew, they are not quite apostolic.

What about the very different John? (Blomberg admits it is quite different; it just doesn't mean anything to him. They're all eyewitness reporting anyway!)[11] It is *so* different from the others, one would expect it to be named for someone even farther from the apostles. And so it was. The opponents of the Gospel of John, who recognized its largely Gnostic character, claimed it was the work of the heretic Cerinthus. As Bultmann showed, the text has undergone quite a bit of refitting in order to build in some sacramental theology as well as traditionally futuristic eschatology.[12] Gnostics rejected both, and so did 'John' originally, though such passages are now diluted by added material. Polycarp (or someone like him) dubbed the newly sanitized gospel *John*, intending the apostolic name as a counterblast against the charge that the book was heretical and thus should remain outside the canon.

This is exactly the same sort of overcompensation we see in the same time period among Jews who debated the canonicity of the racy Song of Solomon (Song of Songs, Canticles, *etc.*). The book does not mention God. It seems to embody old liturgies of Tammuz and Ishtar, and it is sexually explicit. Thus some pious rabbis thought it had no business being considered scripture. The response was to declare it an allegory of the divine love for Israel and to make it especially sacred: "The whole Torah is Holy, but The Song of Songs is the Holy of Holies" (Rabbi Akiba). So you think it is profane, do you? Well, in that case: it's *especially* holy! In the same way a gospel suspected to be Cerinthian becomes a second fully apostolic gospel.

Blomberg is as captive to the scribal traditions of his community as the ancient rabbis were when they named Moses as the author of the Pentateuch and the Book of Job:

> And interestingly, John is the only gospel about which there is some question about authorship… The name of the author isn't in doubt – it's certainly John… The question is whether it was John the apostle or a different John.[13]

University Press, 2000); Trobisch, "Who Published the New Testament?" *Free Inquiry* 28/1 (December 2007/January 2008), pp. 31–33.

11 Blomberg in Strobel, p. 24.

12 Rudolf Bultmann, *The Gospel of John: A Commentary* Trans. G.R. Beasley-Murray, R.W.N. Hare, J.K. Riches (Philadelphia: Westminster Press, 1971), pp. 219–220, 234–237, 261, 471–472.

13 Blomberg in Strobel, p. 23.

It's *certainly* John? Blomberg's exegesis is narrowly sectarian and insular, almost as if we were reading Mormon or Jehovah's Witness scholarship. To anyone even vaguely familiar with modern New Testament scholarship Blomberg's claims are startlingly off-base. If you take a poll of Sunday School teachers and fundamentalist Bible Institute faculty, you will no doubt come up with such a conclusion. But among real scholars, conservative and liberal, the authorship question, as with the closely-related question of the identity of this gospel's 'Beloved Disciple' character, is wide open. And as for this business about John the son of Zebedee versus another John, this is all derived from Eusebius' remarks on the famous Papias passage, just below, in which Eusebius imagined he saw mention of two different Johns, the apostle John and the Elder John.

> I will not hesitate to set down in writing for you whatever I used to learn well from the elders and well remembered, maintaining the truth about them. For not like the many did I enjoy those who spoke the most, but those who taught the truth, not those who recalled the commands of others, but those who delivered the commandments given by the Lord to faith and (coming) from the truth itself. But if by chance anyone came who had followed the elders, I inquired about the words of the elders: what Andrew or Peter said, or what Philip, or Thomas or James, or John or Matthew or any of the Lord's disciples, or what Aristion and the elder John, the Lord's disciples said. For I did not suppose that things from books would help me as much as things from a living and surviving voice.[14]

Eusebius read into this passage a second John, an 'elder,' not an apostle, because he wanted to deny apostolic authorship to the Book of Revelation, which (unlike the gospel) is actually credited to a 'John' *in the text itself*, and which teaches literal chiliasm, or millennialism, which Eusebius rejected. He knew he would not be at liberty to reject and marginalize Revelation if it were the work of an apostle, so he preferred to read Papias as mentioning a *second* John to whom he, Eusebius, might relegate the book. (I might point out, too, that Papias does not actually make the 'disciples' eyewitnesses of an historical Jesus, since he places the unknown, and Greek-named, "Aristion" on a par with Peter, John, James, Thomas, and Matthew. What if they, too, were subsequent-generation

---

[14] Robert M. Grant, ed. and trans. *Second Century Christianity: A Collection of Fragments*. Translations of Christian Literature. Series VI. Select Passages (London: SPCK, 1957), pp. 65–66.

believers to whom commandments were delivered via prophecy? Papias asked, not what the elders said Jesus had said, but what *they themselves* had said, inspired by the truth.)

Revelation's chiliastic teaching is no longer the issue for Blomberg and modern apologists, but the distinction between two Johns has come in handy for a new reason, in that they cannot deny that the Gospel of John and the Book or Revelation come from two different authors, one of whom knew Greek much better than the other. Thus some make the Elder the author of the Gospel, others of the Revelation. But the notion of the two Johns, as on the 2004 Democratic presidential ticket, is tenuous indeed.

Harmonization is one of Blomberg's chief anti-critical axioms, papering over contradictions between and within the texts. Here, for instance, he builds a case on the identification of Matthew as both the man included in the list of apostles and the same man as Levi the publican. The trouble is that, though the evangelist we call "Matthew" does list a disciple/apostle whom he calls "Matthew the tax-collector" (Matthew 10:3), he has combined two prior Markan characters to get him: Matthew the disciple (Mark 3:18) and Levi the converted tax-collector (Mark 2:14; Luke 5:27–28). Mark never equates the two, not does Matthew the evangelist ever say that his combined Matthew, the publican-apostle, was also or previously called Levi.

In the story of the call of the tax-collector to follow Jesus, the evangelist Matthew simply borrows Mark's story and changes one word: the name *Matthew* replaces the name *Levi* (Matthew 9:9). Thus the striking character of the ex-publican Matthew who became a disciple, upon whom so many sermons have been hung, is a literary creation of the evangelist 'Matthew.' And such an artificial character cannot have been the author of anything. The closest you could come to a Matthean authorship claim is that this evangelist created his composite character to use as an implied pseudonym, but I doubt Blomberg or Strobel would be too interested in that option.

Good Question, Bad Answer

Reverend Strobel asks Blomberg a good question about Matthean authorship: "Why… would Matthew – purported to be an eyewitness to Jesus – incorporate part of a gospel written by Mark, who everybody agrees was not an eyewitness? If Matthew's gospel was really written by an eyewitness, you would think he would have relied on his own observations." He receives a bad answer:

> It only makes sense if Mark was indeed basing his account on the recollections of the eyewitness Peter... Peter was among the inner circle of Jesus and was privy to seeing and hearing things that the other disciples didn't. So it would make sense for Matthew, even though he was an eyewitness, to rely on Peter's version of events as transmitted through Mark.[15]

Just about everything is wrong with this. Blomberg is interpreting and evaluating data in the texts according to a decades-later rumor by the unreliable Papias, instead of just letting the texts speak for themselves. If he did the latter, he would have to wonder why Matthew would value Mark above his own recollections, yet venture to correct and rewrite Mark at point after point! He amends Jesus' teaching about divorce (Matthew 5:32; 19:9) as he read it in Mark 10:11–12. He lifts the blame from James and John (Mark 10:35) for jockeying for the chief thrones in the kingdom by having their pushy stage-mother ask Jesus instead (Matthew 20:20).

Where Mark had Jesus rebuke the disciples for failing to understand the parables (4:13), Matthew has him congratulate them for understanding them (13:51–52). Where Mark had Jesus unable to cure those who lacked faith (6:5), Matthew says he merely withheld the healing to punish them (13:58). Mark had Jesus exorcize a single demoniac (5:1*ff*), where Matthew makes it a matched pair (8:28). Where Mark (11:2–7) has Jesus ride a single beast into Jerusalem, Matthew puts him on two, rodeo-style (21:2, 7). Mark had Jesus deflect the praise of the seeker who called him "good master" (10:17–18), whereas Matthew, apparently from Christological anxiety, rewords both the question and the answer so that the seeker no longer addresses Jesus as 'good,' and Jesus no longer comments on it, but on the Torah instead (19:16–17). Mark has the women flatly disobey the young man's command to tell the disciples to meet the risen Jesus in Galilee (16:8), but Matthew has them relay the message after all (28:8). Jesus appeared to the women in Matthew 28:9–10, but he hadn't in Mark. Matthew had Roman troops guarding the tomb (27:65–66; 28:4, 11–15); Mark didn't. Mark had Jesus declare all food henceforth kosher (7:19), a point Matthew conspicuously omits (15:1–20).

And as for Matthew gratefully yielding to the superior inside information from Peter via Mark, we only have to look at the only three places Mark says Peter (with James and John) saw things the others did not—and we find Matthew 'corrects' them, too! The private revelation

[15] Blomberg in Strobel, p. 27.

on the Mount of Olives in Mark 13 grows to twice its length in Matthew 24–25. The Transfiguration in Mark 9 has Jesus' clothing glow eerily (9:3), but Matthew makes Jesus' face (17:2) to shine like the sun as well, in order to make him like Moses in Exodus 34:29–35. Mark has Jairus ask Jesus to heal his daughter while she yet lingers this side of the grave (5:23), only to be subsequently told she has died in the meantime (5:35) while the old bag healed of her menstrual flood has been detailing her whole, long story (5:33). But Matthew has Jairus approach Jesus only once the girl has died (9:18).

It is simply bizarre for Reverend Strobel to conclude "although Matthew had his own recollections as a disciple, his quest for accuracy prompted him to rely on some material that came directly from Peter in Jesus' inner circle."[16] Nonsense: it is obvious Matthew regarded Mark as in need of constant correction. If he knew better, why did he not just follow his own memories to begin with? Why build on a flawed foundation as he must have regarded Mark? Because *Matthew was no eyewitness*, nor close to one. So Mark was the best he could get, and he had to do what he could to improve on it.

'Matthew's' changes nowhere appear to be corrections of fact but rather enhancements of a story, occasionally amending it as a regulatory document that needed updating, sometimes clarifying or abridging it for space. There is no Matthean "quest for accuracy" in evidence at all. Professor Blomberg and Reverend Strobel are shamelessly attributing their own apologetical agenda to these ancient writers.

Blomberg is what R.G. Collingwood[17] calls a "scissors and paste historian," according virtually scriptural authority to whatever scraps of ancient sources he has on hand, trying to credit as many, and therefore to harmonize as many, as he can. He does not ask his ancient authors to justify their claims. He considers them his "authorities" and proof-texts them in the same way a theologian does verses of scripture. And for apologists that is precisely what Papias and Irenaeus have become. They are to be cited and believed. "Papias said it! I believe it! That settles it!" But a critical historian, a historian *period* in the modern sense, is obliged to cross-examine Papias and Irenaeus.

> This, too, the Presbyter used to say: Mark, who had been Peter's interpreter, wrote down carefully, but not in order, all that he remembered

16 Strobel, p. 28.

17 R.G. Collingwood, *The Idea of History* (NY: Oxford University Press Galaxy Books, 1956), pp. 33, 36, 234–235, 257–266, 269–270, 274–281.

> of the Lord's sayings and doings. For he had not heard the Lord or been one of his followers, but later, as I said, one of Peter's. Peter used to adapt his teaching to the occasion, without making a systematic arrangement of the Lord's sayings, so that Mark was quite justified in writing down some things just as he remembered them. For he had one purpose only — to leave out nothing that he had heard, and to make no misstatement about it.
>
> Matthew compiled the Sayings in the Aramaic language, and everyone interpreted/translated them as well as he could. (Eusebius, *Ecclesiastical History* 3.39)

There are serious reasons for not placing absolute faith in Papias as the apologists do. For one thing, *what Papias said does not seem to describe our Gospels of Matthew and Mark.* Matthew was *not* written originally in Hebrew. It is a Greek document, based on a Greek document, *i.e.*, Mark. Matthew is much more than the list of sayings mentioned by Papias, though it is possible Papias is speaking metonymously of our Matthew, which is structured around a five-book Torah design. However, to say this is already to retreat one step into harmonization.

As David Friedrich Strauss pointed out, Jerome for a time thought that the Gospel according to the Nazoreans was the Hebrew original of Matthew. It is possible that Papias was talking about our Greek Matthew and thinking it had come from the Gospel of the Nazoreans and supposed there were several rather different Greek versions of it ("everyone translated as well as he could"). Or since at least one of these Hebrew gospels also claimed to be written by Matthew, Papias may simply be referring to it.

As for Papias' supposed reference to canonical Mark, that, too, is questionable. Strauss saw this:

> On the whole, it would appear that when Papias explains the want of order in Mark from his dependence on the lectures of Peter, who may be supposed to have testified of Jesus only occasionally, he intends to refuse to his narrative the merit not only of the right order but of any historical arrangement whatever. But this is as little wanting in the Gospel of Mark as in any other, and consequently Papias, if we are to understand his expression in this sense, could not have our present Gospel of Mark before him, but must have been speaking of a totally different work.[18]

---

[18] David Friedrich Strauss, *Life of Jesus for the People* (London: Williams and Norgate, 2nd ed., 1879), Vol. I, p. 62

So, for all we know, Papias may not be speaking of our Matthew and Mark at all: he may have in mind something like the *Gospel According to the Hebrews* (Eusebius attributes to that gospel Papias' story about a woman accused of many sins) and the Preaching of Peter, or even the Gospel of Peter. The point is that Papias is not necessarily evidence for our four gospels existing in the first quarter of the second century.

Papias is unreliable: he credulously accepted the wildest legends that he heard, such as the grotesque swelling and exploding of Judas.

> "A great example of impiety was Judas walking about in the world. His flesh was so bloated that wherever a wagon could easily pass through, he could not, not even with his swollen head. For his eyelids were so swollen that he could not see light at all. His eyes could not be made visible even by a surgeon's knife. Such was his decline as to his external appearance. His genitals seemed the most unpleasant and greatest part of his whole disfigurement, and it said that from his whole body flowed pus and worms with violence caused by their own force alone. After many torments and punishments he died on his own property; and because of the smell the spot is deserted and uninhabited even now. But no one can go to that place to this day unless he stops his nostrils with his hands; so great a discharge took place through his flesh and on the land."[19]

He attributes to Jesus a piece of apocalyptic that seems to have come instead from the *Syriac Apocalypse of Baruch*:

> The days will come, when vines will grow up, each having ten thousand shoots, and in one shoot ten thousand branches, and in one branch ten thousand vine-shoots, and in each vine-shoot ten thousand clusters, and in each cluster ten thousand grapes; and each grape when pressed will give twenty-five measures of wine. And when anyone takes one of those holy vine-shoots, another will shout, 'I am a better vine-shoot; take me; bless the Lord through me.' Likewise a grain of wheat will bring forth ten thousand ears; and each ear will have ten thousand grains, and each grain, five two-pound measures of excellent fine flour; and the rest of the fruits and seeds and herbs in harmony follow them; and all the animals, using those foods which are received from the earth, become peaceful and in harmony with one another, being subject to men in complete submission. These things are credible to believers." And Judas the traitor, who did not believe, asked: "How, then, will such creatures be

---

19 Grant, *Second-Century Christianity*, p. 67.

> brought to perfection by the Lord?" The Lord said, "They who come [to those times] will see." (cited in Irenaeus, *Against Heresies* V. 33. 3, 4)[20]

> The earth also shall yield its fruit ten thousandfold and on each (?) vine there shall be a thousand branches, and each branch shall produce a thousand clusters, and each cluster produce a thousand grapes, and each grape produce a cor of wine. (2 Baruch 29:5–6)[21]

One may even question whether Papias would have written such apparent apologetics for *any* written gospels in view of his statement that he *preferred oral tradition to books*, though even this is obviously only a "dangerous supplement"[22] argument on behalf of the superiority of his own written gospel, *Exegesis of the Oracles of the Lord*. In fact, just this sort of "end-run around the canon" argument is used by later Muslim jurists to fabricate a pedigree for their own innovations.[23]

Finally, *Papias has nothing to say of Luke*, which apparently had not yet been written. Bishop Irenaeus of Lyons (*ca.* 180), however, does:

> Thus Matthew published among the Hebrews a gospel written in their language, at the time when Peter and Paul were preaching at Rome and founding the church there. After their death, Mark, the disciple and interpreter of Peter, himself delivered to us in writing what had been announced by Peter. Luke, the follower of Paul, put down in a book the gospel preached by him. Later, John the Lord's disciple, who reclined on his bosom, himself published the gospel while staying at Ephesus in Asia. (*Against Heresies* 3.1.1)

Note that Irenaeus is already parroting the late, Catholicizing party-line about Peter and Paul co-founding the Holy Roman Church. As for Matthew and Mark, Irenaeus is dependent upon Papias, as he elsewhere freely admits. Where then does he get the information about Luke and John?

The idea that Luke was the ghost-writer for a Pauline gospel is simply borrowed from that of Mark as the amanuensis of Peter. Irenaeus just decided to copy the Mark-Peter relation in the case of Luke and a likely

---

20 *Ibid.*, pp. 66–67.

21 R.H. Charles, ed. trans., *The Apocrypha and Pseudepigrapha of the Old Testament* (Oxford at the Clarendon Press, 1913), Vol. II, pp. 497–498.

22 Jacques Derrida, *Of Grammatology*. Trans. Gayatri Chakravorty Spivak (Baltimore: Johns Hopkins University Press, 1976), p. 145.

23 John Burton, *The Collection of the Qur'an* (NY: Cambridge University Press, 1977), pp. 183, 202–203, *etc.*

apostolic sponsor, though it no longer makes sense, as Paul was not supposed to be a beholder of Jesus as Mark's supposed source Peter was! Thus this identification puts Luke at a *greater* distance, not a lesser one, from the eyewitnesses (which is what Luke 1:2 suggests anyway: a chain of tradition, not a reporter's filing).

It is also possible that Irenaeus has derived the Luke-Paul link from the Marcionites, though with an element of reinterpretation. Marcionites claimed that the anonymous gospel underlying canonical Luke was one used (though not necessarily written) by Paul. Irenaeus thinks the author of canonical Luke was actually an associate of Paul, transcribing his preaching.

The connection of John with the fourth gospel was an Eastern tradition he probably received from Polycarp. But let us not be too quick to accept any particular item from Irenaeus. He does not betray himself as quite the purveyor of blarney that Papias does, but he comes pretty close. For Irenaeus seems first to arrive at an opinion theologically, then to claim apostolic tradition and eyewitness memory for it. He does this with the date of Easter and the textual reading 666 in Revelation 13:18. That "this number is placed in all the genuine and ancient copies, and those who saw John face to face provide attestation" (30:1).[24] The Asia Minor presbytery weighed in collectively on a matter like *that*?

More revealingly, Irenaeus reasons from his doctrine of recapitulation (whereby Jesus must have redeemed or sanctified every age of the human span by living through it) that Jesus lived to be nearly 50, then finds this in John 8:57. On this basis he deduced that Jesus was put to death in the reign of Claudius, 41–54!

> All will agree that the age of thirty is that of a young man and extends to the fortieth year, while from the fortieth to the fiftieth one declines into seniority. At this age our Lord was teaching, as the Gospel attests (John 8:56–57), and all the presbyters [*elders*] who came together in Asia with John the Lord's disciple attest that he delivered the same tradition to them; for he [*John*] remained with them [*the elders/presbyters*] until the reign of Trajan. Some of them saw not only John but also other apostles and heard these things from them and attest the fact. (*Against Heresies* 22.5)[25]

24 Robert M. Grant, *Irenaeus of Lyons*. The Early Church Fathers (NY: Routledge, 1997), p. 176.

25 Grant., *Irenaeus of Lyons*, pp. 114–115.

And all this he claimed to have gotten from Asian had heard it not only from John but from other apostles Blomberg is eager to accept this on the basis of attestatio.. chorus of convenient presbyters.

But suppose Irenaeus merely *deduced* the semi-centenarian age for Jesus from studying scripture (as Loisy[26] thought): that only means he was engaging in the same kind of guesswork modern readers are, and his guesses deserve to be treated as nothing more.

Blomberg calls Alexander the Great to the stand, much as King Saul once summoned the shade of Samuel:

> The standard scholarly dating, even in very liberal circles, is Mark in the 70s, Matthew and Luke in the 80s, John in the 90s. But listen: that's still within the lifetimes of various eyewitnesses of the life of Jesus, including hostile eyewitnesses who would have served as a corrective if false teachings were going around. Consequently, these late dates for the gospels aren't all that late. In fact, we can make a comparison that's very instructive. The two earliest biographies of Alexander the Great were written by Arrian and Plutarch more than four hundred years after Alexander's death in 323 B.C., yet historians consider them to be basically trustworthy. Yes, legendary material about Alexander did develop over time, but it was only in the centuries after these two writers. In other words, the first five hundred years kept Alexander's story pretty much intact; legendary material began to emerge over the next five hundred years. So whether the gospels were written sixty years or thirty years after the life of Jesus, the amount of time is negligible by comparison.[27]

That is not my impression: not in the case of Jesus, not even in the case of Alexander. In fact, as to the latter, other scholars sing a much different tune:

> Indeed, the true personality of the man who moved the imagination of posterity as few have done was ultimately lost in legend, buried under an extraordinary body of literature that has nothing to do with history. The Alexander Romance, as it is called, began to form not long after his death and, passing under the name Callisthenes, its eighty versions

[26] Alfred Loisy, *The Origins of the New Testament*. Trans. L.P. Jacks (London: George Allen and Unwin, 1950), pp. 60–62.

[27] Blomberg in Strobel, p. 33.

> in twenty-four languages circulated from Iceland to Malaya. (Charles Alexander)[28]

> It comes as a shock to realize how quickly historians fictionalized Alexander: Onesikritos, who had actually accompanied Alexander, told how Alexander had met the queen of the (mythical) Amazons. (Ken Dowden)[29]

Blomberg is laying the groundwork of a subtext here: he prepares a supposed precedent for reliable gospels by begging the question of whether mythologizing of Alexander began earlier or later. His optimistic, conservative estimate of the Alexander tradition creates a sounding board, in the classic fashion of a literary subtext, against which his subsequent assertions of confidence in the Jesus tradition will seem to ring true. Besides, Plutarch was in the business of *de*-mythologizing. In his essay *Isis and Osiris* he depicts the pair of deities as an early king and queen of Egypt, taking the mythic wind out of them. There is no doubt in this case that his narrative looks a bit less legendary, not because he wrote before legends had accumulated around the divine couple, but because he approached already-developed myths on the (gratuitous, in this instance) assumption that much mythification had already occurred and must be stripped away The same may have been true in his retelling of the Alexander story.

The Gospels: Blind Dates

I fear that quoting Blomberg has opened Pandora's Box. Once we have raised the issue, there is no succinct way to deal with it. The matter is much more complicated than Strobel and Blomberg would like to make it. Thus I must beg the reader's indulgence.

The major focus for dating Mark is usually the 'Little Apocalypse' (Mark 13). Timothee Colani[30] first noticed that it is an independent work subsequently patched into Mark's gospel. Colani thought that Mark 13:4 elicited an answer as to when the temple would fall and that the

---

[28] Charles Alexander, *Alexander the Great* (NY: E.P. Dutton and Company, 1947), p. 233.

[29] Ken Dowden "Introduction" to *The Alexander Romance*, in B.P. Reardon, ed., *Collected Ancient Greek Novels* (Berkeley: University of California Press, 1989), p. 651.

[30] Timothee Colani, "The Little Apocalypse of Mark 13." Trans. Nancy Wilson *Journal of Higher Criticism* (10/1) Spring 2003, pp. 41–47. Excerpted from Colani, *Jesus-Christ et les croyances messianiques de son temps*, 1864, pp. 201–214.

answer came immediately in verse 32, a disavowal that even Jesus knew exactly when. The intervening material, verses 5–31, represent the text of an apocalyptic leaflet Eusebius says was circulated on the eve of the siege of Jerusalem, alerting the Christians to flee the city for safer climes, which they found in Pella. Others think that, while Colani was basically correct, it may be more accurate to picture Mark himself picking up such a document later on, after the fall of Jerusalem and incorporating it into his gospel. In either case, it means one cannot date Mark on the eve of the siege of Jerusalem. If chapter 13 was originally independent, it hardly matters who subsequently added it to the Gospel of Mark: the evangelist himself or a subsequent redactor. The rest of the gospel may have been any number of years or decades after the destruction of Jerusalem in CE 70. And there is evidence that it was.

Notice the bold promise of Mark 13:30: "Truly, I say to you, this generation will not pass away before all these things take place."[31] Mark 9:1 tries to restrict the promise of 13:30 so that Jesus does not predict that the whole generation would see the end-time events, only a few late survivors, because that's all that were left. But then none were left.

This is the stage reached by the composition of the Johannine Appendix, John chapter 21, a subsequent add-on. The scope of the promise had by that time shrunk to include one single known survivor, and now he, too, had expired! So John 21:23: "The saying spread abroad among the brethren that this disciple was not to die; yet Jesus did not say to him that he was not to die, but 'If it is my will that he remain until I come, what is that to you?'"

The same disastrous death occasioned 2 Peter 3:3–4, "scoffers will come in the last days with scoffing, 'Where is the promise of his coming? For ever since the fathers fell asleep, all things have continued as they were from the beginning of creation.'" Once the generation of Jesus' contemporaries all died off, someone added to Mark 13 verse 32, "But of that day and that hour no one knows, neither the angels nor the Son but only the Father" (note the late, formulaic character of "the Son").

At this point, *i.e.*, after at least two stages of delay, Mark offers the Transfiguration as yet another stage of harmonization. He reinterprets the "some standing here seeing the kingdom" to refer to an event that Jesus'

---

31 Let no one pretend this verse means "The Jewish nation will not be exterminated before the end comes." That makes absolutely no sense in the context. Just as bad is the dodge that it means "Whatever lucky generation lives to see these events will live to see them," an utterly pointless tautology, though beloved by harmonizers.

contemporaries could have seen already in their lifetimes. Well, there was the Transfiguration; one might understand it as an anticipation of the heavenly glory of the Second Coming. The only drawback was that, if it had happened already during the earthly lifetime of Jesus, it had happened early enough for the whole generation to have seen it, as per the original Mark 13:30 prediction. Why limit it to only "some"? That is why Mark restricts the vision (without giving any particular reason) to an inner circle of Peter, James, and John (9:2).

The Christians of Mark's day had as poor a track record predicting the Second Coming as Jehovah's Witnesses have in our day. Mark's gospel contains, then, the tree rings attesting a whole series of reinterpretations of a whole series of delays. There is no way it can come from the fifties, even the sixties, much less the seventies.

Matthew has used Mark, so scholars tend to allow a decade between Mark and Matthew. But we may have to allow more time than this simply because of evidence of stratification in the portions of Matthew which are not only added to Mark but based on it (or on Q).

Note that Matthew has based the Sermon on the Mount on the Q sermon from which Luke's Sermon on the Plain also derives, and the added section about the piety of the hypocrites (6:1–18) has itself accumulated other barnacles on prayer and glossolalia (vv. 9–15). Matthew based his mission charge on Mark 6:8–11, but he has added his 'not-so-great commission' in 10:5, which he has superseded in chapter 28.

As Arlo J. Nau shows,[32] Matthew presupposes a pre-Matthean but post-Markan stage of rehabilitation of Peter in the Matthean community, whom Matthew then tries to take down a peg. That is, it wasn't just canonical Mark and then canonical Matthew. We can tell that more than one stage of Matthean (Antiochan) expansion and redaction of Mark took place before our present version hit the stands. That presupposes the passage of time.

Matthew would seem to fall into the class of Nazorean Jewish Christianity descended from Paul's opponents in Galatians. Matthew commands Gentile converts to keep every *yodh* and *tittle* of the Torah. Matthew's *Sitz-im-Leben* is that of later Jewish-Christian polemics, as witness the trumped up nonsense about guards at the tomb, the genealogies seeking to rebut the charges that Jesus was a bastard, and not even a Jew. The trip to Egypt may have something to do with early charges that Jesus

---

32 Arlo J. Nau, *Peter in Matthew: Discipleship, Diplomacy, and Dispraise*. Good News Studies Vol. 36. A Michael Glazier Book.(Collegeville: Liturgical Press, 1992).

went there to learn magic. The very title "The Generations of Jesus" reflects the title of the anti-Christian Jewish gospel the *Toledoth Jeschu.*

Matthew swarms with legendary embellishments, especially all the seismic activity on Easter weekend, plus the enormity of the mass wave of resurrections coincident with the crucifixion of Jesus. This weird scenario is cut from the same cloth as the 'harrowing of hell' mythology we find full-blown in the third-century *Gospel of Nicodemus*. That is some distance from Mark.

Matthew, as a religious leader as well as a writer, was competing with what we call "formative Judaism," in which the use of the titles *Abba* and *Rabbi* is already common (Matthew 23:8–10) and in which scribes sit on the Seat of Moses in synagogues (verse 2), but all this is attested only for the late first or early second century.[33] Strauss notes that Luke the evangelist seems to regard none of his predecessors' works as stemming from apostolic witness, and this includes Mark and Q.

> From this preface [Luke 1:4] we see, first, that at the time when the author of our third Gospel wrote, a considerable evangelical literature was already in existence, to which he referred from a critical point of view. In the second place, as he distinguishes between the "many who had taken in hand to set forth in order a declaration of those things which were surely believed among them," from those "who from the beginning were eye-witnesses and ministers of the word," he appears not to be aware of any Gospel immediately composed by an Apostle; and thirdly, inasmuch as he alleges as his means for surpassing his predecessors, not any exclusive source, like the teaching by an Apostle, but only the fact "that he has followed up, inquired into, all things accurately from the first," there is no appearance of our having before us the companion of an Apostle, though the author of the third Gospel has from the earliest times been considered as such.[34]

Irenaeus' description of a Lukan writing down of Paul's preaching would fit Acts better than Luke. Again, Strauss: "In this case, again, ... the supposition might occur to us that these words must refer to a totally different work; for that the Gospel which Paul preached was neither that or like that which we now have, either in the third or any other Gospel."[35]

---

33 J. Andrew Overman, *Matthew's Gospel and Formative Judaism: The Social World of the Matthean Community* (Minneapolis: Fortress Press, 1990), pp. 44–45, 145.

34 Strauss, *Life of Jesus for the People*, vol. I, p. 63.

35 *Ibid.*, pp. 63–64.

Luke's gospel is not mentioned until Irenaeus includes it among the four gospels he is willing to accept in *ca.* 180 CE. Justin (150?) may refer to Acts, but we are not sure. Marcion (*ca.* 140) had a shorter version of Luke, but no Acts. Adolf Harnack[36] dated Acts at around 60 CE He decided that there was no other way to explain the silence of Acts *re* Paul's death, or at least the outcome of his trial, unless we suppose that Luke wrote during the period of Paul's house arrest in Rome, awaiting trial and preaching the gospel. If Luke knew Paul had been martyred, can we imagine that he would not have made much of it? It cannot be that he is not interested in depicting martyrdoms *per se*, since he does mention that of James son of Zebedee in Acts 12, as well as Stephen's in Acts 8. Blomberg accepts this reasoning.

> Acts ends apparently unfinished – Paul is a central figure of the book, and he's under house arrest in Rome. With that the book abruptly halts. What happens to Paul? We don't find out from Acts, probably because the book was written before Paul was put to death... That means Acts cannot be dated any later than A.D. 62 ... Since Acts is the second of a two-part work, we know the first part – the gospel of Luke – must have been written earlier than that. And since Luke incorporates parts of the gospel of Mark, that means that Mark is even earlier. If you allow maybe a year for each of those, you end with Mark written no later than about A.D. 60, maybe even the late 50s."[37]

Harnack accepted the theory of Luke's dependence upon Mark, and he knew his early dating had to take that into account: Mark and Q must have been early, too. This, however, brought up another problem, in that most scholars regard Luke as having taken the Markan abomination-of-desolation prophecy (Mark 13:14*ff*) and historicized it in light of the actual events of 70 CE (Luke 21:20; *cf.* 19:43). Mark's business about the Danielic "abomination of desolation" probably already reflects the events, but Luke seems to have taken the trouble to renarrate the text in terms of a literal description.

What was Harnack's answer to this? He said that Luke could see the original prophecy denoted a Roman conquest and simply employed his knowledge of typical Roman tactics to describe what would happen.[38]

---

36 Adolf von Harnack, *The Date of the Synoptic Gospels and the Acts*. Trans. J.R. Wilkinson. Crown Theological Library. New Testament Studies IV (NY: Putnam's. 1911), pp. 93–99.

37 Blomberg in Strobel, pp. 33–34.

38 Harnack, *Date of the Synoptic Gospels and Acts*, pp. 122–123.

Similarly, some years later, C.H. Dodd[39] argued that the language of the siege of Jerusalem reflected language typical of the Septuagint (or LXX, the Greek translation of the Old Testament) when it describes city sieges, though scholars have since challenged him. One still has to ask why Luke would have changed Mark in this way *if not to make explicit the fulfillment of the prediction in terms of the Roman siege*.

But is the author of Acts really ignorant of the martyr death of Paul? Most scholars today do not think so. Note that at the end of Acts Luke refers to Paul's two-year imprisonment as a thing completed, a rounded-off episode. "The imprisonment lasted two years." And then what happened? It is indeed puzzling that he does not tell us, but it equally seems that he is assuming something else happened, *i.e.*, the story went on. It may be that he intended to continue the story in a third volume of narrative which would have depicted an acquittal and further travels and finally the death of Paul; or perhaps Paul's death and the ministry of Aristarchus, Barnabas, *etc.* But it may be that the fact of Paul's death was so well known that it would be superfluous to state it. "This is how he came to his famous death. You know the rest." As if a biography of Lincoln ended with: "And thus he entered the Ford Theatre for the 2:15 pm performance, the same one attended by John Wilkes Booth."

Again, it may be that the Acts author, sensitive to the disapproval of Romans in a politically charged climate, where Christians were viewed as subversive and liable to persecution, may have wanted to gloss over the execution of Paul by Rome. He certainly evidences such an apologetic sensitivity elsewhere in both the Gospel and Acts.

But it seems clear, if one will look at all closely, that the Acts author did know the reader knew of the death of Paul as a *fait accompli*. He has Paul predict his martyrdom in pretty explicit terms in Acts 20:25 (v. 22 not withstanding). "You shall see my face no more" — a prediction he could make only if he knew he would soon be dead. In fact, the passage as a whóle, the farewell speech to the Ephesian elders, is an easily recognizable "Last Testament" piece, a common device to put "famous last words" into the mouth of a great man. (see *Crito*, *Testaments of the Twelve Patriarchs*, *Testament of Abraham*, *Testament of Moses*, *Testament of Job*, *etc.*).

Specifically, the 'prediction' (*ex eventu*) of Gnostic heretics emerging later to forage among the churches of Asia Minor seems to be a much later

---

39 C.H. Dodd, "The Fall of Jerusalem and the 'Abomination of Desolation," in Dodd, *More New Testament Studies* (Grand Rapids: Eerdmans, 1968), pp. 69–83.

post-Pauline way of dissociating Paul from the floodtide of 'heresy' that overtook the area by the second century. Luke seeks here to absolve Paul of the blame of it, contrary to the heretics themselves who claimed him as their patron saint.

Also, it is hard to ignore the large-scale series of parallels between the Passion of Jesus and that of Paul. Both undertake peripatetic preaching journeys, culminating in a last, long journey to Jerusalem, where each is arrested in connection with a disturbance in the Temple. Each is acquitted by a Herodian monarch as well as by Roman procurators. Each makes, as we have seen, passion predictions. Is it likely that the Acts author wrote this in ignorance of what finally happened to Paul?

The majority of current scholars date Acts at 80–90 CE. It is simply an attempt to push Luke as far back as possible while admitting that neither Mark nor Luke were written before the death of Paul (62 CE) or the fall of Jerusalem (70 CE), and this in order to keep it within the possible lifetime of a companion of Paul, which is what tradition made Luke, the ostensible author of Acts. The date is itself a function of apologetics, not a prop for it.

The Tübingen critics of the nineteenth century (Franz Overbeck, F.C. Baur, Edward Zeller) dated Luke-Acts in the second century, 100–130 CE More recently Walter Schmithals,[40] Helmut Koester,[41] John C. O'Neill, and Richard I. Pervo[42] have maintained the second-century date. Baur[43] placed Luke-Acts late on the historical timeline because of its 'catholicizing' tendency. That is, he showed how there is a conflict between nationalist Torah-observant Jewish Christianity on the one hand, and more open, Torah-free Hellenistic/Gentile Christianity on the other. The first was led by James, Peter, and the Twelve, while the latter was led by Paul, the Seven, Apollos, Priscilla, Aquila, and others. Baur showed how most of the New Testament documents could be placed on either side of this great divide. On the Jewish side were Matthew, James, and Revelation. On the Gentile side were the four 'authentic' Pauline Epistles (1 & 2 Corinthians, Galatians and Romans 1–14), Hebrews, John, the Johannine Epistles, and Mark.

---

40 Walter Schmithals, *The Office of Apostle in the Early Church*. Trans. John E. Steely (Philadelphia: Westminster Press, 1969), pp. 254–255.

41 Helmut Koester, *Ancient Christian Gospels: Their History and Development* (Trinity Press International, 1990), p. 337.

42 Richard I. Pervo, *Dating Acts: Between the Evangelists and the Apologists* (Santa Rosa: Polebridge Press, 2006).

43 Ferdinand Christian Baur, *Paul, the Apostle of Jesus Christ: His Life and Work, His Epistles and Doctrine*. Trans. A. Menzies (London: Williams and Norgate, 1876).

Later there arose the catholicizing tendency, the tendency to reconcile the two parties. The pseudonymous 1 and 2 Peter either dispense Pauline thought under Peter's name or have Peter speak favorably of Paul while denigrating those who quote Paul against the memory of Peter. Interpolations into the Pauline epistles, as well as pseudonymous epistles attributed to Paul, make him friendlier to Judaism and the Law. Acts attempts to bring together the Petrine and Pauline factions by a series of clever moves: first, Peter and Paul are paralleled, each raising someone from the dead (Acts 9:36–40; 20:9–12), each healing a paralytic (3:1–8; 14:8–10), each healing by extraordinary, magical means (5:15; 19:11–12), each besting a sorcerer (8:18–23; 13:6–11), each miraculously escaping prison (12:6–10; 16:25–26). If one praises God for the work of Peter, then one can scarcely deny him to have been at work in Paul either (and *vice-versa*).

Second, Acts makes Peter a universalizing preacher to Gentiles, *cf.* the Cornelius story and especially the speech of Peter in Acts 15 which echoes that of Paul in Galatians 2, aimed at Peter! At the same time he makes Paul still an observant Jew, claiming still to be a Pharisee (23:6), piously taking vows and paying for those of others (21:20–24), attending Jerusalem worship on holy days. He makes it clear that there is no truth to the prevalent rumors that Paul had abandoned legal observance (Acts 21:24), which is not clear at all from Paul's own writings.

Third, having vindicated Paul as a true and divinely chosen preacher of the gospel, and this conspicuously in the teeth of Jewish Christian opponents, Acts seems to deny him the dignity of the apostolate itself, redefining the office in an anachronistic fashion which would have excluded several of the Twelve, not present at John's baptism, as well (Acts 1:21–22). Paul is subordinated to the Twelve as their dutiful servant. He makes a beeline to them after his conversion, in direct contradiction to Galatians 1:15–19. He does nothing without their approval and preaches of *their* witness to the risen Christ (13:30–31), not his own. In short, Acts has Petrinized Paul and Paulinized Peter, so as to bring their respective factions closer together. All this bespeaks a time well after Paul himself.

The Conz

Hans Conzelmann (who, however, does not place Luke-Acts quite so late) also argued (in *The Theology of St. Luke*, or *Die Mitte der Zeit*)[44] for a date significantly after Paul and presupposing sufficient passage

[44] Hans Conzelmann, *The Theology of St. Luke*. Trans. Geoffrey Buswell (NY: Harper & Row, 1961).

of time that it had become apparent that history had entered a new era. Conzelmann argued that in Luke's day it had become evident that the apocalyptic enthusiasm of the earliest Christians, still evident in Mark, was premature, that the world would keep on going, and that a new era of salvation history had commenced. This is why he wrote Acts: the story of salvation was not yet over. Jesus was the decisive center of it, but not the culmination of it. He rewrote the story of Jesus to 'de-eschatologize' it and make it fit into an ongoing world in which the church had more of a role than merely awaiting the end.

Conzelmann envisioned salvation history as consisting of three great eras. The first was that of Israel. In Luke it would be represented by the first two chapters of the gospel with Zechariah, Elizabeth, Miriam (Mary), Simeon, and Anna as quintessential Old Testament characters (actually modeled on characters in the stories of the infancy of Samuel [Simeon = Eli, Elizabeth = Hannah, *etc.*]). Conzelmann thought that the first two chapters were a later addition to Luke, so he did not make this connection, but it seems to me to fit his theory pretty well.

The second period was that of Jesus. It forms the middle of time, the strategic pivotal zone of history. It culminates the time of Israel and commences that of the church. John the Baptist is the pivotal figure, marking the shift of the aeons (Luke 16:16) from the time when the Law is preached to the time when the Kingdom of God is preached. Within the period of Jesus there is a further breakdown: In the center of it lies the public ministry of Jesus, when the full blaze of heavenly light dispels shadows: wherever Jesus goes evil flees, like the Canaanites before the advancing Israelites. This Conzelmann called the 'Satan-free' period. It begins with Jesus warding off Satan by successfully withstanding the temptations. At the end of this story Luke says Satan "departed from him until an opportune time (*kairos*)" (Luke 4:13). That time comes at the betrayal story when, as in John, Luke says that Satan entered into Judas Iscariot to engineer Jesus' betrayal. Between these two events we see either an editorial elimination of Satan's activity or a continual banishing of his forces from the field.

In the first case, notice that Luke has omitted the rebuke of Jesus to Peter ("Get behind me Satan!") from the Confession of Peter scene. Even Matthew, who doesn't want to make Peter look bad (as witness the "Thou art Peter" material in his version of the scene), retains the rebuke. Why does Luke omit it? The period must have been Satan-free!

In the second case, note that Jesus rides roughshod over the forces of evil, witnessing Satan falling precipitously (Luke 10:18–19) from his position of power in one of the lower heavens ("the powers of the heavens shall be shaken" Luke 21:26b), freeing those oppressed by the devil (Luke 13:16; Acts 10:38) apparently without resistance.

Some see these two motifs as contradictory: how can the period of the ministry be free of the machinations of Satan and yet be the time of unceasing battle between Jesus and Satan? But I think they misunderstand the idea that Satan seems completely unable to reinforce his vanquished troops. Where is he?

Once the Satan-free period is over (and Jesus knows it is over as of the Last Supper) he warns the disciples that it will no longer be so easy as it has been up to this point. Whereas they could travel preaching the gospel unmolested thus far, now they had best carry weapons to protect themselves (22:35–36). It is only now that we learn of Satan's demand to thresh the Twelve like wheat (22:31).

If Conzelmann is right about this, we can detect for the first time the perspective, much like our own, of a distinctly later period, one from which the time of Jesus already looks something like a never-never-land unlike the mundane and difficult time in which we live, a pristine once-upon-a-time of origins. It is, from the standpoint of the reader and the writer, long over. We are now in the third period, that of the church, when the gospel is to be preached and tribulation is to be endured. This is not a work of the apostolic age, it seems to me.

Conzelmann's Luke also tends to push the eschatological fulfillment off into the future. At first this is not obvious, since he retains the passage from the Markan apocalypse in which we are told that this generation will not pass before all these things are fulfilled (Luke 21:32). But we dare not ignore the many subtle changes Luke makes in his sources elsewhere. For instance, in the 'Olivet Discourse,' the false prophets do not merely announce that "I am he," but now also that "The time is at hand!" (21:8; *cf* 2 Thessalonians 2:1–3). Now the events Jesus predicts lead up only to the historical destruction of the Jerusalem temple by Roman troops (21:20), not to the very end of all things, as Mark had expected. The fall of Jerusalem will usher in a new period, the Times of the Gentiles, *i.e.*, apparently times of Gentile dominion over Israel, as in the visions of Daniel 7. Thus there is a distancing buffer between the events of 70 CE and the end, and Luke stands in the middle.

At the Confession story, Jesus predicts that some there will see the kingdom of God, but not "coming in power" as Mark had it (*cf.* Luke 9:27 and Mark 9:1). He wants to avoid the embarrassment that the Twelve all died, and still no second coming (*cf.* 2 Peter 3:4; John 21:23).

At the Trial scene Jesus no longer tells his contemporaries that they will see the Son of Man seated at the right hand of Power (as in Mark 14:62, "you will see"), but rather simply that from now on he will be seated there (Luke 22:69). He wants to avoid the embarrassment that the Sanhedrin are dead and the coming of the Son of Man and the Kingdom of God have not transpired.

Then there are the three impatient questions, all unique to Luke-Acts. First, in Luke 17:20–21 Jesus is asked of signs whereby the arrival of the Kingdom may be counted down (signs such as he himself is presented as giving in the Olivet Discourse). His answer is that no such calculation will be possible. It is not at all the kind of thing that even *could* come that way, since it is an inner, spiritual reality. (Conzelmann didn't say so, but we must wonder if this is where we see Luke's own eschatology emerge most clearly.)

Second, in Luke 19:11*ff* (where Luke has very heavily redacted the parable of the Talents, which survives in something more like its Q form in Matthew 25:14*ff*) Luke makes the point that before the kingdom comes the Son of Man is going to have to go very far away (*i.e.*, heaven—*cf.* Acts 1:10–11) and thus be absent a long time before he can return as king.

Third, in Acts 1:6–7*f*, even after 40 days of 'inside teaching' from the risen Christ himself, the Twelve are still so dense as to expect an immediate theocratic denouement. The artificiality of the scene is plain; hence it is redactional. The point is not to trouble oneself about matters of eschatology but instead to get busy spreading the gospel.

We get the same impression from *the replacement of horizontal with vertical eschatology*: Luke alone among the gospel writers speaks of people going to heaven or hell as soon as they die. The parable of Lazarus and the Rich Man (16:19–31) and the thief on the cross story (23:43) both have such a picture. Also see Luke 20:38b, where Luke adds the idea of present immortality, "for all live unto him," just as in 4 Maccabees 7:19 ("to God they do not die, as our patriarchs Abraham, Isaac, and Jacob died not, but live to God"). Earlier Christians thought of attaining the Kingdom or not. One thinks of going to heaven only when the prospect of an imminent end has faded (1 Thessalonians 4:13–14; 2 Corinthians 5:1–4; Philippians

1:23). The thief on the cross passage is also clearly a Lukan redaction, a development of Mark. And again, the eschatological enthronement of Jesus is replaced by 'going to heaven.'[45] All this expansion of theological history seems to me to require more time than Conzelmann allows. It all implies, I think, *a second-century date.*

After-Apostle Agendas

Charles H. Talbert (*Luke and the Gnostics*),[46] though again without actually holding to a second-century date, showed how Luke shares the agenda and the views of the second-century Apologists Irenaeus, Justin Martyr, and Tertullian. These men faced the challenge of 'heresies' (competing forms of Christianity) which they sought to refute by claiming an exclusive copyright on the 'apostolic tradition.' The Apologists relied heavily, in their polemics against the Gnostics, on the idea of 'apostolic succession' of bishops. That is, the Twelve Apostles had been the apprentices of the Son of God. They alone saw the whole of his ministry and thus were in no danger of taking things he said out of context as, *e.g.*, Irenaeus accused the Valentinians of doing.

In the Pseudo-Clementine *Homilies* and *Recognitions* (fourth-century Christian novels detailing the exploits of Peter, Barnabas, Simon Magus, and Clement, based partly on second-century Ebionite sources including *The Preaching of Peter*) Peter takes Simon Magus to task precisely over this issue: how can the Magus hope to have a correct understanding of Christ and his teaching derived, as he claims, from occasional visions of him? If he were really taught by Christ, he ought to agree with Peter who saw and heard everything the Messiah did and said.

Luke seems already to be setting up the Twelve Apostles as a college of guarantors of the orthodox tradition of Jesus. As Talbert notes, Luke makes explicit in Acts 1:21–22 that he views as an apostle one who has seen and thus can verify all the events of the Jesus story as they are preached elsewhere in Acts, namely the baptism on through the ascension. The artificiality of this is, again, evident from the simple fact that the Twelve cannot all have been present at these events even on Luke's own showing. But he does make the effort, as Talbert shows, to have the disciples miss nothing at least from the point when they join Jesus. For example, while they are away on their preaching tour, there is nothing recorded of Jesus

---

45 Eric Franklin, *Christ the Lord: A Study in the Purpose and Theology of Luke-Acts* (Philadelphia: Westminster Press, 1975.

46 Charles H. Talbert, *Luke and the Gnostics: An Examination of the Lucan Purpose* (NY: Abingdon Press, 1966).

— otherwise the witnesses could not attest it. Jesus would have been a tree falling in the forest with no one there to hear the sound.

Günter Klein has gone one step farther (*Die Zwölf Apostel*)[47] and argued that, whereas we hear from Paul about "the Twelve" and "the apostles," and from Mark and Matthew about "the disciples," the notion of a group of 'the Twelve Apostles' is a Lukan creation to restrict the office of apostle, originally much less specific, to the narrow confines of the Twelve. The one reference to the Twelve apostles in Matthew 10:2 would make sense as a harmonizing interpolation; in Mark 6:30 it seems to be used in a non-technical sense ('the twelve he sent out came back').

Note that Luke has every step of the fledgling church carefully overseen by the vigilant eye of the Twelve who stay magically untouched in Jerusalem even when the whole church is otherwise scattered by persecution (Acts 8:1): They authenticate the conversion of the Samaritans (8:14–16), the ordination of the Seven (6:1–6), the conversion of Cornelius (11:2, 18), even the ministry of Paul (15:2).

The second-century Apologists held that it was the bishops of the Catholic congregations who were appointed by the apostles to continue their work, teaching what they themselves had been taught, as it were, from the horse's mouth. Luke has Paul tell the Ephesian elders that he taught them everything he knew (Acts 20:20 — *i.e.*, against Gnostic claims that he had taught the advanced stuff only to the illuminati, as he says pointedly in 1 Corinthians 2:6*f* that he did), and calls them "bishops" in 20:28, though translations hide it. Compare 2 Timothy 2:2.

Tertullian denied the right of 'heretics' even to quote scripture in their own defense (much as Justin did Jews), claiming that the scripture was meaningless unless interpreted in accordance with the tradition of the apostles. And what was that? Well, whatever the current catholic interpretation happened to be! Even so, Acts is careful to have the Twelve appear as recipients of the Risen Christ's own scriptural exegesis (Luke 24:25, 43–44), which, however, Luke refrains from giving in any detail — writing himself a blank check.

Tertullian fought against the Gnostic idea of a spiritually resurrected Christ as opposed to a physically resurrected one. Is it any accident that Luke has the same concern, as opposed to the presumably earlier view of 1 Corinthians 15:49–50 and 1 Peter 3:18?

The Gnostics claimed that Jesus had remained on earth some eighteen months, even perhaps eleven years, teaching the apostles, from whom,

47 Günter Klein, *Die Zwölf Apostel: Ursprung und Gehalt eine Idee* (Göttingen: Vandenhoeck & Ruprecht, 1961).

incidentally, they, too, claimed apostolic succession (Paul → Theodas → Valentinus; Peter → Glaukias → Basilides). This was of course a way of saying they had the inside stuff, with all veiled language dropped away (*cf.* John 16:25–30, originally part of such a resurrection dialogue as we find in *Pistis Sophia, Dialogue of the Savior, etc.*) It is no wonder that Acts appropriates the Gnostic device of the post-Easter period of teaching, of 40 days, claiming such warrant for whatever the bishops may teach (which is, again, why Luke does not tell you what Jesus taught them!).

J.C. O'Neill (*The Theology of Acts in Its Historical Setting*)[48] argued that Acts belongs in the early second century because its theology has most in common with the writings of that time (again, including the Apologists): first, the view that Jews have forfeited their claim on God and have been shunted to the side is surely impossible before the second century. Had it become clear earlier than this that Jews *en toto* had completely rejected the Christian message? Hardly! Yet in Acts, not only is this a *fait accompli*, but (as Jack T. Sanders, *The Jews in Luke-Acts*,[49] shows) Luke seems to view the Jews of the Diaspora — the only ones he knows as historical entities (as opposed to the Sunday-School-lesson Jews of Jerusalem) — as horned caricatures who oppose the gospel out of base envy. This is a motivation retrojected from a later period in which Christianity has begun to overwhelm Judaism in numbers, surely too late for the lifetime of Paul or one of his companions.

The theology of the supersession of the Temple seen in Stephen's speech is borrowed from post-70 CE Hellenistic Judaism, where, as we see in Justin's *Dialogue with Trypho* and the *Sybilline Oracles*, Jews had begun to make virtue of necessity and to spiritualize temple worship.

The Apostolic Decree (Acts 15:23–29), stipulating that Jewish Christians have every right to observe the ancestral law of Moses (15:21), and the stress on James's securing Paul's public endorsement of the idea (21:20–25), seem to reflect a later period attested in Justin where Jewish Christians were on the defensive against their Gentile Christian brethren, many of whom deemed them heretical for keeping the Law at all, while Justin himself allowed their right to do so if they did not try to get Gentiles to keep it. This dispute seems to provide the *Sitz-im-Leben* for Acts 21, making Luke a contemporary of Justin.

---

48 J.C. O'Neill, *The Theology of Acts in its Historical Setting* (London: SPCK, 1961).

49 Jack T. Sanders. *The Jews in Luke-Acts* (Philadelphia: Fortress Press, 1987)

Similarly, the Decree as set forth in Acts 15 seeks to provide (long after the fact) apostolic legitimization for the cultic provisions attested in second-century sources, but not earlier for the most part. Minucius Felix, the Pseudo-Clementines, Biblis (in Eusebius), the Syriac *Apology of Aristides*, and Tertullian mention that Christians do not eat the blood of animals or the meat of strangled animals. Revelation 2:20 bans eating meat offered to idols. Matthew 5:32; 19:9 forbids consanguineous marriages (*porneia*) to Gentile converts.

The strange thing about this is that *in none of these cases is the prohibition traced back to the Apostolic Decree of Jerusalem,* which, if genuine, must have been treasured as the first ecumenical conciliar decision in the church. Conversely, when Paul's epistles deal with the issues, they never mention the Decree, which would seemingly have been an authoritative way of dealing with the questions. Acts has simply collected these various second-century Christian mores and retrojected them into the Golden Age of the Apostles to give them added weight.

The titles of Jesus, particularly 'Servant of God' (Acts 3:13; 4:27) mark Acts as late, too. Despite the desperate desire of Jeremias and others to trace this back to an imaginary 'Suffering Servant of Yahweh' theology of the earliest church,[50] there is no evidence that such a spectre ever existed. But the title does occur in later documents like the *Didache*, 1 Clement, and the *Martyrdom of Polycarp*. It is *late* Christology, not early.

The natural theology of Acts 17, the Areopagus Speech, reflects that of the second-century Apologists, who sought to make common ground with their pagan audience, *e.g.*, the Christians-before-Christ theory of Justin.

Richard Pervo[51] (*Profit with Delight: The Literary Genre of the Acts of the Apostles*) demonstrates crucial links between Acts and the second-century Hellenistic novels. Acts shares much in common with the popular picaresque novels produced for several centuries, flourishing at the height of popularity in the second century CE These were most often romances

---

50 Walter Zimmerli and Joachim Jeremias, *The Servant of God*. Studies in Biblical Theology, No. 20. Trans. Harold Knight (Naperville: Alec R. Allenson, 1957; rev. 1965). For a devastating critique see Morna D. Hooker, *Jesus and the Servant: The Influence of the Servant Concept of Deutero-Isaiah in the New Testament* (London: SPCK, 1959).

51 Richard I. Pervo, *Profit with Delight: The Literary Genre of the Acts of the Apostles* (Philadelphia: Fortress, 1987); *cf.* Stephen P. Schierling & Marla J. Schierling, "The Influence of the Ancient Romances on Acts of the Apostles" *The Classical Bulletin*, 54, April 1978).

but also sometimes chronicled the travels and miracles of teachers like Apollonius of Tyana.

Rosa Söder notes several features shared by the novels and the Apocryphal Acts of the second century (more on these in a moment). They are also shared with the canonical Acts: first, *travel* (see the apostolic journeys of Peter and Paul), second, *aretalogy*, or tales of miracles and oddities (the apostles do numerous miracles, some quite fanciful, like Peter's healing shadow, Paul's healing hankies, Peter striking Ananias and Sapphira dead with a word); third, *depiction of fabulous and exotic peoples* (see the bull-sacrificing pagans of Lycaonia, Acts 14:8–19, the superstitious natives of Malta, 28:1–6, and the philosophical dilettantes of Athens in Acts 17); fourth, *propaganda*.

Söder adds even more important traits less often found in the Apocryphal Acts but common to the novels. They are found in the canonical Acts as well: first, *sale of the hero into slavery* (see imprisonment of Paul, Peter, Silas, *etc.* Acts 12:6; 16:26; 21:33; 26:29); second, *persecution*; third, *crowd scenes* (*e.g.*, in Ephesus, the Artemis riot); fourth, *divine help in time of great need*; and fifth, *oracles, dreams, and divine commands* .[52] We might add Vernon K. Robbins's[53] observation that the 'We' style of narration associated with sea-voyages is a contemporary novelistic technique, and the shipwreck scene is quite similar to several such in contemporary novels. (If this is true, it renders superfluous the efforts to identify a pre-Lukan 'We–source' or to argue for authorship of the Acts as a whole by a contemporary of the events.) *If the heyday of the novel genre was the second century, it also seems the best period in which to locate Luke-Acts.*

There are similar parallels between Luke-Acts and the apocryphal gospels. Luke is the only New Testament gospel with a story of the childhood of Jesus, but these abound in works like the *Infancy Gospel of Thomas*, the *Infancy Gospel of Matthew*, and the *Arabic Infancy Gospel*. I suggest this shows Luke is intermediate between the two groups of gospels, and thus a second-century work. Luke also seems to have used a version of the Passion which had Jesus tried and condemned not by

---

52 Pervo, *Profit with Delight*, shows both the novelistic character of Acts and how traditional attempts to denigrate its 'apocryphal' relatives have more to do with orthodox canon polemics than with historical judgment.

53 Vernon K. Robbins, "By Land and by Sea: The We-Passages and Ancient Sea Voyages," in Charles H. Talbert, ed., *Perspectives on Luke-Acts*. Perspectives in Religious Studies, Special Studies Series No. 5 (Edinburgh: T&T Clark, 1978), pp. 215–242.

Pilate but by Herod Antipas. This is what happens in the second-century apocryphal *Gospel of Peter*. I suggest Luke's similarity at this point means that it, too, stems from the second century.

Dear and Glorious Paramedic

Traditionally everyone thought the author of Luke's Gospel and the Book of Acts was Luke the 'beloved physician,' the companion of Paul mentioned in Colossians 4:14; 2 Timothy 4:11.[54] As we have seen, Craig Blomberg still thinks so. Or perhaps one ought to say "*believes* so," since it has become fully as much a part of the evangelical Christian party line as believing in the resurrection or the walking on water. But the text itself, like all the gospels, is anonymous. The traditional identification of Luke as the author rests on the assumptions that the 'We' narrative of parts of Acts goes back to an actual eyewitness, and that the letters in question are genuinely Pauline. If some companion of Paul wrote Acts, which one was it? Many names can be eliminated since the author mentions them in distinction from himself among the 'We.' Luke is one of the names he does not mention that *is* mentioned in the epistles. Some have suggested Titus.

The more serious problem facing the traditional ascription of authorship is the divergence between the authentic letters of Paul (provided there are any!) and Acts. The differences are so great that it seems doubtful a companion of Paul could have written Acts. There are chronological problems, too. As John Knox has shown,[55] recently followed by Gerd Lüdemann,[56] if we read the epistles on their own, without trying to fit them into Acts, we come up with a rather different scenario than that of Acts which schematizes the ministry of Paul into three neat missionary journeys. Acts is also irreconcilable with Galatians on the matter of Paul's movements following his conversion. Luke tells precisely the version that Paul expressly repudiates: he *did* go to Jerusalem to consult those who were apostles before him! *Compare Galatians 1:15ff with Acts 9:20–26.*

---

54 Henry J. Cadbury, "The Alleged Medical Language of Luke," in Cadbury, *The Style and Literary Method of Luke* (Cambridge: Harvard University Press, 1920), pp. 39–64, exploded the old notion that Luke employed more technical medical or medicine-derived vocabulary than average, but it seems not to have percolated very far into popular scholarship like Blomberg's in nearly seventy years.

55 John Knox, *Chapters in a Life of Paul* (NY: Abingdon Press, 1950).

56 Gerd Lüdemann, *Paul, Apostle to the Gentiles: Studies in Chronology* (London: SCM Press, 1984).

Worse yet, Acts is un-Pauline in teaching. As Philipp Vielhauer pointed out ("On the 'Paulinism' of Acts"),[57] the author of Acts did not understand Paul's thought at several key points. How then can he have been Paul's bosom companion? In Acts 17, Paul is depicted as granting that pagans are on the right track in their search for God, their only problem being that they have remained stalled without making the connection that there must be one transcendent God. But in Romans 1–3 Paul has a more severe estimate of paganism: none is righteous, and paganism is nothing but a repudiation of the Almighty from the word go. Gentiles are not searching for him but rather are on the run from him. Natural theology is a bridge in Acts, a barrier in Romans. Acts has all humans as "his offspring," unthinkable for Paul. Sin is not hinted at in Acts 17.

Acts has Paul still a Pharisee (23:6; 26:5), while Philippians has him an ex-Pharisee. Acts has him still obeying the Law as his constant custom (21:18*ff*), while 1 Corinthians 9:19–23 allows it as an occasional, opportunistic exception at most. Acts 13 has Paul say that the gospel supplements the Law, expunging offenses for which the Torah made no provision, while for Paul in Galatians, the Law has been superseded by the gospel as a new dispensation. Acts has Paul preach first in the synagogue of each city, turning only reluctantly to the Gentiles after the Jews reject him, something never hinted in the epistles, where Paul is the Apostle to the Gentiles, not to the Jews. Acts 16:3 has him circumcise Timothy, while Galatians 5:2 shows he would have done no such thing. While there are various possible harmonizations at this or that point, these would only be preferable exegeses provided there were some prior, overriding reason to stick with the traditional identification, which there isn't. It seems, as Dibelius[58] suggested, and as Vielhauer seconded (and as Earl Richard[59] and Marion L. Soards[60] have made even clearer recently), the speeches of Acts are all Lukan compositions with no knowledge of what may have been said on the actual occasion (if there was one!).

---

57 Philipp Vielhauer, "On the 'Paulinism' of Acts," in Leander E. Keck and J. Louis Martyn, eds., *Studies in Luke-Acts: Essays presented in honor of Paul Schubert Buckingham Professor of New Testament Criticism and Interpretation at Yale University* (NY: Abingdon Press, 1966), pp. 33–50.

58 Martin Dibelius, "The Speeches in Acts and Ancient Historiography," in Dibelius, *Studies in the Acts of the Apostles* (London: SCM Press, 1956), pp. 138–191.

59 Earl Richard, *Acts 6:1–8:4: The Author's Method of Composition*. SBL Dissertation Series 41 (Missoula: Scholars Press, 1978).

60 Marion L. Soards, *The Speeches in Acts: Their Content, Context, and Concerns* (Louisville: Westminster / John Knox Press, 1994).

Were Luke and Acts written by the same author? J.H. Scholten suggested in the nineteenth century that the two works do not come from the same author. Though there is near unanimity among scholars that the same author *did* produce both works, the opposite hypothesis has been revived by Albert C. Clark[61] (*The Acts of the Apostles, A Critical Edition*, 1933) and A.W. Argyle ("The Greek of Luke and Acts")[62] They both argued on the basis of striking differences in vocabulary. The best solution of the problem is probably that of John Knox (*Marcion and the New Testament*, 1942)[63] who revived the Tübingen argument that Marcionites used an earlier, somewhat shorter '*Ur-Lukas*' (of course they did not call it that), and that a subsequent Catholic redactor (very likely Polycarp of Smyrna) padded it out, adding Acts as a sequel in order to rehabilitate the Twelve alongside Paul. This would neatly account for the thematic continuity between canonical Luke and Acts, as well as the differences in vocabulary.

Synoptic Claim Bake

The Gospel of John is the traditional favorite for apologetics, because there Jesus is represented as magnifying himself in grandiose terms inviting worship, and that is what apologists want of their readers. But why is John so unlike the other gospels, which have no such explicit Christology? Could it be less historically accurate than they are?

Apologists pretend (to themselves) that it doesn't matter. "Even [*in the synoptic gospels, Matthew, Mark, and Luke*], you find Jesus making some very strong claims – for instance, that he was wisdom personified and that he was the one by whom God will judge all humanity, whether they confess him or disavow him."[64] "Jesus says, 'Whoever acknowledges me, I will acknowledge before my Father in heaven.' [Matthew 10:32–33] Final judgment is based on one's reaction to – whom? This mere human being? No, that would be a very arrogant claim. Final judgment is based

---

61 Albert C. Clark, *The Acts of the Apostles: A Critical Edition with Introduction and Notes on Selected Passages* (Oxford at the Clarendon Press, 1933).

62. W.W. Argyle, "The Greek of Luke and Acts." *New Testament Studies* 20 (1973–1974), pp. 441–445)

63 John Knox, *Marcion and the New Testament A Chapter in the Early History of the Canon* (Chicago: University of Chicago Press, 1942). Knox's student Joseph B. Tyson has recently updated and defended the thesis in *Marcion and Luke-Acts: A Defining Struggle* (Columbia: University of South Carolina Press, 2006).

64 Blomberg in Strobel, p. 27.

on one's reaction to Jesus *as God*."[65] Or, as one might put it, to evangelical theology, which is what it really comes down to, for that is what we are reading here, not mere gospel exegesis.

With Craig Blomberg it appears that inherited (I should say *stale*) evangelical apologetics has almost completely displaced any serious attempt to seek the most likely meaning of gospel texts in their own right, in their ancient contexts. Let's examine, as quickly as we can, each of these assertions about Jesus' 'claims' (itself a distinctly apologetical term).

First, what about this notion that the criterion of eschatological judgment will be the inquisitorial question: "What was your reaction to the God named Jesus?" Blomberg jumps right from Matthew 10:32–33 to the historical Jesus, as if Matthew had linked to a *You Tube* video of Jesus saying this. But in fact we can trace the evolution of the saying. We first catch sight of it in Mark 8:38, where it takes this form: "For whoever is ashamed of me and of my words in this adulterous and sinful generation, of him will the Son of Man also be ashamed, when he comes in the glory of his Father with the holy angels."

In this version, the apocalyptic Son of Man mentioned in Daniel 7 ("he") is differentiated from the speaker ("me"). The saying does not identify Jesus with the eschatological, Danielic Son of Man. It only says that on Judgment Day, when the Son of Man comes to even up the score, he will frown on those who have laughed off Jesus' summons to repent. We have nothing here that goes an inch beyond the warnings of John the Baptist: "You brood of vipers! Who warned you to flee from the wrath to come? Bear fruit that befits repentance... He who is coming after me is mightier than I... his winnowing fork is in his hand, and he will clear his threshing floor and gather his wheat into the granary, but the chaff he will burn with unquenchable fire!" (Matthew 3:7–8, 11a, 12).

The point is not whether one has joined the John the Baptist personality cult or the Jesus fan club; the point is: have you repented as these prophets warned you to? The criterion for judgment has to do with the *message*, not the *messengers*.

Matthew has split the saying in two and embellished both halves. First, in the same context in which the saying occurred in Mark, just after Peter's Confession, Matthew 16:27 reads: "For the Son of Man is to come with *his* angels in the glory of his Father, and then he will repay every man for what he has done." (Note that the angels, formerly the Father's, now belong to the Son of Man himself.)

---

65 *Ibid.*, p. 30.

The remainder pops up in Chapter 10, Matthew's Missionary Charge section, verses 32–33: "So everyone who acknowledges me before men, I also will acknowledge before my Father who is in heaven; but whoever denies me before men, I also will deny him before my Father who is in heaven." Now the question has shifted to whether or not one has chosen sectarian allegiance to Jesus. It is no longer the Son of Man but explicitly Jesus himself who is to do the judging. And the shibboleth this time *is* allegiance to Jesus.

We are in a later stage of Christian development here. We can measure the same distance as between Muhammad's own summation of Islam as "belief in God and the Last Day" and the official creed, the Shahada, formulated after his death, when, again, the proclaimer had become the proclaimed: "There is no God but Allah, and Muhammad is the apostle of Allah."

But of all this one will learn nothing from Craig Blomberg: his approach is no more fine-tuned than your average InterVarsity sophomore, quoting any and all gospel verses as infallible proof-texts for the true words and opinions of the historical Jesus. Form and redaction criticism, tradition and composition criticism are of no interest to the raw biblicist.

"In addition, Jesus claims to forgive sins in the synoptics, and that's something only God can do. Jesus accepts prayer and worship." [66] Uh, take a look at the text he is thinking of, Mark 2:1–12:

> And when he returned to Capernaum after some days, it was reported that he was at home. And many were gathered together, so that there was no longer room for them, not even about the door; and he was preaching the word to them. And they came, bringing to him a paralytic carried by four men. And when they could not get near him because of the crowd, they removed the roof above him; and when they had made an opening, they let down the pallet on which the paralytic lay. And when Jesus saw their faith, he said to the paralytic, "My son, your sins are forgiven." Now some of the scribes were sitting there, questioning in their hearts, "Why does this man speak thus? It is blasphemy! Who can forgive sins but God alone?" And immediately Jesus, perceiving in his spirit that they thus questioned within themselves, said to them, "Why do you question thus in your hearts? Which is easier, to say to the paralytic, 'Your sins are forgiven,' or to say, 'Rise, take up your pallet and walk'? But that you may know that the Son of man has authority on earth to forgive sins" — he said to the paralytic — "I say to you, rise, take up your pallet and go home." And he rose, and immediately took up the

---

66 *Ibid.*

> pallet and went out before them all; so that they were all amazed and glorified God, saying, "We never saw anything like this!"

How can Blomberg fail to see that the opponents of Jesus are, as in the Gospel of John, depicted as being all mixed up? Mark does not accept their theological premise. Rather, the whole point is to debunk it. If God allows human agents to lift the penalties he has assigned for sins, this must mean he has concurrently forgiven the sins for which he assigned the ailment as punishment. Which is easier? Merely to *say* the sins are forgiven? Or to *prove* it by nullifying their punishment? Plus the fact that Jesus does not say, "I'm taking it on myself to forgive your sins." He uses the "divine passive":[67] he is telling the man that *God* is forgiving his sins. Matthew certainly understood the text this way; look what he adds to the acclamation of the crowd: "they glorified God, *who had given such authority to men*" (Matthew 9:8). Jesus is one of the "men," not the "God."

Every Mother's Son

This last Matthean comment raises anew the 'Son of Man' question, for it was not always a messianic symbol as in Daniel 7. Sometimes, depending on context, the phrase means to specify human beings as opposed either to the deity on the one side or animals on the other. In this very passage, "given such authority to men" seems to comment on 9:6, "So that you may know that the son of man has authority on earth to forgive sins," *i.e.*, as the deity does in heaven. Jesus can pronounce the deity's absolution on sinners, confident that up in heaven God is freely forgiving them as the chief business of his kingdom — the good news of which Jesus preaches.

Similarly, see Matthew 8:20, "Foxes have holes and birds of the air have nests, but the son of man has nowhere to lay his head." Though here made into a statement about Jesus' itinerant ministry, it is plain the original point was the nomadic condition of the human species, for whom there seems no one natural habitat. Finally, if Mark 2:1–12 means to depict Jesus as claiming godhood, does John 20:22–23 mean Jesus is imparting divinity to the disciples, who can henceforth forgive people's sins thanks to the empowerment of the Holy Spirit? Of course not. They are to forgive sins just as Jesus did: with the delegated authority of their common heavenly Father.

---

[67] Joachim Jeremias, *New Testament Theology, Part One: The Proclamation of Jesus*. Trans. John Bowden New Testament Library (London: SCM Press, 1971), "The 'divine passive,'" pp. 9–14.

And let me linger on Daniel 7's throne room vision for a moment. Blomberg says,

> So look at what Jesus is doing by applying the term 'Son of Man' to himself [from Daniel 7:13–14]. This is someone who approaches God himself in the heavenly throne room and is given universal authority and dominion. That makes 'Son of Man' a title of great exaltation, not of mere humanity.[68]

Strobel adds a disembodied voice from William Lane Craig to shore up the point he was hoping Blomberg would put a tad more strongly: "Thus, the claim to be the Son of Man would be in effect a claim to divinity."[69]

Maurice Casey[70] has demonstrated that no Jewish source known to us ever uses 'Son of Man' as a messianic title, though the text and its scene were invoked as a kind of symbol or metaphor for the coming of King Messiah. That is a fine shade of difference, but it does mean that there was no Son-of-Man title for any messianic claimant to apply to himself. He might quote the passage and say something like, "This day this scripture has been fulfilled in your hearing."

Norman Perrin[71] showed that the gospel (and other New Testament) sayings about the Son of Man taking his seat at the right hand of God, then appearing so that every eye shall see him, *etc.*, originated as a midrashic Christian conflation of Old Testament texts, mainly Daniel 7, Zechariah 12:10, and Psalms 110. Such texts were initially applied to Jesus by Christians, which is why they usually occur in the third person, even when our gospel narrators put them on the lips of Jesus himself. Again, William Lane Craig-Blomberg (the interchangeable apologist!) is oblivious of such 'liberal' scholarship, but if our apologists really loved the text for its own sake, enough to dig beneath the superficial sand-box level at which they play in it, they might be less inclined to attribute so glibly all apocalyptic Son-of-Man sayings as self-references by Jesus.

---

68 Blomberg in Strobel, p. 30.

69 William Lane Craig, *The Son Rises: Historical Evidence for the Resurrection of Jesus* (Chicago: Moody Press, 1981), p. 140, cited in Strobel, p. 30.

70 Maurice Casey, *The Son of Man: The Interpretation and Influence of Daniel 7* (London: SPCK, 1979).

71 Norman Perrin, "Mark 14:62: The End Product of a Christian Pesher Tradition?" in Perrin, *A Modern Pilgrimage in New Testament Christology* (Philadelphia: Fortress Press, 1974), pp. 10–22.

So 'Son of Man' was not precisely a title. But did the phrase still perhaps denote divinity? That is, would someone to whom the passage was applied, like Jesus, therefore be designated 'God'?

There is no evidence the rabbis or the apocalyptists so used it during New Testament times, but if one goes back only a little further into Jewish theological history, one discovers that Daniel may indeed have intended his "one like a son of man" to refer to a god, namely Yahweh himself, the Thunder Cloud Rider, the Mighty Man of War.

Daniel Chapter 7 employs an already ancient creation narrative in which the various chaos monsters (unnamed there, but equivalent to the infamous Rahab, Leviathan, Tiamat, *etc.*) arise from the *tehom* (primordial ocean depth) one by one, only to be destroyed by this young deity, whereupon he becomes co-regent or successor to the elderly deity, El Elyon, the Highest God, the white-haired Ancient in Days. The triumphant god is Yahweh, his father El Elyon.

According to Deuteronomy 32:8–9, Yahweh started out as one of the seventy sons of El Elyon, each of whom was given a nation to rule. Yahweh chose Jacob as his inheritance. But subsequently he triumphed over the threatening dragons (Psalms 74:12–17; 89:5–18, *etc.*) and became universal divine ruler in his father's place—exactly as in the cognate mythologies of Marduk and Enlil, Baal and El, Indra and Varuna, *etc.* Finally, under the influence of the Deuteronomic Reform, the priests and prophets sought to identify Yahweh and El Elyon as the same deity (Genesis 14:17–24). But popular religion still had not accepted monotheism even as late as the battle with the Seleucid Hellenizers when fallen Jewish stalwarts were found to have worn the amulets of Semitic gods (those of Jaffa) into battle (2 Maccabees 12:39–40).

Margaret Barker[72] thinks such grassroots Jewish polytheism survived into the time of Jesus, and that when early Christians identified Jesus ('the Lord') with Jehovah ('the LORD'), they knew what they were doing: they viewed Jesus as a recent theophany among men of Yahweh, the Son of God, *i.e.*, of El Elyon.

Why do I bring this up? Simply to grant a point to the apologists: insofar as anyone identified Jesus as corresponding with the Danielic Son of Man figure, they may indeed have been pegging him as Yahweh on earth. But the apologists beg the question of Trintarianism, as if the earliest Christians, or even the historical Jesus himself, already had prescient knowledge of the Nicene Creed. As if they already took for

---

72 Margaret Barker, *The Great Angel: A Study of Israel's Second God* (Louisville: Westminster / John Knox, 1992), pp. 219–231.

granted what the apologists themselves take for granted: the abstruse third-fourth-century concept of Trinitarian Monotheism! And that is one great historical leap into anachronism, as if one were to say Democritus already thought light behaved sometimes as a particle, sometimes as a wave; or as if Anaximander already knew about natural selection. You see, apologists here as everywhere simply take their nineteenth-century faith for granted and read it into the ancient text. Thus if Christians believed Jesus was divine, they must have been Trinitarians!

But I think the most hilarious absurdity Blomberg propounds, and Strobel credulously swallows, is this one:

> Think of the story of Jesus walking on the water, found in Matthew 14:2–33 and Mark 6:45–52. Most English translations hide the Greek by quoting Jesus as saying, 'Fear not, it is I.' Actually, the Greek literally says, 'Fear not, I am.' Those last two words are identical to what Jesus said in John 8:58, when he took upon himself the divine name 'I AM,' which is the way God revealed himself to Moses in the burning bush in Exodus 3:14. So Jesus is revealing himself as the one who has the same divine power over nature as Yahweh, the God of the Old Testament.[73]

As Jason David BeDuhn explains,[74] this reading of the passage is doubly fallacious. First, there is no evidence that any reader of the Septuagint Greek version of the burning bush passage would have come away with the idea that "I am" was supposed to be the name of God. In the Septuagint, what Yahweh says to Moses is this: "'I am the Being [εγω ειμι ο Ων].' And he said, 'Thus shall you say to the sons of Israel, "The Being has sent me to you."' And God said again to Moses, 'Thus shall you say to the sons of Israel, "The Lord God of our fathers, Abraham's God, Isaac's God, and Jacob's God, has sent me to you."'" (Exodus 3:14–15 LXX).

"I am" (εγω ειμι) does not appear there as a name for God. Even if it did, and even if Greek-reading Jews understood the phrase εγω ειμι to be a divine name, it is comical to take the water-treading Jesus to be "claiming to be God." The terror-stricken disciples see a figure drifting toward them over the waves and they think they are seeing a spook. Not that bad a hypothesis, given the circumstances! Jesus hastens to reassure them, "It's only me! Don't worry!"

---

73 Blomberg in Strobel, p. 29.

74 Jason David BeDuhn, *Truth in Translation: Accuracy and Bias in English Translations of the New Testament* (NY: University Press of America, 2003), pp. 107–109.

If Blomberg is right, the disciples are supposed to hear the familiar words anyone would use for "It's me!" and instead think at once of the Exodus passage and then think, "Oh, I get it! He's Jehovah who has power over nature! Sure! I can calm down now!"

As BeDuhn asks, are we supposed to understand the man born blind to be claiming the divine name when he was asked if he were really the blind beggar and he answered, εγω ειμι, "I am he" (John 9:11)? And just look at Peter's response to Jesus' words: "Lord, if it *is* you, *etc.*" In other words, "If you're really Jesus, as you say, and not some ghost, let *me* walk on the waves, too! *I'm* no ghost, so if I stay afloat, that means you're no ghost either."

Matthew certainly thought Jesus meant "It's me," and that Peter needed some proof. Blomberg slanders translators when he accuses them of "hiding the Greek." Actually, the fault is his for twisting a clear text beyond recognition. This comes close to plain charlatanry.

Oh, and does the synoptic Jesus receive worship from mere mortals? I'm guessing Blomberg is thinking of passages like Matthew 14:33: "Those who were in the boat did him homage, saying, 'Truly, you are the Son of God" (*New American Bible*). But the verb προσκυνεω need mean only "kneel down before someone." However, I would say that the disciples' reverent exclamation does push the implication over the line into Christological worship. As such, it is clearly an artificial, churchly addition intended, along with other redactional changes, to make the story into a lesson of Christian faith, not (as at first) an advertisement for a divine Jesus. What was originally the object lesson has now become a presupposition for the new lesson: to inculcate faithful prayer among Christians,[75] not only because of the choral unison in which they all speak, but because Matthew has added it to Mark's original which merely had, "And they were utterly astounded" (Mark 6:51).

Is Blomberg perhaps thinking of Matthew 28:9, in which the women leaving the tomb meet the risen Jesus and bow before him? Matthew has added the whole episode to Mark. He has also added Matthew 28:16–17, where the disciples bow before the risen Jesus even while doubting it is

---

75 Heinz Joachim Held, "Matthew as Interpreter of the Miracle Stories," in Günther Bornkamm, Gerhard Barth, and Hans Joachim Held, *Tradition and Interpretation in Matthew*. Trans. Percy Scott. New Testament Library (Philadelphia: Westminster Press, 1976), p. 272. See also, in the same collection, Gerhard Barth, "Matthew's Understanding of the Law," pp. 113–114.

Jesus they are seeing, which certainly implies they were not worshipping in the sense Blomberg wants.[76]

And can you claim such scenes as documenting the historical Jesus anyway? A far more appropriate scene enabling us to gauge whether the historical Jesus would have accepted worship is Mark 10:17–18: "And as he was setting out on his journey, a man ran up and knelt before him, and asked him, 'Good teacher, what must I do to inherit eternal life?' And Jesus said to him, 'Why do you call me good? No one is good but God alone!'" So zealous is Jesus that God alone receive all glory, that no flesh should boast, including his, he refuses even the polite flattery of an admirer. One can only imagine what such a Jesus would have made of sophistry like Blomberg's.

Blomberg says, "As you can see, there's all sorts of material in the synoptics about the deity of Christ, that then merely becomes more explicit in John's gospel."[77] What is he really saying? John's gospel is full of divine self-declarations by Jesus, but even Blomberg knows they cannot go back to Jesus verbatim, so thick and idiosyncratic is John's idiom. So, as I used to do when I was still playing the snake-oil game of apologetics, he tries to stretch what synoptic texts he can find to make them look like they say the same thing as John. But the desperate lengths to which he must go reveal plainly enough the futility of the attempt.

The synoptics just do not deify Jesus to anything like the extent John does. On their own, they just are not enough to do the job. What job? Being evangelicals, apologists are not just arguing for traditional, orthodox supernaturalism. They are Pietists whose ultimate goal is to get people to "have a little talk with Jesus." So they want to be able to say that the historical Jesus himself said things amounting to: "I'm your God. Won't you take me as your personal savior? Then I can walk with you and talk with you and tell you, you are my own. How about it? You and me?"

---

76 BeDuhn, chapter 4, "Bowing to Bias," pp. 41–49.

77 *Ibid.*, p. 30.

Chapter Two
Testing the Evidence of the Gospels
Do the Gospels Stand Up to Scrutiny?

Reverend Strobel allows Professor Blomberg a bathroom break, then pitches him more wiffle balls. They take the form of eight 'tests.' I can only call Strobel's glowing appraisal a severe case of grade inflation.

1. The Intention Test: The "Intentional Fallacy"?

> *Strobel:* "Were these first-century writers even interested in recording what actually happened?"
>
> *Blomberg:* "Yes, they were… You can see that at the beginning of the gospel of Luke, which reads very much like prefaces to other generally trusted historical and biographical works of antiquity."[78]

Is Blomberg correct? Here is a relevant snippet from Josephus' exceedingly long preface to his *Antiquities of the Jews*:

> As I proceed, therefore, I shall accurately describe what is contained in our records, in the order of time that belongs to them; for I have already promised to do so throughout this undertaking, and this without adding any thing to what is therein contained, or taking away any thing therefrom. (*Antiquities of the Jews*. Preface, 3)[79]

I invite the reader to compare Josephus' results with his stated intent. Take a look at Josephus' version of the Tower of Babel, and how almost *none* of it actually comes from scripture:

> Now it was Nimrod who excited them to such an affront and contempt of God. He was the grandson of Ham, the son of Noah, a bold man, and of great strength of hand. He persuaded them not to ascribe it to God, as if it was through his means they were happy, but to believe that it was their own courage which procured that happiness. He also gradually

[78] Blomberg in Strobel, pp. 39–40.

[79] William Whiston, trans, *The Works of Josephus* (London: Ward, Lock & Co., n.d.), p. 27.

> changed the government into tyranny, seeing no other way of turning men from the fear of God, but to bring them into a constant dependence on his power. He also said he would be revenged on God, if he should have a mind to drown the world again; for that he would build a tower too high for the waters to be able to reach! and that he would avenge himself on God for destroying their forefathers !
>
> Now the multitude were very ready to follow the determination of Nimrod, and to esteem it a piece of cowardice to submit to God; and they built a tower, neither sparing any pains, nor being in any degree negligent about the work: and, by reason of the multitude of hands employed in it, it grew very high, sooner than any one could expect; but the thickness of it was so great, and it was so strongly built, that thereby its great height seemed, upon the view, to be less than it really was. It was built of burnt brick, cemented together with mortar, made of bitumen, that it might not be liable to admit water. When God saw that they acted so madly, he did not resolve to destroy them utterly, since they were not grown wiser by the destruction of the former sinners; but he caused a tumult among them, by producing in them divers languages, and causing that, through the multitude of those languages, they should not be able to understand one another. The place wherein they built the tower is now called *Babylon,* because of the confusion of that language which they readily understood before; for the Hebrews mean by the word *Babel,* confusion. (1:4:2–3)

The systematic rewriting and embellishing demonstrates quite clearly how loosely his results conform to his intent, or to what he thought it was, or wanted the reader to think it was. To say the very least, when one compares the claims of Josephus with the phenomena of Josephus one finds oneself gazing into quite as wide and deep a ravine as does the little stick-figure in the evangelistic tract ("Steps to Peace with God") at the end of the book. You soon begin to realize that stated intention has little necessarily to do with it. Luke's fidelity to the supposed facts may have been as unconsciously loose as Josephus' was. The similar preface does not prove differently.

> Consider the way the gospels are written – in a sober and responsible fashion, with accurate incidental details,[80] with obvious care and

[80] As we will see in a moment, such details are meant to prime the reader to accept the counter-intuitive, the otherwise-implausible when it appears, by feeding him a steady stream of realism up to the point of disclosure, in the hopes that the outlandish new thing will be accepted more readily, like medicine which goes down easier if buffered with sugar. An uncritical fundamentalist instead of

> exactitude. You don't find the outlandish flourishes and blatant mythologizing that you see in a lot of other ancient writings.[81]

You *don't*? How is Blomberg's scanner calibrated that he does not find it completely outrageous when the gospels depict Jesus as defying gravity as he strolls the surface of Lake Tiberias? When he effortlessly transforms water into wine? When he feeds thousands of the hungry with a single tuna sandwich? When he comes back to life days after death? When he launches into the sky like a booster rocket?

You have to understand something about the device of *verisimilitude*: the real-seemingness of a narrative (or a painting, a film, *etc.*). It is predicated, each and every time, not on what actually seems to be the case in external, public reality (that would be the principle of analogy) but rather on what readers/viewers have come to *expect*. The text, to convince, must seem to reflect the reality the reader *thinks* is real:[82]

Both Blomberg and Strobel (though the latter affects an unconvincing pose as a skeptic) belong to a religious "plausibility structure,"[83] a supportive peer group whose sharing of beliefs and constant allusions to them buttress and fortify each member's faith.[84] The view of things, the map of reality, they share may be called their "cognitive world" or "symbolic universe."[85] Overlaying it atop the events and reports of everyday, the believers possess a comprehensive interpretive paradigm.[86]

---

a critic, Blomberg is happy to be gulled and grifted by this most elementary of literary illusions.

81 *Ibid.*, p. 40.

82 I recall my painting teacher, the late, great Leon DeLeeuw, reminding the class: "Don't tell me, 'But the cloud really *was* shaped that way!' That's not what comes to mind when people think of clouds, so they won't accept this as a good picture of a cloud."

83 Peter L. Berger and Thomas Luckmann, *The Social Construction of Reality: An Introduction to the Sociology of Knowledge* (Garden City: Doubleday Anchor Books, 1967), pp. 154–155; Peter L. Berger, *The Sacred Canopy: Elements of a Sociological Theory of Religion*. (Garden City: Doubleday Anchor Books, 1969), p. 46

84 Thomas V. Luckmann, *The Invisible Religion: The Problem of Religion in Modern Society*. (NY: Macmillan, 1970), p. 65.

85 Berger and Luckmann, *Social Construction of Reality*, p. 95*ff*

86 *Ibid.*, p. 98: "This nomic function of the symbolic universe for individual experience may be described quite simply by saying that it 'puts everything in its right place.'"

Things will seem to them "possible," "probable," "plausible" (or not) depending upon the value assigned in terms of the cognitive universe.

Fundamentalists like Strobel and Blomberg have an ironclad system in which every miracle reported in the Bible, but none outside the canon, seems automatically as plausible as the notion that a presidential election will be held every four years, or that the ingredients of a peach pie, when cooked, will not issue in an apple pie. In short, they are biblical inerrantists. Blomberg would not be allowed to teach in his Conservative Baptist seminary if he did not sign a statement of faith affirming inerrantism. But when he takes such a sectarian cognitive universe, with its distinctive standards, for granted in what purports to be an open discussion on a level playing field, well, let's call it a home team advantage. Blomberg is playing by his own rules and trying to get his opponents to play by them, too, though without noticing.

Despising Prophesying

We find ourselves already deep inside the labyrinth of Fundamentalist apologetics, and not merely of Christian faith. That becomes evident again when we read of Strobel's and Blomberg's distaste for the possibility that the Spirit of the risen Christ produced some or many treasured gospel sayings after the exit of the historical Jesus from the earthly stage. It is strange for a defense of the faith to begin by denigrating faith.

> *Strobel:* "They say that early Christians frequently believed that the physically departed Jesus was speaking through them with messages, or 'prophecies,' for their church ... Since these prophecies were considered as authoritative as Jesus' own words when he was alive on earth, the early Christians didn't distinguish between these newer sayings and the original words of the historical Jesus. As a result, the gospels blend these two types of material, so we don't really know what goes back to the historical Jesus and what doesn't."[87]

This book is called *The Case for Christ*, and it seems like Strobel sees this theory (which he summarizes quite well) as some sort of charge against Christ, some argument against faith in Christ, which he looks to Blomberg to rebut. Why should that be?

Suppose some of the gospel sayings *do* stem from Christian prophecy such as we find on display in the first three chapters of Revelation: why would that make any difference to the pious gospel reader? Must he assume that the early Christian prophets were charlatans or deceivers? Why would it lessen the value of these fine sayings if we were to come

---

87 Strobel, pp. 41–42.

to regard them as spoken by prophets in the name of the risen Jesus? Do we disparage the oracles of Isaiah because Jesus didn't say them? Is 1 Corinthians chapter 13 without value because Jesus Christ did not compose it? What would make such Christian prophecies less valuable than the words of the earthly Jesus?

Strobel is grossly confusing the historian's issues with those of the believer. True, if some or many gospel sayings came from Agabus instead of Jesus, the historian has a lot of hard work ahead of him (though it is fascinating work, and hardly futile in my opinion). But what is the believer's problem? Aren't evangelical Christians committed equally to taking whatever they find between the covers of the Bible seriously? Do we have to prove that Jesus said it? I hope not, because there's no chance he said anything outside the gospels! Is all that material worthless, as Strobel seems to suppose historically secondary 'Jesus sayings' are?

I'm not adopting some pose here. I really do not get it. Unless, again, there is some desire to be able to have Jesus himself making his evangelistic invitation to the reader, since otherwise, the gospel reader will not be having a "relationship with Jesus."

Blomberg seems just as eager to lay that ghost:

> There are occasions when early Christian prophecy is referred to, but it's always distinguished from what the Lord has said. For example, in 1 Corinthians 7 Paul clearly distinguishes when he has a word from the Lord and when he is quoting the historical Jesus. In the Book of Revelation one can clearly distinguish the handful of times in which Jesus directly speaks to this prophet… and when John is recounting his own inspired visions.[88]

Blomberg has not thought the matter through; he has merely inherited one more bogus apologetic. Notice how he completely begs the question: the New Testament Christians *always* distinguished prophecy from historical Jesus quotes. How exactly does Blomberg know this? He thinks he can name a couple of instances in which a writer made such a distinction. That most certainly proves nothing as to whether *all* Christians *always* were so careful. Obviously, it may be that John the Revelator made such a distinction and that some unnamed prophet who coined the powerful saying, "If anyone would be my disciple, let him take up his cross and come after me," did not. Blomberg simply presupposes his conclusion.

But take a closer look. What is Paul saying in 1 Corinthians 7? "Now concerning the unmarried, I have no command of the Lord, but I give

88 Blomberg in Strobel, p. 42.

my opinion as one who by the Lord's mercy is trustworthy." This is verse 25. Paul contrasts *not* a prophetic word of wisdom with a historical Jesus quote, but rather his own sanctified judgment with some kind of "command of the Lord," a vague term that partakes of the very ambiguity Blomberg is trying to dispel. For no one can decide whether Paul means a quote or a prophecy, since he elsewhere speaks even of his own inspired rulings in the exact same terms: "If anyone thinks that he is a prophet or a pneumatic, he ought to acknowledge that *what I am writing to you is a command of the Lord*" (1 Corinthians 14:37).

And how strange that, if Paul was conversant, as apologists apodictically assert he was, with the Synoptic sayings tradition, that he *didn't* have a command of the Lord Jesus on the topic of the unmarried, since Matthew 19:10–12 provides a doozy:

> 19:10 The disciples say to him, "If such is the man's situation with the wife, it is not prudent to marry in the first place!" 11 And he said to them, "Not everyone accepts this saying, 12 for there are eunuchs who were born thus from a mother's womb, and there are eunuchs who were made eunuchs by others, and there are eunuchs who made themselves eunuchs for the sake of gaining the kingdom of the heavens. As for anyone capable of accepting it, let him accept it."

This is why some of us think it more likely that materials from the epistles eventually made their way into the gospels attributed to Jesus, regardless of who originally said them.

Back to 1 Corinthians chapter 7: in verse 10 Paul says, "To the married I give charge, not I, but the Lord, that the wife should not separate from her husband, *etc.*" He seems to fear that what he is about to say may not be taken seriously enough, so he makes sure his readers understand that he is sure he has God's will on the matter and no tentative opinion that they may take or leave as they see fit. To find here a reference either to Christ-channeling or to historical Jesus quoting, much less how to tell the difference, seems like reading an awful lot into the text.

In verse 12 Paul is back to more slippery issues that do not allow absolute answers: "To the rest I say, not the Lord, that if any brother has a wife who is not a believer, but she is wiling to live with him, *etc.*" Does it not seem apparent that what we are dealing with here is simply a matter of levels of certainty depending upon the clarity of the situation? When things are inherently 'iffy' one cannot simply lay down the law. But in clearer matters, one can, with divine authority. What Jesus of Nazareth may or may not have said is not in view.

Blomberg appears confused about Revelation as well. He says... what? That John the Revelator distinguished between "the words of the Son of God whose eyes are as a flame of fire" and the visions he saw of angels and devils, Beasts and catastrophes? Well, sure. Is Blomberg afraid someone will think Jesus narrated the whole thing to John? Again, his own words belie the distinction he is trying to preserve.

The death blow to this dull apologetical saw is the mere fact of the mass of Gnostic gospels. What are these but proof in black and white that Christians who believed they spoke the revelations of the ascended Christ had no hesitation about ascribing their own revelations to Jesus back on earth? They had no more scruples about doing it than Elizabeth Claire Prophet (her real name!), Helen Schucman, and others today who dare to fill whole books with unreadable gibberish which they attribute to Jesus. They had no more reticence than fundamentalist propagandists who post highway billboards with inspirational slogans like "Count my wounds to see how much I love you" and put Jesus' name underneath them, as if he had said them in some ancient gospel. None of these instances ever occurs to apologists, because for them the whole game board is the canon of scripture, and nothing else counts.

But the worst is yet to come.

1. The Intention Test and the Intentional Fallacy

Blomberg plays what a number of evangelicals seem to consider the trump card against form-criticism.

> But the strongest argument [*against Christian prophecies having been ascribed to the historical Jesus*] is what we never find in the gospels. After Jesus' ascension there were a number of controversies that threatened the early church – should believers be circumcised, how should speaking in tongues be regulated, how to keep Jew and Gentile united, what are the appropriate roles for women in ministry, whether believers could divorce non-Christian spouses. These issues could have been conveniently resolved if the early Christians had simply read back into the gospels what Jesus had told them from the world beyond. But this never happened. The continuance of these controversies demonstrates that Christians were interested in distinguishing between what happened during Jesus' lifetime and what was debated later in the churches.[89]

---

[89] *Ibid.*, p. 42.

Blomberg sounds like a Creationist (and to scholars, I'm afraid that is a very dirty word) denying the existence of transitional forms when in fact there are plenty to choose from. According to form critics, there are numerous places where the concerns of the early church have snuck back into the gospel tradition, allowing one party to the dispute (sometimes both!) to pull rank on behalf of their opinion. In fact, it is the very fact that we can see these issues still debated outside the gospels among the early Christians that tells us their occurrence *in* the gospels is anachronistic! *If Jesus were known to have addressed these questions, why would there still be debate?*

Was Jesus not retroactively made to mouth someone's opinion on the issue of whether Gentile converts must eat only kosher food, as in Galatians 2:12–14? That must be the point of Mark 7:14–19, where we find an echo of Romans 14:14: a rationalistic repudiation of the idea that non-kosher food renders one unclean. Must they accept circumcision? That must be the point of Thomas 53: "His disciples say to him, 'Is circumcision worthwhile or not?' He says to them, 'If it were, men would be born that way automatically. But the true circumcision in spirit has become altogether worthwhile.'"

You say the gospels do not make Jesus address the issue of the legitimacy of a gospel mission to Gentiles, debated in Acts 10 and 11? As Peter's vision shows, the sticking point was the necessity of Jewish missionaries eating Gentile food. But Jesus addresses it plainly in Luke 10:7, where the seventy, in contrast to the twelve (in other words, future missionaries to the Gentiles), are told to "eat and drink what they set before you." The Gentile Mission as a whole? What do you think the Great Commissions (Matthew 28:19–20; Mark 16:15; Luke 24:47–48; John 20:21), not to mention the distance-healings of the children of Gentiles (Mark 7:24–30; Matthew 8:5–13), are all about?

Table fellowship with Gentiles, as in Antioch? That's why Jesus is depicted as dining with sinners. Eating meat offered previously to idols? Someone must have realized that Jesus could not plausibly be pictured addressing this in Jewish Palestine, so they left this one in the form of a post-Easter prophecy (Revelation 2:20), a concern for verisimilitude not often observed. Paul is concerned that Gentile Christians not cause Jewish converts (neophytes, babes) to stumble by railroading them into disregarding lingering Jewish dietary scruples (Romans 14:13). The same language, and I think, implicitly the same issue, occurs in Mark 9:42. The role of women in the community is the point of Luke 10:38–42, where, depending on how one understands it, the issue is either women serving the Eucharist (Martha)[90] or women embracing the stipended, celibate life as 'widows' and 'virgins' (Mary).[91] Speaking in tongues? Matthew 6:7 ("When you pray, do not say '*batta*" as the heathen do.") is against it; the late Mark 16:17 ("they will speak with new tongues.") is for it.

If these issues had really been settled by Jesus, we should expect to find them in the gospels *but not in the epistles*. The fact that they occur in the epistles means they were being hashed out by Christians with no directive from the historical Jesus. In fact, these issues couldn't even have surfaced in his day! They only wind up in the gospels because somebody got the bright idea of ascribing their opinion to Jesus via prophecy and so nuking his opponent. But then the opponent produced his own Jesus-prophecy! Who wins? The two prophets are locked in a stalemate, since neither can prove his word from Jesus is more than a subjective impression.

The prophetic arms race next escalated to producing 'forgotten' or hitherto-silenced sayings alleged to have been spoken by Jesus while on earth but somehow unknown or forgotten till now (the point, I suspect, of Matthew 10:27 ["What I say to you in the dark, repeat it in the light of day. And what you hear whispered in your ear, proclaim from the housetops."] or Luke 12:3 ["Therefore, whatever you said under cover of darkness will be heard in the light of day and whatever you whispered in someone's ear in the private rooms will be proclaimed from the roof tops."]).

This was objective! Jesus had said this with others there to hear it! But then nothing was stopping the clever opponent from fabricating his own newly-discovered Jesus-saying! And that is how we ended up with the gospel Jesus offering two opinions about divorce, three about fasting, two about calculating the signs of the end, *etc.*[92]

2. The Ability Test: Orality—Or Reality?

> [T]he definition of memorization was more flexible back then. In studies of cultures with oral traditions, there was freedom to vary how much

---

[90] Elisabeth Schüssler Fiorenza, *In Memory of Her: A Feminist Theological Reconstruction of Christian Origins* (NY: Crossroad, 1984), p. 165.

[91] Origen, *Scholia in Lucam* 353.

[92] "It soon became evident that each point of view, each party, each proponent of a doctrine gave the form of hadith to his theses, and that consequently the most contradictory tenets had come to wear the garb of such documentation." Ignaz Goldziher, *Introduction to Islamic Theology and Law*. Modern Classics in Near Eastern Studies. Trans. Andras and Ruth Hamori (Princeton: Princeton University Press, 1981), p. 39.

> of the story was told on any given occasion – what was included, what was left out, what was paraphrased, what was explained, and so forth. One study suggested that in the ancient Middle East, anywhere from ten to forty percent of any given retelling of ancient tradition could vary from one occasion to the next. However, there were always fixed points that were unalterable, and the community had the right to intervene and correct the storyteller if he erred on those important aspects of the story."[93]

Well, this is really a remarkable admission! If this is how Blomberg thinks the gospel tradition was transmitted, where does he still differ from the form-critics? He has opened a door that swings wide, and it should henceforth be impossible to catch it and reduce it to the mere crack the rest of his apologetics are willing to leave open. Tell me, if you can, just which those non-negotiable points are, where no variation would be allowed? I suppose they would be those on which we find no variation. And what are those? That Jesus existed? That he was a male? That he performed miracles in general but none in specific? That he was crucified at some point? That he rose from the dead and appeared to somebody or other in varying circumstances? This tactic backfires, reducing the "reliable gospel tradition" to Spartan, practically Kierkegaardian, proportions.

But maybe we do not need to worry about it. It is all, once again, highly circular anyway. Blomberg simply ignores manifest signs of differences between the gospels being the result of literary redaction, at the mercy of editorial creativity and answerable to no audience of children who must have the bedtime tale told identically every night. He simply asserts that the Balkan coffeehouse poets recorded by Albert Lord,[94] Milman Parry,[95] and their students, used the same practices as the hypothetical gospel tradents. Who knows?

Blomberg betrays the fallacy of his argument when he says, incredibly, that "One study suggested that in the ancient Middle East," so-and-so happened. How was this study undertaken? With the aid of a time machine? No, all orality studies (a growth industry these days) can do is to suggest models that *might* parallel the way they did things centuries ago. One dare not simply assume the gospel tradition was passed on the same way as Balkan coffee shop singers and hillside shepherds plied their trade.

---

93 *Ibid.*, p. 43.

94 Albert Lord, *The Singer of Tales* (Cambridge: Harvard University Press, 1960).

95 Milman Parry, *The Making of Homeric Verse: The Collected Papers of Milman Parry* (NY: Oxford University Press, 1987).

And I don't know why Blomberg and other recent apologists want to in the first place! Goodbye gospel accuracy!

We weren't there, so we don't know what the unknown passers-on of the gospel traditions may have done. But there is a possible analogy much closer in space and time than these Balkan Starbucks bards, and that is the propagation among early Muslim savants of spurious hadith of the prophet Muhammad. Here is a case which seems closely to match that of the early church: the great prophet has departed, leaving behind a community cherishing his words and, especially as times change, thirsty, if possible, for further guidance from the same source. So the holy men fabricated vast oceans of false hadith, 'traditional' sayings, ostensibly oral reports of what Muhammad did or said on some point not explicitly dealt with in the Koran.

It became clear to Muslim scholars themselves that their Prophet could not possibly stand at the beginning of all this material, so they began to sift them, in the process compiling six major collections of supposedly authentic hadith. But each is still a continent of material, simply too much material. There is no doubt that these were holy men, as witnessed by the teaching contained in the very hadith they created. It was a generally accepted legal fiction.

"In nothing do we see pious men more given to falsehood than in 'Tradition,'" *i.e.*, *hadith.*[96] It was, I think, not some precocious zeal for historical accuracy that motivated the traditionists abu Muslim, al-Bukhari and the others to issue their compilations, but rather the same as that which had caused Caliph Uthman to collect, collate, and standardize all extant copies of the Koran: a concern to provide a uniform source of authority and so to narrow the hitherto-impossible range of intra-Muslim debate. They needed a smaller game board and fewer pieces, or no one could ever win the theological game.

The history of the rapid, massive fabrication of hadith in the name of the Prophet provides an exact parallel to the scenario envisioned by the form-critics. I think that what is known to have happened in the one

---

[96] So said Asim al-nabil, who died in the 212th year after the Hegira, and, almost verbatim, by Yahya ibn Said, who died in the 192nd year. In Alfred Guillaume, *The Traditions of Islam: An Introduction to the Study of the Hadith Literature* (London: Oxford University Press, 1924), p. 78. See also Goldziher, *Introduction to Islamic Theology and Law*, pp. 38–39; G.H.A. Juynboll, *Muslim Tradition: Studies in Chronology, Provenance and Authorship of Early Hadith.* Cambridge Studies in Islamic Civilization (NY: Cambridge University Press, 1983); Edward Sell, *The Faith of Islam* (London: SPCK, rev. ed., 1907), pp. 98–99.

case may very well have happened in the other in a very similar religious milieu.

We're the Telephone Company. We Don't Care. We Don't Have to.

Apologists are stung when they hear people compare the process of oral transmission of Jesus' sayings to the common party game Telephone. In this game the first player whispers a sentence to the next, who whispers it, as well as he can recall it, to the next, and so on around the circle, until the last one repeats the message aloud. Typically it bears little resemblance to the original. I cannot see what is wrong with the analogy, except insofar as participants in the game might make no real effort to repeat what they were told, but I assume they do; otherwise, what's the point of the game? Naturally, Blomberg cannot afford to let the analogy stand. He somehow knows that the early tradition process was not like this.

> The community would constantly be monitoring what was said [*of Jesus and his teaching*] and intervening to make corrections along the way. That would preserve the integrity of the message... And the result would be very different from that of a childish game of telephone.[97]

Where, one may ask, is the evidence, *any* evidence, for *this*? It is sheer assertion, the way apologists *wish* it had been. And, ironically, *it is a case of Blomberg doing the very thing he is arguing the earliest Christians did* not *do: manufacturing history' to meet their theological needs.*

3. The Character Test: Your Cheatin' Art

Strobel winds up and lobs another softball to Blomberg, who has put down his caffeine and is holding his comfortable old catcher's mitt, its shape long since accommodated to the familiar shape of the ball. Strobel lets it waft: "Was there any evidence of dishonesty or immorality that might taint their ability or willingness to transmit history accurately?"

Blomberg lets it nest in his welcoming palm: "We simply do not have any reasonable evidence to suggest they were anything but people of great integrity... In terms of honesty, in terms of truthfulness, in terms of virtue and morality, these people had a track record that should be envied."[98]

97 Blomberg in Strobel, p. 44.

98 *Ibid.*, p. 45.

Blomberg is so practiced at circular arguments, he ought to list his religious preference as 'Whirling Dervish.' His glowing estimate of the moral perfection of the New Testament tradents and writers reduces to his controlling belief in biblical inerrancy. It is just another way of putting the same dogma. It *has* to be, because there is no evidence. What does he think we know about the moral consciences and behaviors of these ancient people? He 'knows' they were great truth tellers because they told us what is in the Bible, which we believe to be inerrantly true. The only evidence we have of their truth-telling is our evaluation of what they wrote, and you can see Blomberg needs no convincing on that score. He is whirling.

Consider what we know (or do not know) about the New Testament Christians. It is virtually nothing. Well, let's see: James and John are said to have wanted to summon fire from heaven to roast Samaritans who withdrew the welcome mat. That would imply they were hopelessly insane (picture somebody actually thinking they could call down heavenly fire…!), but they still might be sincere in thinking they could do it. John told an itinerant exorcist to cease and desist using the trademarked name of Jesus, but that has nothing to do with honesty or dishonesty. But there is Peter who lies a blue streak about not knowing Jesus. Ah!, Blomberg will protest, that was before he was reformed by the Holy Spirit! So then we can trust such Christians when they write scripture because they must have done so under the divine afflatus of the Holy Spirit? Around and around goes Blomberg: he is only asserting inspiration and consequent inerrancy yet again.

Paul tells us Peter, Barnabas, and other elders of the Antiochene Church were carried away with hypocrisy when James' representatives arrived to see them eating with Gentiles (Galatians 2). His whole argument in Galatians is based on his charge that the Pillars (John bar Zebedee, James the Just, and Simon Peter) reneged on their original agreement that Gentiles need not keep kosher. Paul is always referring to the insincerity of false brethren who seek to make trouble for him, to spy out and sabotage Christian freedom (Galatians 6:12–13; Philippians 1:15–17). It is not hard to imagine that some of these Christians and their transmission of Jesus-traditions might be subject to these dubious motives and character flaws.

Oh, Blomberg will assure us, these foes of Paul, villains though they were, were not New Testament tradents or writers, so they don't count. Sheer supposition, I say! In fact, whoever had Jesus insist that Christians were wrong who taught freedom from the Law (Matthew 5:17–19) belongs among the very ranks condemned as false brethren in Galatians, for this was their chief 'sin.'

If one is not wearing the smoked goggles of inerrantism and apologetics, one begins to detect fairly important signs of imposture in the gospels. For instance, it is easy to explain why Josephus would not have taken much notice of Jesus if all the public knew of him was his healings and exorcisms, since such deeds were as common then as they are now on certain cable networks.

The public is not said ever to have witnessed spectacular scenes such as Jesus multiplying food (it never says they knew where it came from); walking on water, being transfigured, stilling the storm, or appearing alive after his execution. So one can hardly blame Josephus for not knowing of these things and mentioning them.

But… *wait* a second! Is this coincidence? *Or are these things said to have happened in private precisely in order to explain away the lack of evidence resulting from their never having happened in the first place?*

It was an embarrassment to Christians that, if their man was truly the Messiah, Elijah had not appeared to prepare his way, as Malachi predicted. One apologetic argument was that he *had* appeared, only figuratively, in the form of John the Baptist. The trouble here was that 'Elijah's' coming thus became itself a matter of faith instead of evidence for faith. This lame apologetic was soon replaced by the assertion that the selfsame Elijah, the hirsute old Tishbite himself, *had* appeared in person — only he was seen by no more than four people, and that for only a few minutes!

I guess you had to be there. Too bad you weren't.

Even Christians must have found this disturbing: "Why didn't I ever hear of this before? If I had, I'd never have tried to convince anyone that Elijah's return was fulfilled in John! What gives?" Oh, uh, er, you see, Jesus told the disciples to keep the matter to themselves for the foreseeable future! Yeah, *that*'s the ticket.

When fanciful Gnostic texts claim to represent secret teaching vouchsafed only to, say, Matthias, Thomas, and Bartholomew, apologists, like all scholars, have no trouble seeing through the claim as a fraudulent gimmick later Gnostics used to pin their own innovations on Jesus. Surely the same thing is going on in the case of the Transfiguration.

And let's not forget Mark's Empty Tomb story. How does Mark know what the young man at the tomb said to Mary and the other women? He himself says very clearly that they told no one of the young man and his words. *Mark knows it because he invented it.* He is the 'omniscient narrator'—of fiction. Now fiction is not fraud, but he does add fraud on top of fiction when he puts the story forth with the women's silence as a way of explaining why no one had ever heard of the Empty Tomb story until his late date.[99]

Of course I realize Blomberg will be able to offer his own harmonizations in order to reconcile this surely apparent chicanery with his dogmatic assumption that Mark must have been at least honest if he was to be inerrant. But I think any impartial reader will see for himself what the 'keep-mum' element of both stories, the Transfiguration and the Empty Tomb, naturally implies. And the same goes for the appearances of the risen Jesus — in locked rooms, behind closed doors, to small groups of friends and sympathizers! Too bad you weren't there! You'll just have to take my word for it! Instead, I say, "Be wise as serpents" so you can tell when someone is not being "as innocent as a dove."

Second Peter is not a gospel, but it does contain a gospel scene, the Transfiguration again, and the writer's pants were certainly smoldering! He claims to be Peter yet later (3:2) speaks of the apostles as being figures of the remote past who prophesied the events current at the time of his writing. He knows not merely Pauline teaching but the collected letters of Paul ("all his letters") and considers them "scripture." He tries to explain his way out of the delay of the second coming in view of the death of the whole founding generation of Christians (of which he is ostensibly a member!). His Greek is impossibly different from that of 1 Peter to which he claims to be penning a sequel, not to mention way too complex for a rude Galilean fisherman (Acts 4:13).

Second Peter is a pious fraud if ever there was one. And there have been many. No one with any knowledge of early or medieval Christianity can be unaware of the almost conventional use of pious frauds, holy forgeries, aimed, ironically, to buttress faith. Now I am not begging the question by referring here to biblical documents. I mean, aside from that.

Take the spurious Donation of Constantine, or the Letter of Lentullus describing Jesus' personal appearance, or the Letter from Heaven,[100] ostensibly by Jesus himself! And once we see that, there is just no reason to deny that well-meaning Christians could commit forgery, if they would

---

99 Alfred Loisy, *The Birth of the Christian Religion*. Trans. L.P. Jacks (London: George Allen & Unwin, 1948), p. 91: "The concluding statement 'they said nothing to any man, because they were afraid,' has the simple and very evident object of explaining how the discovery of the empty tomb was unknown to anybody until the moment here recorded by him."

100 Edgar J. Goodspeed, *Famous Biblical Hoaxes, or Modern Apocrypha* (Grand Rapids: Baker Book House, 1956), Chapter Eight, "The Letter from Heaven," pp. 70–75.

even have considered that word appropriate. In fact, I would (forgive me for saying so) point to the opportunistic special pleading of Christian apologists themselves as blatant cases of people who consider themselves to be good, honest Christians, saying whatever they think they have to in order to attain a higher end: the conversion of their hearers.

Blomberg imagines we know much, *much* more about the disciples than we do. Keep in mind that the very names of the supposedly so-important Twelve do not quite agree from one gospel to another, and that by far most never emerge from those lists to become anything more than mere names. What do we know of Simon the Zealot? Had he been a member of the revolutionary Zealot faction? Or does the epithet merely denote he was a "zealot for the Law" (Acts 21:20). We have nothing but the name to go on. Who was "Judas not Iscariot"? Who was Thaddaeus? Lebbaeus? Or were they all three different names for the same man? Who was Matthew? Bartholomew? Nathaniel? Apologists merely assert that Nathaniel equals Bartholomew because one takes the other's place from one list to another. And James bar Alphaeus—? Was Philip the same as Philip the Evangelist? Who was this Andrew?

Simon Peter occurs only as a literary foil for Jesus. He is like Ananda, the Buddha's dim-witted chief disciple who always comes up with a bright idea which the Buddha must correct. Peter is Doctor Watson, whose thick-pated questions occasion Holmes's patient explanations — for the benefit of the reader! All such stories are the equivalents of those cloudy, dotted-line thought balloons in comic strips, or echoing voice-overs in old movies. They are nothing but literary devices for glossing the text.

This means that *none of them are historical*! So we really know not a darn thing about Peter. Not even that he denied Jesus. As Loisy reasoned long ago, it is very likely that the story was simply an anti-Petrine slur put about by his ecclesiastical rivals.[101]

Consider the naiveté of apologists who insist that the preservation of Peter's moment of shameful weakness proves the honesty of the accounts: who else could the story [*if we suppose it true*] have come from except Peter himself? And if he was willing to be so ruthlessly honest about his own failure, why not trust him on everything else? But we do not know where this story came from. It does not matter if our Sunday School

[101] Loisy, *Birth of the Christian Religion*, pp. 82, 102: "Exegetes have made it a merit in Peter that he himself revealed his weakness, which the world would never have known if he had held his tongue. There are better grounds for believing that the incident is in line with other fictions invented to belittle an apostle who became the grand authority of Jewish Christianity" (p. 102).

teacher told us it came from Peter; there is simply no way to know. What an apologetical corner!

Either the story is trustworthy, in which case Peter's credibility is hopelessly shot; or it is a slander from enemies, in which case we can no longer cite it as attesting Peter's later honesty!

Blomberg's praise for the sterling character of these people, who for us are but names on a list (on inconsistent lists, at that!), is sheer imagination. It reduces to yet another form of the old circular argument, "The Bible is true, because it says so in the Bible." Just substitute "Bible writers are by definition trustworthy, so we know they told the truth about Jesus. And how do we know they were so honest? Hey, they wrote the Bible! They had to be!"

To the Death!

"They were willing to live out their beliefs even to the point of ten of the remaining disciples being put to grisly deaths, which shows great character."[102] Just like Joseph Smith, right? He was lynched in the Nauvoo jail. His teaching and practice of polygamy as well as his attempt to suppress a (Mormon!) newspaper criticizing him for it, led to his terminal neck-tie party.

We know how and why Joseph Smith died. What do we know about how the disciples met their ends? Acts 12:1–2 tells us that Herod Agrippa put James son of Zebedee to death. Mark 10:39 tells us implicitly and Papias explicitly that John, James' brother was executed alongside him, though later legend has John live on for decades, as indeed he may have, since our evidence is contradictory. We just don't know. Tertullian thought that persecutors tried to boil John in oil but that to him it was only a warm bath. You can see already that we are not on firm ground.

Were not Peter and Paul both martyred in Rome at Nero's command? Maybe, maybe not. Here is our earliest (dated variously between 80 and 140 CE) witness, make of it what you will:

> Let us set before us the noble examples which belong to our generation. By reason of jealousy and envy the greatest and most righteous pillars of the Church were persecuted, and contended even unto death. Let us set before our eyes the good Apostles. There was Peter who by reason of unrighteous jealousy endured not one but many labors, and thus having borne his testimony went to his appointed place of glory. By reason of jealousy and strife Paul by his example pointed out the prize of patient

102 Blomberg in Strobel, p. 45.

> endurance. After that he had been seven times in bonds, had been driven into exile, had been stoned, had preached in the East and in the West, he won the noble renown which was the reward of his faith, having taught righteousness unto the whole world and having reached the farthest bounds of the West; and when he had borne his testimony before the rulers, so he departed from the world and went unto the holy place, having been found a notable pattern of patient endurance. (1 Clement 5:1–6)

I would suggest that, not only is this report pretty skimpy, as well as based on what little we learn in the New Testament (*i.e.*, not incorporating any outside knowledge or memory), but, contrary to popular exegesis, *it does not even say Peter and Paul were martyred*, only that, having worked much and endured much, they finally went to their heavenly reward. So where do we get the idea of Peter and Paul perishing in the Neronian persecution? Here is our earliest account, from the second-century *Acts of Paul*:

> Then Paul stood with his face to the east and lifted up his hands unto heaven and prayed a long time, and in his prayer he conversed in the Hebrew tongue with the fathers, and then stretched forth his neck without speaking. And when the executioner struck off his head, milk spurted upon the cloak of the soldier. And the soldier and all that were there present when they saw it marveled and glorified God which had given such glory unto Paul: and they went and told Caesar what was done.
>
> And when he heard it, while he marveled long and was in perplexity, Paul came about the ninth hour, when many philosophers and the centurion were standing with Caesar, and stood before them all and said: Caesar, behold, I, Paul, the soldier of God, am not dead, but live in my God. But unto thee shall many evils befall and great punishment, thou wretched man, because thou hast shed unjustly the blood of the righteous, not many days hence. And having so said Paul departed from him. But Nero hearing it and being greatly troubled commanded the prisoners to be loosed, and Patroclus also and Barsabbas and them that were with him.
>
> And as Paul charged them, Longus and Cestus the centurion went early in the morning and approached with fear unto the grave of Paul. And when they were come thither they saw two men praying, and Paul betwixt them, so that they beholding the wondrous marvel were amazed, but Titus and Luke being stricken with the fear of man when they saw Longus and Cestus coming toward them, turned to flight. But they pursued after them, saying: We pursue you not for death but for life, that ye may give it unto us, as Paul promised us, whom we saw just now

> standing betwixt you and praying. And when they heard that, Titus and Luke rejoiced and gave them the seal in the Lord, glorifying the God and Father of our Lord Jesus Christ.

So, let's get this straight: Paul was beheaded, causing a jet of milk to spurt up. Then he rose from the dead and appeared to Nero, then to a couple of his own disciples. This is our earliest source for the martyrdom of Paul. And the other Apocryphal Acts and even later church-foundation legends are even more fantastic. I submit to you that we really have no evidence about the final fates of the disciples, whoever they may have been.

4. The Consistency Test: Harmonizing and Homogenizing

Apologists, it seems to me, are constantly engaged in a double game, a game of "Heads I Win, Tales You Lose," especially when it comes to the vexing business of intergospel contradictions. Listen to the famous Vaudeville team of Strobel and Blomberg (though we might quote almost the same argument from many apologists, who have it from common tradition).

Mister Interlocutor: "Ironically, ... if the gospels had been identical to each other, word for word, this would have raised charges that the authors had conspired among themselves to coordinate their stories in advance, and that would have cast doubt on them."

Mister Bones: "That's right... If the gospels were too consistent, that in itself would invalidate them as independent witnesses. People would then say we really only have one testimony that everybody else is just parroting."[103]

Strobel fancies himself a Robin Hood of crusading reporters, but Blomberg is supposed to be a highly trained seminary professor of New Testament. Yet here he has reverted to Sunday School. Surely he knows about basic source criticism and redaction criticism? Even Plymouth Brethren member and evangelical New Testament scholar F.F. Bruce (who wrote his own share of apologetics) accepted the Two Document Hypothesis, or Markan Priority, to wit: Matthew and Luke overlap Mark and each other to such an exact degree (most differences appearing to be intentional edits) that they must be interdependent documents. They are anything but "independent witnesses." If Blomberg supposes they are, then he is more deeply entrenched in sectarian 'rabbinics' than I had thought.

---

103 Strobel, p. 45.

The Synoptic gospels *are* way too close to be independent witnesses. There is just no way their vast verbal similarity (and the editorial character of their differences) could be the result of a process of oral transmission such as Blomberg himself describes.

Here we glimpse a rare, off-guard moment of honesty, where the apologist at least alludes to what his genuine, default convictions are, no matter what he may seem to believe in order to ape the scholarly lingo for public relations reasons. Yes, after all, the evangelists *are* like four different witnesses to an auto accident, *yada yada yada.*

Usually they wait to bring this old saw into play when discussing the contradictions in the resurrection narratives. And the utter hypocrisy of their approach, whether in the case of Easter or the whole Synoptic Problem, is that, while 'on stage' they celebrate the contradictions among the evangelists as signs of independence, they will, after the show, reassure one another, as inerrantists, that the gospel contradictions are only 'apparent,' and they even have in their back pocket a schema to harmonize all of them. They feel entitled to twist the text into pretzels in this manner because they believe the gospel writers *did* collude with the Holy Spirit who virtually dictated what they must write.

But then why did he inspire these seeming contradictions? One must suppose it was for the same reason God created the discrete animal species with false signs of inter-species evolution: to test our faith. The apologists, who congratulate themselves on the spotless ethical purity of Christians, which rules out the possibility of gospel deceptions, are like the imaginative but unscrupulous 'eel wrigglers' against whom the Buddha used to debate.

One can only gape in astonishment to see Blomberg actually take whip and chair in hand and step into the cage with one of these threatening contradictions. Thinking he has successfully domesticated the lion into a housecat, Blomberg emerges from the circus cage a head shorter than when he entered. He makes what he thinks is short work of the gross contradiction between Matthew's and Luke's genealogies.[104]

Blomberg blithely adopts an old Roman Catholic apologetic that Matthew gives us Joseph's ancestry, while Luke gives us Mary's! Too damn bad Luke explicitly traces the line through *Joseph*, just as Matthew does! Blomberg says that Matthew decided to give Joseph's family tree since Joseph was the legal, adoptive father. Why would he do this? Try to

---

104 Blomberg in Strobel, pp. 47–48.

imagine someone claiming Davidic, Messianic credentials for a would-be king if all he could produce was the lineage of an *adoptive* father!

But suppose we were willing, as Blomberg is, to gulp this swill against our better judgment. We'd still have to explain what on earth *Mary's* genealogy is doing credited to Joseph instead! Blomberg doesn't even raise the question, much less answer it. And that's too bad, since it would be an edifying spectacle seeing him trying to explain how and why it is good for Luke to have said it is Joseph's genealogy when in fact it is not.

It's not that the Bible doesn't make mistakes; for the apologist the Bible makes *good* mistakes, like that little kid in the *Twilight Zone* episode "It's a Good Life":[105] "It's *good* you destroyed the wheat crop, Anthony!" Witness the sickening obsequiousness of the fundamentalist as he grovels before his paper idol. Is this supposed to be the truth that makes you free?

5. The Bias Test: A Biased Test?

Reverend Strobel asks an obvious (but no less important) question about what kind of objectivity in reporting one might be able to expect from the New Testament evangelists: "They were not neutral observers; they were his devoted followers. Wouldn't that make it likely that they would change things to make him look good?"[106]

If I were Blomberg, I should have replied that the very suspicion that the evangelists engaged in disingenuous spin or even in starry-eyed hero worship, though not unreasonable, carries no weight at all, since it implies some prior knowledge on our part that there must have been something about Jesus they needed to suppress or to 'spin,' and that is just the point at issue. That is why you would never catch me, as a gospel critic, making such a charge. But what does Blomberg actually say?

> Well, I'll concede this much...; it creates the potential for this to happen. But on the other hand, people can so honor and respect someone that it prompts them to record his life with great integrity. That's the way they would show their love for him. And I think that's what happened here.[107]

105 Adapted by Rod Serling from a story of the same title by Jerome Bixby.

106 Strobel, p. 48.

107 Blomberg in Strobel, p. 48.

Yet Blomberg's answer partakes of the same futile circularity as Strobel's question: *how would we know* the evangelists' love for Jesus prompted them to tell his story accurately, warts and all, if there are no warts in it? Blomberg does have a point, and it explains why some biographers of Dr. King, plainly his admirers, did not flinch at recording his embarrassing marital discretions. They admired him precisely because he showed superhuman courage for a mere human being, and it only reinforces their admiration (as it ought to) when one keeps in mind the foibles he shared with other mortals. It is what Roland Barthes describes as a kind of incarnation paradox.[108]

What? You mean even the great ruler (or the great movie star or the great artist) *brushes his teeth*—and even more amazingly, sometimes skips it—just like little old me? Wow! The fact is, though, of Jesus we have no dirty linen preserved; that might be because Jesus' spin doctors hid the mess, or because Jesus made no mess. I wouldn't presume to say. The whole thing is a wash.

At one point, however, Blomberg shows himself to be naïve: "Besides, these disciples had nothing to gain except criticism, ostracism, and martyrdom. They certainly had nothing to gain financially."[109]

I bid the reader to take a second look, as Reimarus[110] did, at Acts 4:34–5:11, the story of Barnabas, Ananias, and Sapphira. Barnabas is the *good* example to emulate: he sold his property and brought the proceeds to the apostles. Ananias and Sapphira are the *bad* examples: they kept back part of the profits and said they had donated the whole sum. They died by Peter's voodoo curse. This is a cautionary tale pure and simple,[111] and it paints a disturbing picture of the early Christian apostles as cult-overlords whom one must not defy, since to defy them is to defy the god they claim to represent.

> If we may be allowed to take a premonitory glance at the after-conduct of the apostles, the sequel shows that they really did tread in the paths

---

[108] Roland Barthes, "The Writer on Holiday," in Barthes, *Mythologies*. Trans. Annette Lavers (NY: Hill and Wang. 1972), pp. 29–31.

[109] Blomberg in Strobel, p. 48.

[110] Hermann Samuel Reimarus, "Concerning the Intention of Jesus and His Teaching," in Charles H. Talbert, ed., *Reimarus: Fragments* Trans. Ralph S. Fraser. Lives of Jesus Series (Philadelphia: Fortress Press, 1970), pp. 247–248, 259–260.

[111] Alfred Loisy, *The Origins of the New Testament*. Trans. L.P. Jacks (London: George Allen and Unwin, 1950), p. 173.

> leading to influence and aggrandizement, and gleaned from them as much power over the minds of ignorant people as they possibly could.[112]

Of course this is not evident to Blomberg—because he is a member of the cult and sees nothing untoward in the scenario. He dares not see anything amiss, or there will be reprisals (whether from his god or his employers — the same thing?). If Yahweh can be excused for butchering Canaanite babies, why bother straining out this gnat? But there has always been money to be made by starting, and controlling, a religion.[113]

Please understand: I do not take these Acts texts as evidence that Christianity began as an apostolic con game. I do not think it did. These texts must stem from a later period of institutional consolidation. But, thinking as he does, that Acts presents an accurate account of the dawn of Christianity, Blomberg has reason to wonder.

If I may introduce a related point which Strobel and Blomberg treat under their next 'test,' Blomberg is similarly naïve as to why a man-made religion might contain severe, guilt-inducing teachings. "If I were inventing a religion to suit my fancy, I probably wouldn't tell myself to be as perfect as my heavenly Father is perfect, or define adultery to include lust in my heart."[114]

Dostoyevsky's Grand Inquisitor was shrewder than Blomberg; he knew the power of inducing perpetual guilt into the tender consciences of one's flock (clientele) by imposing impossible demands. They would serve to keep the conscientious under a cloud of guilt from which they would futilely seek relief by supplicating the very institution that had imposed the burden to begin with. It is as if the American Medical Association invented some disease so they could drum up business offering a cure for it. Only not a very effective cure, since they wanted the poor sufferers to keep coming back for another dose of medicine, in this case sacramental absolution.

I am in no position to know if this approximates the origin of Christian doctrine, and of the 'hard sayings' of Jesus. I only mean to point out that it is by no means difficult, as the naïve Blomberg imagines, to posit a self-seeking reason for such inventions.

---

112 Reimarus, p. 247.

113 J. Duncan M. Derrett, "Financial Aspects of the Resurrection," in Robert M. Price and Jeffrey Jay Lowder, eds., *The Empty Tomb: Jesus beyond the Grave* (Amherst: Prometheus Books, 2005), pp. 393–409.

114 Blomberg in Strobel, p. 49.

6. The Cover-up Test: "Except to Be Exposed"

This very good criterion is what John Dominic Crossan calls "the Damage Control criterion." Reverend Strobel asks Blomberg, "Did the gospel writers include any material that might be embarrassing, or did they cover it up to make themselves look good? Did they report anything that would be uncomfortable or difficult for them to explain?"[115]

Blomberg's response is astonishing and implies he has never bothered even to consider seriously either form-criticism or redaction-criticism. I am sorry to say so, but he comes across more like a Campus Crusade for Christ staff worker than a New Testament Ph.D.

> There's actually quite a bit along those lines...For instance, Mark 6:5 says that Jesus could do few miracles in Nazareth because the people there had little faith, which seems to limit Jesus' power. Jesus said in Mark 13:32 that he didn t know the day or the hour of his return, which seems to limit his omniscience. [*This can be and has been explained: in human form, Jesus had human limitations.*] But if I felt free to play fast and loose with gospel history, it would be much more convenient just to leave out that material altogether... Jesus' baptism is another example. You can explain why Jesus, who was without sin, allowed himself to be baptized, but why not make things easier by leaving it out altogether? On the cross Jesus cried out, 'My God my God, why hast thou forsaken me?' It would be in the self-interest of the writers to omit that because it raises too many questions."[116]

Has Blomberg never noticed that in *each and every one* of these cases, one gospel writer *does* rewrite the work of his predecessor, and apparently for the very reasons Blomberg posits? Mark thinks nothing of limiting Jesus' healing power. Why shouldn't he? Hadn't Jesus told his patients, "Let it be done to you in accordance with your faith" (Matthew 9:29) and "Your faith has healed you" (Mark 5:34)? It was ultimately up to them. But Matthew falls victim to a later Christological anxiety of which Mark was innocent. So Matthew pointedly rewrites the scene (Matthew 13:58), eliminating the element of Jesus' being surprised at their lack of faith,

115 Strobel, p. 49.

116 *Ibid.*

then having Jesus simply not heal them, avoiding any suggestion that he couldn't have if he'd wanted to.

Jesus' admission that he knew nothing of the day or hour (Mark 13:32) is itself a piece of damage control. It is meant to patch the hole left by Jesus' failed prediction, only a verse before, that the world would come to an end in his contemporaries' own generation. It was too late to change the wording of that well-known prophecy, so Mark (or some predecessor) merely added this disclaimer to 'correct' it.[117]

The baptism of Jesus? Mark seems not to have had a high enough Christology to find any difficulty in the notion that Jesus, precisely as a saintly man, should have felt the need for a baptism of repentance, no doubt grieving over what no one else would even consider sins. Had he accidentally stepped on an ant? Said something innocently which he later realized another might have taken offense at? As Kant[118] remarked, it is only the righteous who thinks to repent; the real sinner is heedless. But Matthew, again with the later eye of sophisticated and abstract theology, finds the scene embarrassing and inserts John's attempt to dissuade Jesus (Matthew 3:14), who assures him it all is copasetic (Matthew 3:15) for unexplained reasons. The real reason doesn't matter anyway: the point Matthew wants to make is: Jesus didn't have any sins to have forgiven. God forbid!

And once John the Baptist's followers began denigrating Jesus as their own guru's inferior, that, too, became an issue, one that had not troubled Mark. So Luke (3:21–22) has Jesus baptized during a flashback relegated to a subordinate clause, almost leaving the reader to think that he had been baptized by unknown persons after John's arrest! You have to read it carefully to void that impression.

And John? He did just what Blomberg said a butt-covering evangelist might do but that none did: he simply *omits* the baptism (and the desert temptation) altogether! John endorses Jesus (John 1:15, 29–36), certainly, but there is not a word about John baptizing Jesus in the fourth gospel.

Were Jesus' last words from the cross so disturbing that a conniving gospel writer would have changed them? Does Blomberg not remember his gospels? Luke *does* omit this quote from Psalms 22:1 and substitutes

---

117 Ironically, Jesus' failed prediction in verse 31 is a good example of what Blomberg claims: a passage left intact despite its scandalous nature, only Blomberg would reject it as an example, refusing to believe Jesus was wrong and twisting the text in some way to avoid admitting it!

118 Immanuel Kant, *Religion within the Limits of Reason Alone*. Trans. Theodore M. Greene and Hoyt H. Hudson (NY: Harper & Row Torchbooks, 1960), p. 68.

another from Psalms 31:5, "Into your hands I commit my spirit." For John, he said, "It is finished."

In each of these cases, we have seen how there was nothing necessarily embarrassing or offensive to Mark, but that the later sensibilities of the subsequent evangelists had led them to do just what Blomberg said they did not do. And, of course, if Mark and his contemporaries found no problem in Jesus getting in line for John's baptism, in his inability to heal unbelieving ingrates, in his quoting Psalms 22:1 from the cross, and his denying any inside knowledge of the eschaton, this means Mark (or a predecessor) might have fabricated these stories or sayings.[119] At least you can't invoke the 'damage-control' factor to prove he didn't.

Blomberg sounds like he might have more of a case when it comes to the 'hard sayings' of Jesus: turning the other cheek, giving away property and money, shunning home and family, forgiving enemies, daring persecution. We tend to ignore these annoying sayings, or to reinterpret them beyond recognition.

Who would have made them up if Jesus hadn't actually said them? But Blomberg forgets (or never grasped) the basic axiom of form-criticism: *nothing was passed down that did not have some utility,* that was not in someone's eyes "profitable for doctrine, reproof, correction, and instruction."

Gerd Theissen[120] figured out that the preservation of such sayings implies there *was* a group who found it advantageous to quote (or, possibly, to fabricate?) these sayings. Remember, we are talking here — Blomberg is talking here — about that theoretical period before the written gospels when the repetition of gospel sayings preserved (some of) them till they could be recorded for posterity. And if the early Christians had all been like us, fat and happy, at ease in Zion, or wanting to be, then, quite simply, these sayings would just have dropped out of circulation.

No one would have needed to censor them. No, it is just that people would not have mentioned or preached on these sayings. We don't either! But, unlike these early Christians, we are stuck with them because they are in printed Bibles. My point is, even if Jesus had said these things, we

119 I'd say there are actually pretty good reasons for thinking these texts have been fabricated, but for this I will have to refer the reader to my book *The Incredible Shrinking Son of Man*. It doesn't matter given our topic here.

120 Gerd Theissen, "The Wandering Radicals: Light Shed by the Sociology of Literature on the Early Transmission of Jesus Sayings," in Theissen, *Social Reality and the Early Christians: Theology, Ethics, and the World of the New Testament*. Trans. Margaret Kohl (Minneapolis: Fortress Press, 1992), pp. 33–59.

would not know of them anymore — unless they were repeated habitually by some Christians who found it served their interests to repeat them.

Now there *was* such a group: the itinerant charismatics, the prophets and apostles of the early church. These were, obviously, the ones who used the Synoptic Mission Charge (Mark 6:7–11; Matthew 10:5–23; Luke 9:3–5; 10:2–16) as their marching orders. These are the ones whom Diotrephes banned from his church (3 John). These are they whom the *Didache* (chapter 11) allows to conduct the Eucharist as they wish. These are those to whom Jesus promised prophetic authority: "Whoever hears you hears me." These men were very pleased to quote these daunting sayings of sacrifice and self-abnegation, because it gave them great clout: unlike the mass of their audience, *they had done it*. They had left all for Jesus, and this lent them great clout. And if one had the motivation to *repeat* the hard sayings, one had the motivation to *create* such sayings, perhaps under 'prophetic inspiration.'

Here is a contemporary parallel: if it were up to the rest of us, or to the mainstream of evangelical Protestants and to Roman Catholics, can you imagine anyone would be giving any air time to Mark 16:18a ("they will pick up serpents.") or to Luke 10:19 ("Behold: I have given you authority to stamp on serpents and scorpions, to trample underfoot all the power of the Enemy; and nothing can harm you.")?

These verses are, to put it more bluntly than anyone else will, an embarrassment. If we were not stuck with them in printed copies of the Bible, they would have vanished long ago since we would have been quite happy to forget them. But they would have survived anyway, because these texts, hard as it is to believe, do have their fans, their partisans: the snake-handling churches of the Appalachians.[121] If you had the guts to pass around the rattlers and the cottonmouths, and the luck to survive it, I guarantee you would be quoting these two texts every chance you got as a way of boasting of your feat. And so it was with the hard sayings about letting goods and kindred go. They came in mighty handy if you had done it, because they gave you clout over the majority who hadn't.

One of the oldest apologetical arguments for gospel accuracy is the contention that the apostles would sooner have passed over material depicting them in an unflattering light. So if we find such material (and we do), this means the apostolic authors were great truth tellers. But the

---

[121] Weston LaBarre, *They Shall Take up Serpents: Psychology of the Southern Snake-Handling Cult* (NY: Schocken Books, 1969; Robert W. Pelton and Karen W. Carden, *Snake Handlers: God-Fearers? Or Fanatics?* (NY: Thomas Nelson, 1974).

argument *presupposes* that the authors of the gospels were eyewitnesses of Jesus and are to be identified as the bumbling, cowardly, or venal characters in the stories. In that case, yes, it was awfully big of them to let themselves be held up to cold scrutiny. As Reverend Strobel comments, "There's plenty of embarrassing material about the disciples." Blomberg finishes his sentence for him:

> Absolutely ... Mark's perspective on Peter is pretty consistently unflattering. And he's the ringleader! The disciples repeatedly misunderstand Jesus. James and John want the places [*of honor*] at Jesus' right and left hand ... They look like a bunch of self-serving, self seeking, dull-witted people a lot of the time. [122]

There goes the whirling dervish again! Blomberg's argument depends on the very premise he is seeking to defend: the gospels were written by self-effacing eye-witnesses of the events described. It simply does not occur to him that the author of Mark may have had it in for the Twelve Disciples because his loyalty was with a different, competing leadership faction. Mark is like Marcion, as Theodore J. Weeden has demonstrated, with exegesis much more detailed and thorough than the tosses Blomberg aims at the broad side of a barn (which usually miss even then!), that Mark the evangelist ascribed to the Twelve a triumphalistic Christology that he found heretical and sought to correct with his own emphasis on the cross.[123]

Mark's attitude toward Peter and the others was virtually Marcionite. Richard J. Arthur believes Mark's gospel was actually the same as the gospel of Marcion,[124] which the Church Fathers claimed was an abbreviated version of Luke. He may be right; he may be wrong. In any case, it should be obvious that it is easy to envision the anti-Twelve, anti-Peter perspective as polemical.[125] This never occurs to Blomberg because he would rather base his view of Mark's gospel on some rumor promoted by the gullible Papias than on close scrutiny of the text itself. Loisy

122 Strobel and Blomberg in Strobel, p. 50.

123 Theodore J. Weeden, *Mark: Traditions in Conflict* (Philadelphia: Fortress Press, 1971).

124 Personal conversation with Robert M. Price.

125 Alfred Loisy, *The Birth of the Christian Religion*. Trans. L.P. Jacks (London: George Allen & Unwin, 1948), p. 46: "On this we may remark, but only by way of a probable hypothesis, that the revision of Mark thus characterized by ill will to these apostles was the work of parties in Rome devoted to the memory of Paul."

suggested long ago that the infamous narrative of Peter denying Jesus (an action normally considered to be irreversible apostasy) must have been an anti-Petrine libel circulated by his ecclesiastical enemies.[126]

Blomberg cuts to the chase:

> But here's the point: if they didn't feel free to leave out stuff when it would have been convenient and helpful to do so, is it really plausible to believe that they outright added and fabricated material with no historical basis?[127]

Again, Blomberg argues within the option-narrowing parameters of the assumption of eyewitness, apostolic authorship of the gospels. Gospel materials stemming from their enemies, as I have just argued, could include just about anything. But let's grant apostolic authorship of the gospels, as gratuitous as the assumption is, just for the sake of argument. Even then it is quite easy to imagine the writers possessing the same self-abnegating humility predicated of John the Baptist when he says of Jesus, "He must increase, and I must decrease" (John 3:30), or felt by any pious Christian today for that matter. As the Psalmist said, "I know my transgressions, and my sin is ever before me. Against you, and you only, have I sinned, and done that which you regard as evil, so that you are justified in your sentence and blameless in your judgment" (Psalms 51:3–4). "But if through my falsehood God's truthfulness abounds to his glory, why should I still be condemned as a sinner?" (Romans 3:7).

The humble Christian might indeed rejoice to recount his own foibles and follies *if it meant glorifying Jesus by contrast.* Joyce Meyers's whole preaching style is built on this sort of Christian self-ridicule. And there is nothing in this obsequious fawning that is inconsistent with telling tall tales to glorify one's precious Lord. *One notices no deception, because every inch of exaggeration and embellishment is the same amount of glorification of one's savior.* Remember the wisdom of George Costanza: "It's not a lie if you believe it."

---

126 Loisy, *Birth of the Christian Religion*, p. 82.

127 Blomberg in Strobel, p. 50.

7. The Corroboration Test: Imaginary Confirmation

Blomberg offers us the empty assurance that

> We can learn through non-Christian sources a lot of facts about Jesus that corroborate key teachings and events in his life. And when you stop to think that ancient historians for the most part dealt only with political rulers, emperors, kings, military battles, official religious people, and major philosophical movements, it's remarkable how much we can learn about Jesus and his followers even though they fit none of those categories at the time these historians were writing.[128]

Again we find Blomberg blatantly engaging in the very sort of embellishment he denies the conscientious early Christians would have practiced, for here Blomberg's imagination has run away with him at light speed. What historians is he talking about? He gives no specifics whatever. But we know whom he must have in mind: the usual gang of suspects, Josephus, Tacitus, Suetonius, and Pliny Secundus (Pliny the Younger). But none of these pass muster. Let's take them one by one. First, Josephus:

> Now there was about this time Jesus, a wise man, if it be lawful to call him a man, for he was a doer of wonderful works, a teacher of such men as receive the truth with pleasure. He drew over to him both many of the Jews, and many of the Gentiles. He was the Christ; and when Pilate, at the suggestion of the principal men amongst us, had condemned him to the cross, those that loved him at the first did not forsake him, for he appeared to them alive again the third day, as the divine prophets had foretold these and ten thousand other wonderful things concerning him; and the tribe of Christians, so named from him, are not extinct to this day. (Josephus, *Antiquities of the Jews* 18.3.3)

Josephus, a non-Christian Jew who considered, virtually ordained, the Roman Emperor Vespasian as the messiah of Israel, could not have written this passage. Nor, in fact, did he. Origen was reading a much earlier copy of Josephus than those surviving today, and he comments that Josephus "did not accept Jesus as Christ" (*Commentary on Matthew* 10.17). It is pretty obvious that the text did not contain what our Josephus text says about Jesus. Who knows what it may or may not have said about him?

---

128 *Ibid.*, pp. 50–51.

Schlomo Pines[129] drew attention to another, Arabic version of the passage in Agapius' *Book of the Title*. Its author was a tenth-century Christian Arab and a Melkite bishop of Hierapolis, Papias' old stomping grounds.

> Similarly Josephus, the Hebrew. For he says in the treatises that he has written on the governance (?) of the Jews: "At this time there was a wise man who was called Jesus. His conduct was good, and (he) was known to be virtuous. And many people from the Jews and other nations became his disciples. Pilate condemned him to be crucified and die. But those who had become his disciples did not abandon his discipleship. They reported that he had appeared to them three days after the crucifixion, and that he was alive; accordingly he was perhaps the Messiah, concerning whom the prophets have recounted wonders.

Apologists like to claim this Arabic version as representing something closer to what Josephus originally wrote, but that is futile. It is apparent that Agapius' version is simply an abridgment of the longer, familiar version. For instance, the concluding reference to the wonders predicted for the messiah seems to refer back to some earlier reference to Jesus doing miracles. There is no such antecedent in Agapius' version, but there it is in the Greek *Testimonium Flavianum*. No doubt the passage originated with the fourth-century church historian Eusebius, the first to 'quote' it. It is amazing, if the text were actually authentic to Josephus, that no Christian writer before Eusebius should mention it. The passage shares Eusebius' literary style, not so much Josephus'.

Then again, the whole business is cast in a new light once we realize the chances are excellent that the Markan Passion narrative is based on Josephus' narrative of the interrogation and flogging of the Jerusalem prophet Jesus ben Ananias. Weeden has made a very strong case for a Josephan origin of the Markan Jesus story.[130] Whoever looked over his copy of Josephus and saw a major gap where some mention of Jesus

---

129 Pronounced 'penis,' poor devil. See his *An Arabic Version of the Testimonium Flavianum and its Implications*. (Jerusalem: Israel Academy of Sciences and Humanities, 1971).

130 Theodore J. Weeden, *The Two Jesuses* (*Foundations and Facets Forum* New Series 6/2; Fall 2003). Steve Mason (*Josephus and the New Testament* (Peabody: Hendrickson, 1992) revives the view of a less timid scholarly generation, arguing that Luke-Acts made significant use of Josephus, too, not merely paralleling it. See his Chapter 6, "Josephus and Luke-Acts," pp. 185–225.

should have gone did not realize Jesus was there all right, or rather his literary prototype, Jesus ben Ananias, brought up by the Sanhedrin to the Roman procurator, flogged for daring to predict the destruction of the temple, giving no reply, and dying during the Roman siege. Josephus, then, could hardly have been referring back to a 'historical Jesus' who had not finished being invented yet.

Cornelius Tacitus (*Annals* 15:44), writing about 125 CE, asserts that Nero blamed Roman Christians for setting the great Roman fire, only to divert suspicion from himself. In case his readers were unacquainted with Christianity, Tacitus explains they were a sect founded by one 'Christus' who had run afoul of the Prefect Pontius Pilate and been crucified. These are the only two historians Blomberg even might have in mind, and it is certain neither corroborates what the gospels say Jesus said, nor add to it. What can Blomberg be (wishfully) thinking? These two writers, even supposing their Jesus-snippets to be authentic, cannot be shown to be doing any real reporting. They need only be relaying the Christian story as noised abroad in their times.

Pliny Secundus (*ca.* 112 CE) reports that Christians in Bithynia, where he was the governor, "sang hymns to Christ as to a god." This tells us nothing about any historical Jesus, only about Christian worship. One might as well convey the bulletin that one's local Presbyterian church worships Jesus; it would add nothing to our knowledge of a historical Jesus. But ultimately, that is what is going on here anyway: the apologist's 'knowledge' of Jesus is but an extrapolation of his faith and his church allegiance.

Some even drag poor Suetonius into this brawl, pointing to his note that Claudius expelled Jews from Rome because he was tired of the riots instigated there by "one Chrestus" (*The Twelve Caesars*, Claudius 5:25:4). Well, I suppose this might be a reference to "Jesus Chrestus" (as Marcionites called him) if Irenaeus was right in claiming that Jesus lived to age forty-nine and was crucified during Claudius's reign. Otherwise, forget it.

The Adverse Witness Test: Mumbling beneath the Muzzle?

Lee Strobel is 'grilling' Craig Blomberg about as strenuously as a kid on Santa's lap. He is asking him for the pre-packaged answers he wants to hear. And if he did not already know Blomberg would be dispensing them like a Good Humor man, he would not be asking for them. Indeed, Strobel has cast himself in the role of Peter in the gospels: a straight man who asks artificial, planted questions just to solicit the prescribed answer for the reader's benefit. He is, in short, not only a shyster but a shill. Forgive me such language if it offends you, but I refuse to dignify this sham by treating it with the polite respect with which I would analyze a genuine scholarly theory with which I differed. To lend Strobel an undeserved respect is to contribute to the pseudo-intellectual scam he is pulling.

Essentially repeating the 'hostile-eyewitness' argument from the previous chapter, Reverend Strobel asks Blomberg, "Were others present who would have contradicted or corrected the gospels if they had been distorted or false? In other words, do we see examples of contemporaries of Jesus complaining that the gospel accounts were false?"[131]

Why don't you let me take this one, Craig?

Un, no, we do not hear of such—*for the simple reason that no gospels were written while contemporaries of Jesus were still alive!* The war with Rome had darn near depopulated Jerusalem and Galilee, after all. Plus, one must remember that the gospels were circulated among Christian communities, not sold on drugstore racks. Would early critics of Christianity even have known of the gospels?

If you are willing to push the dates up, allowing time for hostile readers to read and rebut the gospels, there is the third-century *Acts of Pilate*, which must have been pretty unflattering to Jesus since, once they got the chance under Constantine, the bishops suppressed and replaced it with their own *Acts of Pilate*, also called the *Gospel according to Nicodemus*.

Among Jews there circulated from early centuries polemical narratives eventually gathered and published as (more than one version of) the *Toledoth Jeschu*, a derisive anti-gospel. Earlier than this, the Talmud contains notices of Jesus as a deceiver and a sorcerer. But, as surviving copies with whole passages blotted out show, Jews censored many of these readings for fear of Christian reprisals. None of this preserves any independent evidence of Jesus: it only shows that there were anti-gospel texts—and that we have only rare specimens that somehow survived known attempts to burn all such criticisms. There might have been more—who can say? But one is hardly justified saying what Blomberg does, that there is a deafening silence of criticism against the gospels.

Blomberg adds that the gospels make Jesus' scribal critics concede that he performed miracles since, instead of denying them or debunking them, they attributed them to sorcery (Mark 3:22). Blomberg seems not to realize

131 Strobel, p. 51.

Jesus' peanut gallery was not a first-century CSICOP[132] chapter, trying to refute all claims of paranormal events. They were fellow supernaturalists, and it scored more points to brand one's rival as a *houngan* in league with the devil than to make him a mere pickpocket and sleight-of-hand artist.

Besides, they were engaged in a kind of tit-for-tat polemical game[133] in which one's opponent declared, "Okay, I'll see your exorcism and raise you a sorcery charge! Ready to fold?" Have it your way, pal! It was a miracle all right—of Satan! We see the same style of can-you-top-this argumentation on display in Matthew's empty-tomb narrative, where Jews have rebutted the Christian empty-tomb story by granting it, then one-upping it: charging that the disciples stole the body. Christians upped the ante by fictively posting Roman guards at the tomb to prevent it.

Again, a third-century rabbi, Simeon ben Lakish, was willing to admit that Jesus raised himself from the dead — by means of black magic.[134] The much later Yezidi sect[135] taught that it was Satan who raised Jesus from the tomb! Is there any chance Rabbi Simeon had independent eyewitness knowledge of the resurrection? Does his willingness to grant the resurrection for the sake of argument imply he was in a position to know whether Jesus really rose? Of course not. The same with the Yezidis: it was way too late for them to be independently attesting the resurrection albeit in a back-handed manner. They were simply taking the Christian claim and parodying it.

If anyone still needs proof that Lee Strobel approached his allegedly Diogenes-like quest for the truth with his mind made up already, listen to this

> Could this Christian movement have taken root right there in Jerusalem – in the very area where Jesus had done much of his ministry, had been crucified, buried, and resurrected – if people who knew him were aware that the disciples were exaggerating or distorting the things that he did?[136]

---

132 Committee for the Scientific Investigation of Claims of the Paranormal. They've recently changed their name to something shorter but duller.

133 Robert E. van Voorst, *Jesus outside the New Testament: An Introduction to the Ancient Evidence* (Grand Rapids: Eerdmans, 2000), p. 121.

134 "Resh Lakish has said, woe to him who recalls himself to life by the Name of God" (Sanhedrin 106a).

135 Isya Joseph, *Devil Worship: The Sacred Books and Traditions of the Yezidis* (Boston: Gorham Press, 1919), pp. 59–60.

136 Strobel, p. 51.

Talk about a loaded question! Let's see: we can take for granted that Jesus had been crucified, buried, and resurrected in Jerusalem. And then we ask, theoretically, how the local witnesses could have let the Christian preachers get away with exaggerations. Ah, exaggerations of *what*? Does Strobel mean to ask how, if *none* (not all) of these things had happened under the noses of the Jerusalemites, Christian preachers of the death and resurrection could have been taken seriously there? If this is what he means, he is still no better off.

Imagine, if you will, Annas (or Caiaphas or Malchus) hearing Peter preaching the resurrection of Jesus. He might interrupt and insist, "Hey! *I* didn't see any risen Jesus! Did any of the rest of you?" The crowd is silent. Peter answers, I suspect a tad sheepishly, "Er, uh, that's because he appeared just to us disciples, and behind locked doors! I guess you just had to be there!"[137] Isn't that what he *does* say in Acts 10:40*f*?

> [10:40]This man God raised on/after the third day and granted him to become visible, [41]not to all the people, to be sure, but to witnesses previously appointed by God, to us who ate with him and drank with him and accompanied him for forty days after he got up from the dead.

It got off the ground the same way all faith-movements do — especially once the gospel hit Gentile soil, where no proof could have been asked or supplied. Strobel might as well ask, "How did Mithraism get off the ground unless plenty of people witnessed the god slaying the celestial bull?"

Reverend Strobel has raised a very good question, albeit in a confused manner. Merrill P. Miller[138] raised it clearly: why should we accept Acts' story of bold apostolic preaching of the death and resurrection of Jesus right under the noses of the same murdering tyrants who had killed Jesus and could have no more scruples about killing his apostles, especially in order to stop all their libelous accusations? If Jerusalem figured into the early days of Christianity at all, things must have been quite different from the way Acts presents them, at least on the surface. But there are undercurrents that may be traces of an earlier, less dramatic version.

---

137 I know one might want to bring up the 500 brethren who saw the risen Jesus in 1 Corinthians 15:6, but then we have to ask, if this encounter had really taken place, why is there no mention of it anywhere else? Ancient apologists would certainly have made as much use of it as their modern counterparts do had it been available to them. It is, alas, a later interpolation.

138 Merrill P. Miller, "'Beginning from Jerusalem…': Re-examining Canon and Consensus," *The Journal of Higher Criticism* 2/1 (Spring 1995): pp. 3–30.

For instance, Gamaliel's warning to his fellow councilmen not to risk opposing Jehovah by persecuting a new sect that might conceivably be his genuine planting (Acts 5:33–39) does not refer to or presuppose a month-old conspiracy by those present to execute a dangerous champion of the people. Rather, they seem like the American Catholic bishops trying to decide the most responsible way to deal with the Charismatic Movement in their churches, or like the Vatican deliberating what stance to take on some possibly fanatical Marian apparition in some desolate corner of the world.

Similarly, what is the Sanhedrin upset about in Acts 4:1–2? Charges that they knowingly murdered the very Son of God? No, simply that the quasi-heretical doctrine of resurrection, so lately borrowed by the Pharisee sect from Persian Zoroastrians,[139] was getting a new airing. That's the reason the Jesus business annoyed them, as an occasion to spread that silly stuff again.

What was so objectionable in Stephen's preaching? His opposition to the Jerusalem temple and the perpetuity of the Torah, an opinion he might easily have held simply as a function of his Hellenism, a cosmopolitan stance transcending the boundary-anxiety of mossbacks like the Hasmoneans and their successors the Sadducees. When Stephen's assimilationist party was exiled and punished, how could the original Twelve have evaded the Sanhedrin's wrath (Acts 8:1)[140] if the sticking point between Jews and Christians centered on the death of 'God's Christ'? This cannot have been much of an issue. Nor was it when Paul addressed the Sanhedrin in Acts 23:6–9.

The issue is again the resurrection of the dead in principle, and Jesus is important merely as an angel or ghost (two forms, besides bodily resurrection, in which some thought a person might survive death, *cf.* Acts 23:8) whom Paul was claiming, perhaps correctly as the Pharisees present urged, verified belief in survival. None of this has anything to do with the charged atmosphere of the murder of the Messiah and who bears the guilt for it, as the conventional picture of apostolic preaching in Jerusalem envisions things. Was the original Jerusalem Christianity something much, much closer to Judaism, something that did not yet involve any dying and rising savior or martyred Christ?

---

139 T.W. Manson, *The Servant Messiah: A Study of the Public Ministry of Jesus* (Cambridge at the University Press, 1961), pp. 19–20.

140 Oscar Cullmann, "Dissensions within the Early Church," in Richard Batey, ed., *New Testament* Issues (NY: Harper & Row / Harper Forum Books, 1970), pp. 122–123.

In the end, it turns out Craig Blomberg has quite a bit of faith in floating oral tradition, let us say, *usable* oral tradition, from his standpoint:

> I'll tell you this: there are plenty of stories of scholars in the New Testament field who have not been Christians, yet through their study of these very issues have come to faith in Christ. And there have been countless more scholars, already believers, whose faith has been made stronger, more solid, more grounded, because of the evidence – and that's the category I fall into.[141]

Frankly, I am willing to bet that this first assertion, the one about non-Christian New Testament scholars coming to Christian faith as a result of their studies, is arrant nonsense. How many individuals, do you suppose, enter the complex field of biblical scholarship without the prior motivation of Christian belief that the Bible is authoritative scripture? Very, very few, I am sure. I have known some Jewish scholars (*e.g.*, Robert Eisenman, Amy-Jill Levine, Hyam Maccoby) and known the work of others (Hugh J. Schonfield, Hans-Joachim Schoeps, Samuel Sandmel, David Flusser) whose interest stems from analogous faith concerns (*e.g.*, ecumenicity, history of Jewish sectarianism). *But none of these became Christians as a result.* There may be a few somewhere, but I can't imagine there are many.

As for the second avowal, that Christian scholars have had their faith strengthened through the course of New Testament studies, again, I doubt it seriously. Blomberg invites us to take him as a case study. Well, in that case, it becomes clear he has flushed away any close acquaintance he ever possessed with serious New Testament criticism and found his "faith strengthened" by accepting a load of vacuous InterVarsity apologetics arguments. That is hardly the same thing as studying New Testament scholarship. In his works that are not even supposed to be apologetical in nature, he is constantly doing apologetics anyway. He just doesn't know the difference, except insofar as he seems to understand, without admitting it, that *real* scholarship is his enemy.

It is no surprise that Blomberg does not tell Strobel the rest of the story: that most critical, professional New Testament scholars, both in the past and today, began as pious fundamentalists seeking better to understand and apply the inerrant 'Word of God,' and then discovered there was no such critter.[142] Then there are those who came up through evangelical

141 Blomberg in Strobel, p. 53.

142 For examples, see the autobiographical accounts of Dewey M. Beegle, Dennis Ronald MacDonald, John William Colenso, and Henry Preserved Smith in Edward T. Babinski, ed., *Leaving the Fold: Testimonies of Former Fundamen-*

apologetics, somehow imagining that apologetics *was* New Testament scholarship (like the misguided novice who mistakes Christian Science for medicine), and decided to pursue a sheepskin for respectability's sake.

Strobel himself wears a different stage mask from Blomberg's:

> As for me, I had originally been in the first category – no, not a scholar but a skeptic, an iconoclast, a hard-nosed reporter on a quest for the truth about this Jesus who said he was the Way and the Truth and the Life.[143]

Sorry, but I don't believe that one for a second. Look at the way he describes his supposedly risky, courageous, and open-ended quest: he already assumes what critical scholarship will never tell him, but which apologists, in default mode, repeat from Sunday School: that Jesus' words in the Gospel of John (in this case, 14:6) are genuine quotes from a historical Jesus. If this is what he says he started out searching for, it's no surprise that he found it. He stacked the deck from the start.

I don't know about you, dear readers, but as far as I'm concerned, the interview with Dr. Blomberg has turned out to be every bit as much a waste of time as when I publicly debated him some years ago at the University of Colorado in Colorado Springs.

---

talists (Amherst: Prometheus Books, 1995) as well as Bart D. Ehrman, *Misquoting Jesus: The Story behind Who Changed the Bible and Why* (San Francisco: Harper One, 2005).

143 Strobel, p. 53.

Chapter Three
The Manuscript Evidence
Do We Have What the Evangelists Originally Wrote?

Bruce Metzger, Reader's Digest Version

Our roving reporter next tracks down the saintly (and now, sainted) Dr. Bruce Metzger at Princeton Theological Seminary. Reverend Strobel was truly fortunate to have managed to interview him, shortly before Dr. Metzger's sad passing in 2007. I couldn't believe the luck when I got the chance to take a summer course with Dr. Metzger on the Sermon on the Mount back in 1977. Metzger was everything Strobel says he was: "thoroughly kind, surprisingly modest and self-effacing, with a gentle spirit."[144] Strobel is right again, I am happy to say, when he says Dr. Metzger "is held in the highest regard by scholars from across a wide range of theological beliefs."[145]

But I must question his judgment when he places Metzger "on the cutting edge of New Testament scholarship."[146] And don't think I am demeaning Dr. Metzger's memory when I say so. For the last place on earth evangelical scholars want to be found is on the cutting edge of biblical scholarship. Their enterprise is quite explicitly to dull that edge, to turn it back. They wish things were as they used to be, say, at the time of the Protestant Reformation, when Christians could simply debate exegeses of the text and no one doubted its authority, no one questioned its authorship. The last thing Evangelicals want is, God forbid, novelty. That is understandable: this is why they are called "conservatives." I don't think I am in any way caricaturing their position. Isn't it what they stand for?

Only sometimes they pretend otherwise. My friends Paul Eddy and Greg Boyd, authors of the recent text *The Jesus Legend*[147] (fine fellows both) delve as deeply as they can in subjects like postmodernity and orality studies. Why? To find tools with which they hope to turn back the clock,

---

144 *Ibid.*, p. 58.

145 *Ibid.*

146 *Ibid.*

147 Paul Rhodes Eddy and Greg Boyd, *The Jesus Legend: A Case for the Historical Reliability of the Synoptic Jesus Tradition* (Grand Rapids: Baker Academic, 2007).

to undo and debunk all of modern biblical criticism. Is it not so? They are like Billy Graham when Reinhold Niebuhr criticized him for "setting Christianity back a hundred years." Graham replied, "Only a hundred? I'd like to set it back two thousand years!"

I believe Bruce Metzger is a perfect example of a type pegged by James Barr:[148] evangelicals who love the Bible (I know and still share the feeling) and decide to pursue a degree in graduate biblical study, only they take refuge in either marginal or even adjacent fields of biblical scholarship, especially textual criticism or biblical languages and grammar. With the Higher Criticism, biblical criticism proper, they want nothing to do. They fear these fields are subject to the vagaries of unbelieving, naturalistically biased, and, in short, unbelieving enemies of the true faith.

If they stick to Greek grammar or textual criticism, they think, they will be able to avoid being corrupted or confused by such insidious speculations. They will have stuck to more 'objective' matters. And this focus in turn will give them a privileged perspective from which to weigh in on critical debates from (what they imagine is) the superior position of the outsider. "Why, *we* would never waste our time with such fancies for five minutes!" In the meantime, like C.S. Lewis, they simply take for granted traditional, which is to say pre-critical, positions on authorship and accuracy. What they miss is that Old and New Testament criticism have developed new questions and new tools for trying to answer them, having found that the issues are not cut and dry. The smug certainties of those who count manuscripts and weed out copyist errors are simply not appropriate in a field that involves admittedly speculative reconstructions of an unobtainable past.

It is almost funny to read, *e.g.*, the constant appeals to scholars like Adrian Nicholas Sherwin-White,[149] the Roman historian, who confesses his puzzlement that form-critics should find it a trickier matter to reconstruct a historical Jesus than a historical Julius Caesar. Sherwin-White (himself an evangelical, and thus hardly a disinterested referee with Olympian objectivity), like the pious Metzger, can't see why the life-of-Jesus critic cannot construct Jesus the way they do the United Bible Society Greek New Testament: by simply adding up verses. And to that I can only oppose

---

148 James Barr, *Fundamentalism* (Philadelphia: Westminster Press, 1977), pp. 128–131.

149 A.N. Sherwin-White, *Roman Society and Roman Law in the New Testament*. Twin Brooks Series (Grand Rapids: Baker Book House, 1992).

a maxim I saw posted on the door of my college English Lit professor, Dr. Paul Hanson: "Thoughtful uncertainty is better than cocksure ignorance."

The apologists are speaking out of self-imposed ignorance, as if Lower Criticism (textual criticism) were the only game in town, the paradigm for all the rest. Historical criticism is not the same thing as textual criticism, and I fear Dr. Metzger, like Reverend Strobel, failed to grasp the distinction. Worse yet, they both fail to see the critical historical issues underlying textual criticism, which may be a less secure perch than they imagine.

For instance, apologists and conservative textual critics[150] love to boast about the vastly greater number and age of the extant New Testament manuscripts as opposed to the mere hand full of copies of the *Iliad* and *Odyssey*, or the plays of Sophocles and Euripides. (Pardon me if I wonder if that differential has something to do with the literary tastes and censorship habits of post-Constantinian bishops who naturally kept scribes busy copying scriptures for church use but frowned on pagan drama as vestiges of a false religion.) They scoff at skepticism being directed at the fidelity of New Testament manuscripts — suspicions that they have been doctored.

Here come all the Sherwin-Whites again: we should consider Classicists insane if they doubted the integrity of the ancient plays and epics. But isn't it evident that the early Christian environment was charged with theological disputations that made it mighty tempting to alter biblical texts to safeguard orthodoxy (or heresy!) in early debates?[151] As we will see, early Muslims found the same situation in their frustrating debates over texts of the Qur'an that varied — no doubt edited to make it easier to

---

150 Let no one imagine that all text critics are conservative, even if the establishment is. Examples of more daring, less theologically/apologetically restrictive textual criticism would include Winsome Munro, *Authority in Paul and Peter: The Identification of a Pastoral Stratum in the Pauline Corpus and I Peter*. Society for New Testament Studies Monograph Series 45 (NY: Cambridge University Press, 1983) and J.C. O'Neill, *Paul's Letter to the Romans*. Pelican Commentaries (Baltimore: Penguin Books, 1973); O'Neill, *The Recovery of Paul's Letter to the Galatians* (London: SPCK, 1972).

151 Bart D. Ehrman, *The Orthodox Corruption of Scripture: The Effect of Early Christological Controversies on the Text of the New Testament* (NY: Oxford University Press, 1993). Cf. Wayne C. Kannaday, *Apologetic Discourse and the Scribal Tradition: Evidence of the Influence of Apologetic Interests on the Text of the Canonical Gospels*. Society of Biblical Text-Critical Studies, Volume 5 (Atlanta: Society of Biblical Literature, 2004).

win! If we had reason to posit something like this in the case of the New Testament, it would mean all bets are off.

But all this never occurs to the evangelical text critics like Metzger and Gordon Fee. For them textual criticism is no different from the geologist digging through layer after layer of soil to get to the stony bedrock beneath. And they imagine they have done it. Strobel quotes apologists (never a critic!) Norman L. Geisler and William E. Nix on the point: "The New Testament, then, has not only survived in more manuscripts than any other book from antiquity, but it has survived in a purer form than any other great book – *a form that is 99.5 percent pure*."[152]

So, apologists tell us, we are that close to the goal. There remain a few cases, all insignificant, in which we are not yet sure how the original texts read. Sometimes these are mere variances in word order. Sometimes a sentence or a clause is at stake. Did Jesus pray from the cross, "Father, forgive them; they know not what they do"? Did he say, "The son of man came to save men's lives, not to destroy them"? And so forth. It would be good to know, and we don't. But that's a measly point five percent!

But not so fast! John Beversluis[153] notes the circularity of the argument:

> Since there are thousands of surviving copies, we can study them and thus arrive at a "close approximation" to the originals. However, this seemingly authoritative explanation leaves the most important question unanswered. Since the *autographa* have not survived and nobody has laid eyes on them for 2,000 years, how could anybody possibly know what was in them — much less, which copies approximate most closely to them? Since there is nothing to which existing manuscripts can be compared, the very ideas of the *original* manuscripts and which manuscripts *approximate most closely* to them are useless ideas and should be abandoned. I can judge that a photo is a good likeness of you if and only if I have seen you and know what you look like. If I have not, then I am the last person on earth to ask. The situation is not improved

---

152 Norman L. Geisler and William E. Nix, *A General Introduction to the Bible* (1968; rpt. Chicago: Moody Press, 1980), p. 367, quoted in (with emphasis added by) Strobel, p. 65. Neither author is a professional biblical specialist. Geisler is a philosopher and Christian ethicist (in which field he does, in my opinion, fine work), while Nix is an educational consultant of some kind.

153 John Beversluis, *The Gospel according to Whom?* (forthcoming). Beversluis, the author of *C.S. Lewis and the Search for Rational Religion*, is also a philosopher, like Geisler, but making a helpful logical point here.

by assuring me that there are thousands of photos of you. The fact is that I have never seen *you*, so ten million photos would not help.

Metzger, Geisler, and Fee would no doubt reply that, to maintain such suspicion, one must posit some conspiracy by which another's portrait has been substituted, and that we are being tricked into believing all the other pictures really represent you. But where is the evidence for any conspiracy on the part of early Christians so to hide and misidentify the true nature of the New Testament text?

As it happens, there *is* reason to question the optimistic estimate of the evangelical text-apologists. For the evidence for how the text once read comes to a screeching halt at about 200 CE, with the conjecturally dated Chester Beatty Papyri. *Before that, there is no textual evidence, no manuscripts at all.*

Either, as the Tübingen critics and the Dutch Radical critics held, the New Testament documents in their final, heavily redacted and rewritten forms, were written quite close to that date, leaving no real tunnel period, or the previous manuscripts were systematically destroyed and replaced in a purge and standardization analogous to that of the Qur'an under Caliph Uthman. William O. Walker, Jr., suggests:

> the surviving text of the Pauline letters is the text promoted — and perhaps produced — by the historical winners in the theological and ecclesiastical struggles of the second and third centuries... [I]t is certainly possible that the emerging "orthodox" leadership of the churches might have "standardized" the text of the Pauline corpus in the light of its own views and practices, suppressing and even destroying all deviant texts and manuscripts. Thus, what Wisse characterizes as a "remarkably unified text without a hint of major editing" may well point not to a uniform transmission of the text from the very beginning but rather to such a deliberate standardizing of the text at some point(s) in its transmission. This would explain why it is that we have no manuscripts dating from earlier than the latter part of the second century and why all of the surviving manuscripts are remarkably similar.[154]

Again, back in the early days of Islam there were more and more scriptural disputes ending in stalemate since the opposing sides found

[154] William O. Walker, Jr., *Interpolations in the Pauline Letters*. Journal for the Study of the New Testament Supplement Series 213 (London: Sheffield Academic Press, 2001), pp. 52–54.

their copies of the Qur'an did not agree. This unrest reached the ears of the Caliph Uthman, who decided it would be best to collect all known copies of the Qur'an and have a team of scholars come up with a standardized text, an 'authorized version' or *textus receptus*. Once the job was complete, he replaced the collected copies, the ones swimming in variants, with the brand new ones that all agreed. When they got them back, various Muslim theologians found that their proof texts had been yanked out from under them. The texts now sided with one side, not the other, in every dispute. Indeed: hadn't that been the whole point of the exercise? The same thing may well have happened in the case of Christian scripture.

And this nicely clears the ground for apologists. There can be no smoking gun if all guns have been confiscated. Apologists[155] demand that one must show manuscript support for any proposed interpolation from that crucial early period *from which none of any kind survives*. And then we realize: this is precisely why none survives.

Benjamin B. Warfield used the same Catch-22 to defend inerrancy, by setting up a gauntlet he dared any proposed biblical error to run. Any alleged error in scripture must be shown to have occurred in the original autographs, which, luckily, are no longer available.

After such a scrubbing of the text, the only evidence remaining as to a possible earlier state of the text will be *internal* evidence, namely *aporias* — contradictions, stylistic irregularities, anachronisms, redactional seams. And this is precisely the kind of thing our apologists scorn. As we know by now to expect from an apologist (don't they explicitly admit it, after all?), their way of dealing with such loose ends is *not* to unravel them, as is the way of critics who want to understand the warp and woof of the text by deconstructing it, but rather harmonization of 'apparent contradictions.' Here is the axiom: "Designating a passage in a text as a redactional interpolation can be at best only a last resort and an admission of one's inability to account for the data in any other way."[156] In other words, any clever connect-the-dots solution is preferable to admitting that the text in question is an interpolation.

Before we shift gears to consider Metzger's astonishing remarks on the New Testament canon, let us pause for a revealing glimpse of his theological thinking. Strobel asks him if any Christian doctrine loses its

---

155 Frederik W. Wisse, "Textual Limits to Redactional Theory in the Pauline Corpus," in James E. Goehring, Charles W. Hedrick, Jack T. Sanders, and Hans Dieter Betz, eds., *Gospel Origins & Christian Beginnings: In Honor of James M. Robinson* Forum Fascicles 1 (Sonoma: Polebridge Press, 1990), p. 167–178.

156 Wisse, p. 170.

footing because of textual criticism (of the conservative sort he practices: straining out jots and tittles, no more). After all, even Metzger must admit that 1 John 5:7b ("There are three that bear witness in heaven: the Father, the Word, and the Spirit, and these three are one.") is a spurious interpolation into the Latin Vulgate, unattested in any ancient Greek manuscripts. That would have been one meaty proof text for Trinitarianism, which of course is why it was interpolated in the first place. Never fear, Metzger reassures us:

> That does not dislodge the firmly witnessed testimony of the Bible to the doctrine of the Trinity. At the baptism of Jesus, the Father speaks, his beloved Son is baptized, and the Holy Spirit descends on him. At the ending of 2 Corinthians Paul says, "May the grace of the Lord Jesus Christ, and the love of God, and the fellowship of the Holy Spirit be with you all. There are many places where the Trinity is represented.[157]

Again, this is Sunday School stuff. How could Metzger, with his depth of knowledge of church history, telescope the fascinating development of Trinitarian doctrine in this manner?[158] The doctrine of the Trinity is a complex philosophical model (whether ultimately successful, *i.e.*, coherent, you decide.). It stipulates that there is a single divine nature (*ousia*) shared in common by three distinct persons (*hypostases*). It attempts to steer a course between Tritheism on the one hand and Modalism on the other.

Tritheism is the belief that Father, Son, and Spirit are distinct deities, their common divine 'nature' referring merely to the common category in which they belong, just as Tom, Dick, and Harriet may be said to share a single human nature. They do not constitute some three-headed freak.

Modalism lays greater emphasis on the unity of God, making Father, Son, and Spirit three different functions, offices, or modes in which a single God acts and manifests himself. Trinitarian theologians have always rejected Modalism as cheating the threeness aspect, and condemned Tritheism for minimizing the oneness. But all are viable, conceptually meaningful ways of associating threeness with God.

It ought to be obvious that no New Testament verses, certainly not those Metzger cites, actually *teaches*, *i.e.*, spells out, the doctrine of the Trinity. Even Tertullian is not so clear on the matter because it was still being defined. The doctrine may indeed be a true belief, but it is preposterous,

157 Metzger in Strobel, p. 65.

158 For a judicious, historically sophisticated treatment of just how far any New Testament text bears on what would become the doctrine of the Trinity, see Arthur W. Wainwright, *The Trinity in the New Testament* (London: SPCK: 1975).

so long as one has any historical sense at all, to say that Peter or Matthew or Mark ever thought of such a thing. A mere reference to 'three' does not a Trinity make. Whatever it was the New Testament authors had in mind in these 'three-passages' (which obviously they do not stop to explain to our satisfaction), it may have contributed to Trinitarian thinking at some point. If you could get into a time machine and explain Trinitarianism to Paul or Peter, they might well have been willing to sign on the dotted line, but there is no evidence they had already thought of it or taught it.

Why did Metzger indulge in such confusion, such unwitting falsification? Because his default mode was sheer fundamentalism where one believes there is a direct, one-to-one link between Bible verses and today's Christian beliefs. In short, proof-texting. His method is circular: do we really know Mark, author of the baptism narrative, believed Jesus was already divine, prior to the descent upon him of the Spirit? Or was it the descent of the dove that empowered him, made him a demigod? And does it mean nothing that the 2 Corinthians benediction Metzger quotes mentions not "Father, Son, and Holy Spirit," but rather only "God, Lord Jesus Christ, and Holy Spirit"? The word 'Son' does not appear in this verse and Metzger is unconsciously making the equation *Son = Jesus Christ.* The verse separates Son and Spirit, whatever its author thought of them, from 'God.' Is there any reason to believe such an author meant to include Spirit and Christ (=Son) in the term God? Only if one begs two questions.

Strobel and Metzger move on from text criticism to discuss the canon of the New Testament. First, why is Metzger interested in both? *Because they are essentially the same question for him.* Textual criticism seeks to delimit the specific verbal shape of the text, exactly what statements are to be included in the official version of each New Testament book, while canon apologetics does the same thing with reference to the larger units, whole books.

Metzger explains to his straight man, Reverend Strobel, for the benefit of us ignorant readers, just how the early church picked the New Testament books.

> First, the books must have apostolic authority – that is, they must have been written either by apostles themselves, who were eyewitnesses of what they wrote about, or by followers of apostles. So in the case of Mark and Luke, while they weren't among the twelve disciples, early

tradition has it that Mark was a helper of Peter, and Luke was an associate of Paul.[159]

You already know what I think about this. Let me just ask myself, "How could Dr. Metzger have been satisfied with this?" Paul was not one of the original disciples, either. What does it matter if Luke was the associate of this stranger to the historical Jesus? And surely the professor knew well enough that the authorship of every single New Testament book is up in the air, and has been for generations, among critical scholars. It is by no means even particularly likely that these anonymous books were written by the New Testament characters Matthew, Mark, Luke, and John.

How can Metzger simply disregard all this, for it is plain in context that he deems these canon-criteria quite legitimate. Beyond this, there are many Christian writings that were refused canonization even though they bore the names of apostles with as little historical justification. How did the early Church (and how did Metzger) know the *Apocryphon of John*, the *Apocalypses of James* and *Peter* and *Thomas*, and *Paul*, and the *Gospels of Peter*, *Thomas*, *etc.*, do not have at least as much claim to apostolic authorship—in all cases, a pretty tenuous one—as the books that made it into the canon? Barr, it seems, was right: evangelicals retreat into textual criticism because they do not want to have to wrestle with genuinely critical issues. This way they can say they are New Testament scholars and just work from their default mode of college apologetics.

Metzger goes on: "Second there was the criterion of conformity to what was called the rule of faith. That is, was the document congruent with the basic Christian tradition that the church recognized as normative?"[160] Note the question-begging use of the term "the church." It is safe to say Metzger (like those who originally propounded this criterion) had already dealt the Gnostics, Ebionites, *etc.*, out of the game. They were "heretics" and thus their preferences did not make any difference at all. Thus it is no surprise that many early texts, not arising from within Catholicism, were not welcomed by it. "Those who discerned the limits of the canon had a clear and balanced perspective of the gospel of Christ."[161]

Yes, whoever they were, we know they were the right men for the job of choosing the books for the canon, since they chose the right books! Does Lee Strobel really mean for us to believe he found arguments like this convincing enough to become a Christian? I don't believe it. No one

159 Metzger in Strobel, p. 66.

160 *Ibid.*

161 *Ibid.*, p. 67.

swallows arguments like these unless he is looking for rationalizations for a decision he has already made—probably on some emotional basis.

Two other points: *First*, it is obvious that the first criterion ('apostolicity') reduces to this one: it *cannot* go back to an apostle if does not promote the teaching of the Catholic canonizers. Thus the *Gospel of Peter* has to be a forgery. What more proof do you need?[162] Giving it an apostolic name-tag was giving it a ticket into the canon. You gave them to the books you liked. Rejecting an apostolic name claim, calling the book a forgery, was to reject it from consideration, which you did for other, theological, reasons. *Second*, the criterion implies that the prospective biblical book owes its presence in the canon to a consistent orthodox interpretation (often requiring extensive harmonistic reading if not rewriting). If one dares to reopen the question of whether specific texts really do march goose-step to orthodoxy, one reopens the whole question of canonicity, as Schleiermacher[163] wanted to do, and one makes it dependent upon the Higher Criticism, whose province it is to weigh precisely such questions as authorship, date, *etc.* And since such issues are never susceptible to final, definitive solution, neither is the question of the canon. "It's, ah, quite *probably* the word of God…!"

"And third, there was the criterion of whether a document had continuous acceptance and usage by the church at large."[164] Again, *which* church at large? The large one, the Catholic one. And this criterion was honored in the breach as much as in the observance, since few had heard of Jude or 2 and 3 John, while we possess copies and citations of the Gospel of Thomas from far-flung quarters of the ancient world. But the 'right' Christians weren't reading it. It is all contrived institutional spin. And, sad to say, Dr. Metzger was almost as much of a spin doctor as Lee Strobel. I revere the man's memory and am sorry to have to pronounce such a judgment. Forgive me.

Metzger speaks as if the whole canonization process were more than the sum of its parts. To put it in plain speech, that is another way of saying the reasons adduced are inadequate to explain the phenomenon. And that in turn implies the criteria were mere rationalizations. Metzger nearly says as much when he admits the work of church councils was simply to ratify (*i.e.*, rationalize) the choice already made by the Christian community.

---

162 "Much in every way!"

163 Friedrich Daniel Ernst Schleiermacher, *The Christian Faith.* Paragraphs 126–172 Trans. Hugh Ross Mackintosh (Edinburgh: T&T Clark, 1928), p. 603.

164 *Ibid.*, p. 66.

> The canon is... the separation that came about because of the intuitive insight of Christian believers. They could hear the voice of the Good Shepherd in the gospel of John; they could hear it only in a muffled and distorted way in the Gospel of Thomas... When the pronouncement was made about the canon, it merely ratified what the general sensitivity of the church had already determined. You see, the canon is a list of authoritative books more than an authoritative list of books. These documents didn't derive their authority from being selected; each one was authoritative before anyone gathered them together. The early church merely listened and sensed that these were authoritative accounts.[165]

This idealized personification of "the early Christians," as opposed to some hierarchical potentates, matches the thinking (ironically) of the early form-critics, who posited a poetically sensitive, anonymous 'creative community' responsible for the fabrication of sayings and stories of Jesus.[166] But it was not the Christian Church in general, which Metzger seems to picture as the indefectible Mystical Body of Christ, that served as the conduit of incarnation for the inspired canon, as the Virgin Mary did for Jesus. The real factors have been hidden, and Metzger does a fair job hiding them from himself. The fact is, the leaders of the victorious party succeeded in banning and burning the books cherished by those they considered heretics. Is it simply divine Providence that issued in the preservation of the now-canonical writings but only a single copy (three at the most) of the Nag Hammadi revelations and gospels? No, I have to think it had something to do with the grinding boot-heel of human, all-too-human, ecclesiastical politics.[167]

---

165 *Ibid.*, p. 69.

166 Actually, I think they were basically right, but the creative community was not anonymous so much as the products of early Christian prophets and tradents *wound up* anonymous, collectively attributed to a 'Jesus Christ' who was functionally the same as 'the Torah' or 'our sages' in Mishnaic Judaism. To remove the names of individual religious geniuses reinforced the notion that what they said was simply to be identified with an abstract, divine Truth. Again, it is a matter of reification: the ideas of mortals in history are mystified into seeming like eternal verities occurring in nature. See my chapter "Messiah as Mishnah" in my book *Deconstructing Jesus* (Amherst: Prometheus Books, 2000), pp. 97–112.

167 By his denials, Metzger only admits the truth of what he desperately denies: "you have to understand that the canon was not the result of a series of contests involving church politics" (p. 69). Of course that is exactly what it *was*. Metzger is like Vatican spokesmen who attribute the selection of a new pope merely to the Spirit's guidance, as if the preceding weeks of ecclesiastical machinations had not made their contribution!

"William Barclay said it this way: 'It is the simple truth to say that the New Testament books became canonical because no one could stop them doing so.' ... The Gospel of Thomas excluded itself!"[168] Metzger's pious rhetoric implies again and again that the books *canonized themselves*. Ask yourself: how could Metzger know that all the early Christians (the ones he counts as such) felt the way he says they felt reading the canonical works? How does he know they had such Wesleyan heart-warming experiences as they read these and no other books? He has no evidence for such statements. No, for him, this is the way it *must* have happened, working backward from his preferred Protestant theology. Protestant theologians do not want to make the choice of biblical books contingent on the authority of the church or of church tradition. They want the canonical boundary of the Bible to be based, like all Protestant dogmas, directly on the Bible, the product of the Bible itself. Hence all this strange talk about the Bible canonizing itself. This is not so strange as a *theological* argument, as I have just tried to show. It is, however, exceedingly strange as an *historical* judgment which is what Strobel and Metzger imagine it to be.

In fact, we may say Metzger's self-canonization rhetoric is a perfect example of religious mystification, or reification whereby a piece of history, an invention in history, by human beings, a product of *culture*, becomes transformed (in illusory fashion) into an unalterable piece of *nature*, established from all eternity and thus prior to human invention. Therefore humans have no business gainsaying it. Thus does the product of the first generation, since it predates the second generation of the community, appear to be pre-human, and so superhuman. Henceforth it has a status superior to that of its ancient creators and present-day worshippers.[169] The point of such language from Metzger, a defender of orthodox Protestantism, is to warn the reader: "Pay no attention to that man behind the curtain!"

A Note on a Scrap

Isn't there at least one very important piece of New Testament text that can be dated to before the third century? What about the John Rylands Papyrus fragment, $\mathfrak{P}^{52}$, traditionally dated to between 125 to 160 CE? Metzger attributes a slightly earlier date (100–150) to the fragment.[170] It is from a copy of the Gospel of John, and we must allow some years between the original composition and the initial circulation of copies (like this one).

168 Metzger in Strobel, pp. 67–68.

169 Berger and Luckmann, *Social Construction of Reality*, 58–61.

170 Metzger in Strobel, p. 62.

This might place John's gospel within spitting distance of the time (*ca.* 90 to 100) at which tradition had placed the book. Strobel fairly dances a jig with delight when Metzger informs him that, thanks to 𝔓52, the "skeptical" Tübingen critics of the nineteenth century, who had speculated a second-century date for John's gospel, must be "blown out of the water." This dating, he thinks, vindicates the early and reliable character of the Gospel of John.[171] Indeed, it is customary to see evangelical apologists whip out 𝔓52 like a cop brandishing a traffic manual to issue a speeding ticket to a reckless driver. Only the apologist says, "Hold on, there buddy! You're going too *slow* in dating that gospel! Speed it up, or I'm afraid I'm going to have to run you in!" But the tide has turned, endangering the "assured results" of apologetics.

Brent Nongbri[172] concludes that

> any serious consideration of the window of possible dates for 𝔓52 must include dates in the later second and early third centuries. Thus, 𝔓52 cannot be used as evidence to silence other debates about the existence (or non-existence) of the Gospel of John in the first half of the second century. Only a papyrus containing an explicit date or one found in a clear archaeological stratigraphic context could do the work scholars want 𝔓52 to do. As it stands now, the papyrological evidence should take a second place to other forms of evidence in addressing debates about the dating of the Fourth Gospel.[173]

Likewise Walter Schmithals: "The early dating of 𝔓52 is arbitrary, however, and with newer discoveries and investigations it has proven untenable."[174]

---

171 Strobel, p. 62.

172 Brent Nongbri ("The Use and Abuse of P52: Papyrological Pitfalls in the Dating of the Fourth Gospel." *Harvard Theological Review* 98 (2005), p. 48.

173 Plus, as Darrell J. Doughty observed in a class lecture, the smirking refutation of conservatives fails to reckon with the fact that critics from Bultmann to Raymond E. Brown all agreed that John's gospel was composed and reedited in various stages. There must have been several versions of the gospel. 𝔓52 is so tiny, containing so few words, that we have no reason at all to rule out the possibility that it is a fragment of some earlier version or source of the gospel.

174 Walter Schmithals, *The Theology of the First Christians*. Trans. O.C. Dean (Louisville: Westminster John Knox Press, 1997), p. 330.

Chapter Four
No Corroborating Evidence
No Reporters Covered the Jesus Beat

Flubbed Opportunities

Edwin M. Yamauchi is another great scholar. I have been privileged to meet him a couple of times and to correspond with him a bit. I have much enjoyed his writings, though rather more back when I agreed with them! Still, he is a man of impressive and deep erudition. I am no mind-reader, so I certainly do not know his motivation, but it would not surprise me if he were one of those intellectually gifted evangelicals who seek out the path of learning on a course that will enable them to steer clear of the Slough of Despond, the challenge of genuine historical criticism. For Dr. Yamauchi has gone into a field adjacent to the New Testament, namely Mandaean studies. In this field he is a leading figure, though I remain unpersuaded by his (apologetical?) efforts to make Mandaeanism even *less* adjacent to the Christian scriptures.

Mandaeans ('Gnostics' in Mandaean Aramaic, though they also call themselves "Nazoreans," another name for both early Jewish Christians and a pre-Christian Jewish sect of roving, Gypsy-like carpenters) are the only surviving Gnostic sect. They dwell in the marshes of Iraq, claiming their ancestors fled there from Judea centuries before in a time of persecution. They venerate John the Baptist as an incarnation of one of the archangels and vilify Jesus as a false prophet. As Bultmann shows in great detail, the parallels, both broadly conceptual and strictly verbal, between the Gospel of John and the Mandaean scriptures are startlingly close. Bultmann argues that the Mandaean claim of descent from the New Testament-era sect of John the Baptist ought to be accepted, and that the Johannine similarities to Mandaeanism stem from the fourth evangelist's prior membership in that sect.

More recent scholars, like Kurt Rudolph, still accept the Mandaeans and their scriptures as good evidence that Christianity, like the kindred Baptist sect, emerged from Jewish baptizing Gnosticism in the Jordan valley. History-of-Religions scholars believe that many important Christian themes, such as the very incarnation of the Son of God, were learned from pre-Christian Gnosticism. Radical critics have suggested that Christianity even began in Alexandria as a mystical, allegorizing type of Judaism.[175]

Evangelicals do not much relish the very notion of pre-Christian Gnosticism. They are used to thinking of Gnosticism as a wildly distorted Christian heresy, not as a source of Christianity, which they imagine would undermine the revealed integrity of their faith. So they much prefer to interpret the Gospel of John in connection with similar sets of parallels (and there certainly are some) with the Dead Sea Scrolls,[176] a set of Jewish works. This enables them to feel they are sticking closer to the Old Testament, a more direct from-the-Old-to-the-New-Testament growth model, which is of course the traditional, orthodox model.

Dr. Yamauchi argues at length that there is no evidence for pre-Christian Gnosticism,[177] including Mandaeanism. Some suggest the link that Mandaeans claim with John the Baptist is a medieval addition to their creed in order to get out of a tight spot: to avoid Islamic persecution, they had to slip in under the line as a 'people of the book,' *i.e.*, possessing some connection with the larger biblical tradition, so they chose John the Baptist as a (fictive) patron. I don't buy this, because this theory does not begin to explain the strange business of glorifying John and vilifying Jesus. That, I think, simply demands a *Sitz-im-Leben* (originary context) in which there was polemical rivalry between Christians and Mandaeans. Otherwise, why risk the ire of Muslims who consider Jesus the sinless, virgin-born Messiah and prophet of Israel? Yamauchi seeks to dismiss Bultmann's claim for Mandaean influence on the Gospel of John[178] by pointing to the spotty textual tradition of the Mandaean scriptures: they are a bit of a mess, with few extant copies, and all quite late.[179] But, again, as we saw in the previous chapter, one cannot point to an utter absence of textual evidence and take that to prove there was an absence of texts for the same period. We have exactly the same situation in regard to the Zoroastrian scriptures (an undateable chaos) and their proposed relation to late Old Testament and Pharisaic and Essene doctrines.[180] In such cases, the correct strategy

---

175 L. Gordon Rylands, *The Beginnings of Gnostic Christianity* (London: Watts, 1940).

176 Edwin M. Yamauchi, *The Stones and the Scriptures*. Evangelical Perspectives (NY: Lippincott/Holman, 1972), p. 137–138.

177 Edwin M. Yamauchi, *Pre-Christian Gnosticism: A Survey of the Proposed Evidences* (Grand Rapids: Eerdmans, 1973).

178 Bultmann, *Gospel of John*, pp. 8–9, 17–18.

179 Yamauchi, *Pre-Christian Gnosticism*, pp. 30–34, 126, 170–171.

180 Walter Schmithals, *The Apocalyptic Movement: Introduction and Interpreta-*

is to examine the parallels and, if they are striking enough, to *suggest* dependence, and then see what you get when you apply this theoretical model to the wider evidence. All such experiments are tentative.

As it happens, Old Testament scholars have had great success with the theory that Persian Zoroastrian significantly enriched Judaism with themes that would go on to become central in Orthodox Judaism, Christianity, and Islam: the periodization of salvation history, a supernatural deliverer, end-time resurrection and judgment, an evil anti-god and his angelic minions, *etc.* The case seems the same to me with regard to Mandaeanism and the Gospel of John. The parallels are much more detailed, extensive, and strict between them than any comparable parallels between John and the Dead Sea Scrolls.

As for pre-Christian Gnosticism in general, Yamauchi rightly points out that non-Christian Gnosticism is not the same thing as pre-Christian Gnosticism.[181] The Nag Hammadi texts present us with Gnostic texts that are only superficially Christianized.[182] Some make Jesus into a later-day return or avatar of Seth, Melchizedek, or Zoroaster! But Yamauchi warns that, though these Gnostics have added Jesus onto a system they had embraced before becoming Christians (of a sort), it does not follow that the sects to which they had belonged were themselves pre-Christian. True enough, but I side with Kurt Rudolph on this one. The appearance of a long and developed theological tradition, complete with liturgies and angelologies, *etc.*, and with Old Testament patriarchs as their revealers,[183] seems to place these texts alongside the Jewish Pseudepigrapha. They make the same sort of experimental ventures beyond late-BCE Judaism, where they employ biblical themes, as the Pseudepigrapha do. There is no real reason to try to deny a pre-Christian origin.

I see in the attempt to do so the same implausible defensive tactic Yamauchi and others take toward the issue of pre-Christian Greek and

---

tion. Trans. John E. Steely (NY: Abingdon Press, 1975), pp. 115–118; Norman Cohn, *Cosmos, Chaos and the World to Come: The Ancient Roots of Apocalyptic* (New Haven: Yale University Press, 1993), pp. 220–226.

181 *Ibid.*, pp. 181–184.

182 Kurt Rudolph, *Gnosis: The Nature and History of Gnosticism.* Trans. R.McL. Wilson, P.W. Coxon, and K.H. Kuhn (San Francisco: Harper & Row, 1983), p. 51.

183 Rudolph, *Gnosis: The Nature and History of Gnosticism*, p. 277; *cf.* Walter Schmithals, *Apocalyptic Movement*, pp. 15, 95, 125; Schmithals, *The Office of Apostle in the early Church.* Trans. John E. Steely (NY: Abingdon Press, 1969), pp. 116–118

Anatolian dying-and-rising god myths.[184] These, too, seem to many critics not only to be the antecedents but the sources of Christian resurrection-belief. The sheer notion that such beliefs were widely available to Jews at the dawn of Christianity seems to undermine faith in a historical resurrection of Jesus. To posit such a thing seems utterly superfluous if Christianity could easily have arisen by a simple process of adapting a pre-existing set of myths and rituals, which is what I believe happened. For obvious reasons, conservatives don't like this possibility very much either, and they (absurdly, to my way of thinking) try to believe that pagans borrowed the resurrection of a savior god *from Christianity*!

Never mind the tangible, datable evidence supplied by ancient texts, monuments, and shards that these gods and their Easters predated Christianity; ancient Christian *apologists themselves* admitted the pre-Christian dates of the pagan parallels when they argued (somehow with a straight face) that the pagan versions were Satanic counterfeits *before the fact!* Yes, Satan knew what was coming, so he planted false versions of it before the real thing came along, so that pagans would hear Christian preaching and say, "Yeah, yeah. So what else is new?" No Christian would have argued in such a suicidal way if he didn't have to. By contrast, the alternate strategy to disarm the bomb, the attempt to assign the pagan resurrection parallels a post-Christian date, is fully as ludicrous as the scene in *Star Trek V: The Undiscovered Country* in which Warlord Chang growls out what he claims is the "original Klingon" text of Hamlet's To-be-or-not-to-be soliloquy.

All right, I am commenting on subjects Strobel does not even ask Dr. Yamauchi about in *The Case for Christ*. And that is my first complaint. I do not agree with Yamauchi's positions or his general approach, as is obvious, but he is a scholar with notable opinions that need to be addressed if one wishes to engage the subject of Strobel's book. And yet Reverend Strobel asks Dr. Yamauchi about none of this. Instead, we are treated to yet more dismal nonsense about extra-biblical attestations of a historical Jesus, as if there were any. He already quizzed Craig Blomberg about this, and Dr. Yamauchi adds nothing, not only because there is nothing new to say on the subject after Blomberg has said his piece, but also because the apologetical line is utterly vacuous, whether it is Blomberg or Yamauchi who parrots it.

---

184 Yamauchi, Edwin M. "Easter: Myth, Hallucination, or History?" *Christianity Today* Vol. XVIII, No. 12 (March 15, 1974): 660–663; Yamauchi, "Tammuz and the Bible," *Journal of Biblical Literature* 84 (1965): 283–290.

Is No News Good News?

I am not going to repeat the whole business about Josephus here. Let me just note the rich irony of the position taken by apologists like Yamauchi, Blomberg, and John Meier when it comes to the spurious *Testimonium Flavianum* passage. They scream "Foul!" if a critic proposes interpolations in scripture without benefit of first- or second-century manuscript evidence,[185] but in the case of Josephus they are willing to let the beloved patient undergo the risky surgery. They would really rather claim the whole Jesus-Christ-boosting passage *as is*, for apologetics. But no one will listen to them if they do. So they have to trim away some of the juiciest bits in order to save a somewhat less useful carcass. Still, they figure, it's better than nothing. And so they suggest certain phrases be surrendered as Christian interpolations, yes, the best ones, but better to save the patient's life. Better to cut off an offending limb and hobble into the kingdom than be tossed, whole and sound, into the *post mortem* magma pit. But all that is going on is a negotiation. It is an attempt to make a bad bit of evidence into a good one by trimming away the tell-tale signs of spuriousness.

There is a second passage in Josephus' *Antiquities* (20:9:1) in which he describes the death of a certain James, saintly brother of a certain Jesus, considered the Anointed.

> And now Caesar, upon hearing of the death of Festus, sent Albinus into Judea, as procurator. But the king deprived Joseph of the high priesthood, and bestowed the succession to that dignity on the son of Ananus, who was also himself called Ananus. Now the report goes that this eldest Ananus proved a most fortunate man; for he had five sons who had all performed the office of a high priest to God, and who had himself enjoyed that dignity a long time formerly, which had never happened to any other of our high priests. But this younger Ananus, who, as we have told you already, took the high priesthood, was a bold man in his temper, and very insolent; he was also of the sect of the Sadducees, who are very rigid in judging offenders, above all the rest of the Jews, as we have already observed; when, therefore, Ananus was of this disposition, he thought he had now a proper opportunity [to

185 Never mind that some of the same writers take refuge in precisely such proposals when they are the only remaining expedient for denying an error in the Bible: "Oh yeah? Prove this error was in the original autographs! Go ahead! It must have been a scribal alteration." *¡Ay Caramba!*

> exercise his authority]. Festus was now dead, and Albinus was but upon the road; so he assembled the Sanhedrin of judges, and brought before them the brother of Jesus, who was called Christ, whose name was James, and some others, [or, some of his companions]; and when he had formed an accusation against them as breakers of the law, he delivered them to be stoned: but as for those who seemed the most equitable of the citizens, and such as were the most uneasy at the breach of the laws, they disliked what was done; they also sent to the king [Agrippa], desiring him to send to Ananus that he should act so no more, for that what he had already done was not to be justified; nay, some of them went also to meet Albinus, as he was upon his journey from Alexandria, and informed him that it was not lawful for Ananus to assemble a Sanhedrin without his consent. Whereupon Albinus complied with what they said, and wrote in anger to Ananus, and threatened that he would bring him to punishment for what he had done; on which king Agrippa took the high priesthood from him, when he had ruled but three months, and made Jesus, the son of Damneus, high priest.

Recently some have suggested that this incident, as originally related by Josephus, intended no reference to James the Just, the "brother of the Lord." It would make a lot of sense if the ambushed James was James, son of Damneus, the brother of Jesus, son of Damneus. The implied scenario would be one in which Ananus arranged to have a rival for the priesthood eliminated on trumped-up charges but did not get away with it. Once his crime was known, he was thrown out of office, and the brother of the murdered James was awarded the office Ananus had sought to render secure for himself. In this way, the slain James was avenged at least insofar as his surviving brother, Jesus, received the office James had been cheated out of.

The reference we now read to "Jesus called Christ" might originally have read (or denoted, even if it read as it does now) "Jesus, called/considered high priest." In both Daniel 9:26 and in the Dead Sea Scrolls, 'an anointed one' (which is what Josephus has here, no definite article denoting "the Messiah") means 'high priest.' It is easy to see how early Christian copyists might have confused all this, quite innocently taking a passage about the assassination of James son of Damneus, brother of Jesus who followed him into the priestly office after the scheming Ananus was eliminated, and unwittingly making it into a passage about Jesus Christ and James the Just.

The Tacitus passage, as I said in the previous chapter, represents no reporting on Jesus by a contemporary; it only tells us what we already knew anyway: Christians believed Jesus, crucified at the order of the Prefect Pontius Pilate, was the resurrected Christ, and Tacitus was aware that they did. I really don't see what the fuss is all about on this one. And I am, frankly, amazed at what Dr. Yamauchi thinks to squeeze out of it. "How can you explain the spread of a religion based on the worship of a man who had suffered the most ignominious death possible? Of course, the Christian answer is that he was resurrected."[186]

The thinking here is surprisingly confused. Not even Burton L. Mack suggests that Christianity was ever propagated as the story of a man who was crucified and then eaten by buzzards, end of story. That might indeed have been a tough product to sell (though people have lined up to buy weirder ones!). What Yamauchi seems to be struggling to say is that a crucifixion story without a heroic reversal where God raises Jesus would have garnered few converts outside the Cross Makers Union. The important point, however, is not that a resurrection actually happened, but that the *story* culminated that way.

How would people in the second generation (or even in the first) have known whether the story were true anyway? They were already stuck with faith instead of sight. But as these things go, it is by no means hard to imagine people being attracted to the *tale* of a good man being crucified for crimes he did not commit, then rising from the dead. After all, this sort of reversal-of-fortunes story, played out in a salvation ritual (such as Christianity also offered) was already fantastically successful in the Hellenistic world.

Poor Attis had castrated himself and bled to death. (Didn't you know? That's why the violets are deep purple: his blood soaked them.). Then he rose after three days. His religion was quite popular, even though his death was, if anything, more disgusting than crucifixion. Adonis was gored to death by a boar, as was the Cretan Zeus/Dionysus. Dionysus was dismembered and eaten alive, then reborn. Osiris was suffocated in a coffin, then brought back to life without his penis!

---

186 Yamauchi in Strobel, p. 82.

Spartacus and Cleomenes had already become famous as crucified martyrs. There was nothing disgraceful in martyrdom, then or now. Yamauchi's point would be a good one had Jesus been condemned as a child molester or for bestiality, but being a martyr to Rome was by no means a shameful death.

Next we have the question, how exactly does Dr. Yamauchi envision the miraculous nature of the (allegedly improbable) spread of this religion? I assume he has in view, however vaguely, the spread of Christianity up till Tacitus' time of writing, nearly a century after Jesus. Where does the supernatural come into play here?

Did all these Christians for about a century after Easter have their own resurrection appearances, like Joseph Smith and Oliver Cowdery experienced inside the new Mormon temple in Kirtland, Ohio, April 3, 1836? Or does he mean that the Holy Spirit hypnotized people, forcing them to believe despite the improbability? Or does he mean merely that the first century's worth of evangelists, if we judge by their success, made a case stronger than we are able to make today, and that we ought to believe that whatever extra-convincing evidence they had would convince us, too, if only we knew what it was?

But how can we know it would have been convincing if we don't know what it said? Even to raise such an argument is suicidal, implying that the best apologetics one can offer today are pathetically vacuous in comparison with whatever superior reasons and warrants Christians were able to offer in ancient times. Until we know what they were, why not admit we have no really compelling or even convincing "Case for Christ" to make?

Darkest Africanus

In the section of a chapter titled "The Day the Earth Went Dark," Yamauchi cites a certain Thallus to support the Gospel claim that the world went dark at the time of Jesus' crucifixion: "Thallus, in the third book of his histories, explains away the darkness [*at the time of the crucifixion*], as an eclipse of the sun – unreasonably, as it seems to me." So said Church Father Julius Africanus in 221 CE. He does not quote whatever he was reading, nor does he indicate which of three known ancient figures named Thallus he refers to, whether the mid-first-century Thallus or one of the later ones. We don't know which one authored the history Africanus was reading. Africanus does not even say for sure that Thallus mentioned that this darkness coincided with Jesus' crucifixion, only that he mentioned some strange darkness which he reasoned must be an eclipse. Africanus may simply *suppose* it to have been the darkness of Good Friday, perhaps inferring this from whatever date Thallus mentioned, and so rejects the naturalistic explanation. We do not know what Thallus said or meant.

Pilate the Pussycat?

How can a brutal, Jew-baiting dictator like Pontius Pilate (as Josephus and Philo have made him out to have been) have had the slightest compunction against throwing Jesus to his accusers like a piece of meat to a cage of hungry lions? Scholars have long considered the whole sequence of Pilate zealously undertaking to free Jesus to be apocryphal—part of a general early Christian attempt to shift the burden of 'Christ-killing' guilt from the Romans to the Jews. It is just hard to depict Pilate either caring about Jesus, the confused soothsayer (as he must have seemed to Pilate), or knuckling under and surrendering him to his enemies if he did not want to. Thus the gospel portrait looks doubly implausible. But not according to Yamauchi. Referring to Paul Maier's book on Pilate,[187] he explains that Pilate's

> protector or patron was Sejanus and... Sejanus fell from power in A.D. 31 because he was plotting against the emperor... Well, this would have made Pilate's position very weak in A.D. 33, which is most likely when Jesus was crucified... So it would certainly be understandable that Pilate would have been reluctant to offend the Jews at that time and to get into further trouble with the emperor. That means the biblical description is most likely correct.[188]

Or not.

Imagine Caesar's reception of the news that Pilate had, to mollify a crowd of the native rabble, condemned a man he had already acquitted, and that instead he had released a convicted insurrectionist and killer of Romans (Mark 15:7)! Was Pontius Pilate such a fool?

Bragging Rites?

As in his fascinating booklet *Jesus Zoroaster Buddha Socrates Muhammad*[189] Dr. Yamauchi gives us a brief but fact-packed tour of what

187 Paul Maier, *Pontius Pilate* (Wheaton: Tyndale House, 1968). Another of Barr's evangelicals, erudite in the margins of biblical studies.

188 *Ibid*., p. 85.

189 Edwin M. Yamauchi, *Jesus Zoroaster Buddha Socrates Muhammad* (Downers Grove: InterVarsity Press, 1972).

we know (or what evangelicals think we know) about the five saviors listed in the comma-less title.[190] It is plain that he indulges in unconscious special pleading, happily incorporating the results of critical study of the non-Christian traditions and documents yet excluding all Jesus scholarship except evangelical apologetics for the gospels. He provides a quick repeat performance, which has by now become something of a ritual repetition, for Lee Strobel:

> But the fact is that we have better historical documentation for Jesus than for the founder of any other ancient religion… For example, though the Gathas of Zoroaster, about 1000 B.C., are believed to be authentic, most of the Zoroastrian scriptures were not put into writing until after the third century A.D. The most popular Parsi biography of Zoroaster was written in A.D. 1278. The scriptures of Buddha, who lived in the sixth century B.C., were not put into writing until after the Christian era [began], and the first biography of Buddha was written in the first century A.D. Although we have the sayings of Muhammad, who lived from A.D. 570 to 632, in the Koran, his biography was not written until 767 – more than a full century after his death.[191]

But is this really the point? Granted, there is no solid footing for the historian or biographer researching the other religion founders. The sources are very late and no doubt corrupt. We can see this from the numerous anachronisms, from the internal contradictions implying more than one writer, one correcting his predecessor, from interruptions in narrative logic, manifest borrowing (Muhammad on record as composing the Lord's Prayer, for example), differences in style, *etc.* For sure, their documentation has grown very confused.

The relevant point, however, is *how long this process takes*. Did it require all the centuries Yamauchi measures out disdainfully between the Buddha or Zoroaster and their scriptures? (And why not include the great historical distance between Moses and the grossly contradictory stories about him and laws ascribed to him?) Would there have to be a gap of centuries between Jesus and his records for them to have become subject (in either oral or written transmission) to corruption and embellishment? Hardly!

The kind of close scrutiny biblical critics have been engaged in for the last three centuries (while apologists have sat on the sidelines carping:

---

190 The author himself had christened the piece "Notes on the (In)comparable Christ" when it originally appeared in *Christianity Today* magazine (October 22, 1971), pp. 7–11.

191 Yamauchi in Strobel, p. 87.

"Throw the bums out!") has revealed the same sort of phenomena in the gospels that scholars have found in the various Buddhist, Islamic, and Zoroastrian texts Yamauchi invokes. Such corruption doesn't take long in the first place. But, as James Barr anticipated, apologists wouldn't know about all this for the reason that they don't bother with such things. They sit on their perches of textual criticism or theology or Greek grammar or biblical Hebrew or Assyriology, and they pontificate on how, judged by standards alien to the field, the gospel writers "couldn't have" or "wouldn't have" done this or that. They don't want to be confused with the facts. They know already what could and could not be there. Who the heck needs form-criticism when we know *a priori* that there could be no secondary growth of the tradition? Who needs to look through Galileo's telescope when Aristotle already told us what the moon must look like?

Chapter Five
The Stones Keep Mum
How Biblical Archaeology Digs Up a World without Jesus

In all the discussion of faith and history such as that expertly explored in Van A. Harvey's classic *The Historian and the Believer,*[192] archaeology inevitably comes to the fore as the source from which surprises threaten to emerge. What might upset faith's apple cart? Many things might (including genetic research, as Mormons recently found out the hard way), not to mention the critical study of historical documents, but believers are adept at fending off evidence of that kind. For such thought experiments one usually imagines the delver's spade turning up some gross inconvenience such as the bones of Jesus or the bone box of his brother. And yet it is the entire *absence* of evidence that has wrought great devastation to the credibility of the Bible.

Old Testament minimalism[193] has torn from our grasp the once-firm hold we thought we had on the historical character of ancient Israelite narrative. Who'd have guessed Davidic Jerusalem was only a crossroads with a gas pump? Solomon's temple little more than a Vegas wedding chapel (if even that)? I do not see in evangelical apologetical literature any attempt to come to grips with this new biblical archaeology. Apologists seem still content to rest on the laurels of the William F. Albright era when any structure found in more or less the area the Bible mentioned a city or structure existing must be that site. They still imagine that archaeology has vindicated Old Testament accuracy.

Similar debates occur in the New Testament field, especially as concerns synagogues in Galilee. The gospels and Josephus mention synagogues throughout Galilee, but as yet no evidence of synagogue

---

192 Van A. Harvey, *The Historian and the Believer:The Morality of Historical Knowledge* (NY: Macmillan, 1966).

193 Thomas L. Thompson, *The Mythic Past: Biblical Archaeology and the Myth of Israel* (NY: Basic Books, 1999); Keith W. Whitelam, *The Invention of Ancient Israel: The Silencing of Palestinian History* (NY: Routledge, 1996); Niels Peter Lemche, *The Israelites in History and Tradition* Library of Ancient Israel (London: SPCK / Louisville: Westminster John Knox Press, 1998); Philip R. Davies, *In Search of 'Ancient Israel.'* Journal for the Study of the Old Testament Supplement Series 148 (Sheffield: Sheffield Academic Press, 1992); Marc Zvi Brettler, *The Creation of History in Ancient Israel* (NY: Routledge, 1995).

structures has yet been unearthed. Of course, we know of open air meeting places (Acts 16:13) in the first century CE, but numerous references in the gospels imply Jesus entering a special building: Matthew 6:5; Mark 1:21, 23, 29, 31; 3:1; 6:2; 12:39; 13:9; Luke 4:15, 16, 20, 28; 7:5; 13:10; 21:12; John 6:25, 59; 9:23, 42; 16:2; 18:20. None of these sounds right to me if we try to substitute "private gathering" or "lawn party." And when we hear of a benefactor bank-rolling the construction of a synagogue, or of the religious peacocks angling for the podium seats in the synagogue, or floggings of heretics there, I just can't imagine the evangelists were thinking of anything but discrete synagogue buildings. And there is no evidence of any, which means the evangelists simply assumed things had been as they were in their own day.

No Nazareth

Now we have to ask ourselves: Can any good news come out of Nazareth? That all depends on where one stands, but René Salm[194] has shown that we have an utter void of archaeological vestiges of the Galilean home town of Jesus. At least there was no such town in the early part of the first century. The area had indeed been inhabited in the Iron and Bronze Ages, but by the time of Jesus it had been empty and windswept for some eight hundred years. It *began* to be repopulated about the middle of the first century CE, twenty years after Jesus' ostensible death.

Salm examines every bit of known evidence from the Nazareth Plateau. What a disparity between his results (none of them methodologically dubious, none controversial except in implication) and the blithe generalizations of certain well-known Bible encyclopedias and handbooks! These authors write as if there were enough evidence not only to establish a Jesus-era Nazareth but even to characterize it in various ways. A great deal of the confusion inherited by these 'experts' stems from the schizophrenic researches of Roman Catholic diggers and taggers charged by Rome to find out what they could about Nazareth. To them it seemed that Church tradition and Gospel narrative deserved to be considered evidence equal in importance to the yield of the ground. Their procedure was exactly like that of B.B. Warfield and his fellow inerrantists who insisted on giving equal weight to both the "claims" and the "phenomena" of scripture. The result is inevitably, even intentionally, skewed.

---

[194] René Salm, *The Myth of Nazareth: The Invented Town of Jesus* (Cranford: American Atheist Press, 2008).

Salm's archaeological outcome does fit quite well with other literary considerations, namely the entire silence of both Josephus and the Mishnah when it comes to Nazareth. More than this, it seems to confirm a long-standing critical theory that 'Jesus the Nazorean/Nazarene' first denoted a sectarian label, reflecting the Nazorean sect(s) catalogued by various Jewish, Christian, and Muslim heresiologists, notably including the still-living Mandaean (Nasorean) sect of Iraq. Jesus was considered to be a member, or at least a pious Jew of that type (Nasoreans were itinerant carpenters, among other things). It was only later, once those with a higher Christology had begun to feel uneasy with notions such as Jesus receiving instruction from John the Baptist or even from village tutors, that some preferred to understand "Nazarene" to mean "of Nazareth." And by this time, there *was* a Nazareth, which the gospel writers were only too happy to retcon,[195] or retroject, into the first century BCE.

In Frank R. Zindler's ground-breaking essay "Where Jesus Never Walked,"[196] Zindler, anticipating Salm, argues that there was no village of Nazareth in the ostensible time of Jesus. Reverend Strobel's interviewee John McRay appeals to the work of James F. Strange to refute Zindler: "Archaeologists have found a list in Aramaic describing the twenty-four 'courses,' or families, of priests who were relocated, and one of them was registered as having been moved to Nazareth. That shows that this tiny village must have been there at the time."[197] McRay does not, however, mention the fact that the "list" in question is a fragmentary inscription—in which the beginning of the Hebrew word read as 'Nazareth' is missing—from a synagogue in Caesarea that is datable to the end of the third or beginning of the fourth century CE![198]

Salm, moreover, reminds us that no exodus of priests followed the Roman victory of 70 CE, since, as Emil Schürer notes,[199] it took a long

195 "Retconning" is a term created by comic book fans for what happens when a character or story-line is rebooted and overhauled, necessitating the retroactive rewriting of the back story to adjust it to the new "continuity."

196 Frank R. Zindler, "Where Jesus Never Walked," in *American Atheist*, Winter 1996–97.

197 McRay in Strobel, p. 103.

198 Jack Finegan, *The Archeology of the New Testament: The Life of Jesus and the Beginning of the Early Church*, Revised Edition (Princeton: Princeton University Press, 1992).

199 Emil Schürer, *A History of the Jewish People in the Time of Jesus Christ* (Peabody: Hendrickson, 1989), 1.2.272., cited in Rene Salm, *The Myth of Nazareth: The Invented Town of* Jesus (Cranford, NJ: American Atheist Press, 2008), p. 277.

time before Jews accepted the inevitable, that worship would no longer be possible at the temple or its ruins. This is why the Temple Tax continued to be collected long after 70. Jews were, however, forced to leave the city after the Bar Cochba revolt in 136. Richard A. Horsley estimates that the resettlement of Jewish priests in Nazareth took place "well into the second (or even the third) century."[200]

So Strange has pre-dated the list. It does not after all attest a Jesus-era Nazareth. Strange also points to "Herodian" era oil lamps and tombs in Nazareth, but his dating was premature on these, too. The tombs are all *kokh* tombs, having a central chamber, branching out into shafts, and these were not adopted in Nazareth till after 50 CE[201] Likewise with the oil lamps. The single example (out of 13) not definitively datable to after 50 CE, may date to a few years earlier, but there is no way to be sure.[202]

Some of McRay's other reassurances are not so definite: "Two tombs contained objects such as pottery lamps, glass vessels, and vases from the first, third, *or* fourth centuries."[203] Ian Wilson is quoted: "Such findings suggests that Nazareth *may* have existed in Jesus' time."[204]

Acts and Accuracy

Strobel and his informant John McRay happily trot out a long series of governmental offices mentioned by the author of Acts, showing that each one is correct. The author correctly places politarchs in Thessalonika, Asiarchs in Ephesus, *etc.*, a veritable almanac of ancient Mediterranean civics. Good for the author of Acts. F.F. Bruce[205] goes through the same list. It is a familiar litany by now.

What is the point? Our apologists make a bizarre leap at this point, and like Dickens's ghosts, they invite us to hold their hand to find ourselves magically upheld as we fly through the air with them, leaving historical method vanishing in the mist far beneath us. For what can it profit a man

---

200 Richard A. Horsley, *Galilee: History, Politics, People* (Valley Forge: Trinity Press International, 1995), p. 110. See also, D. Trifon, "Did the Priestly Courses (Mishmarot) Transfer from Judea to the Galilee after the Bar-Cochba Revolt?" *Tarbits* (1989–1990)

201 Salm, p. 160.

202 *Ibid.*, pp. 168–169.

203 McRay in Strobel, p. 103, italics mine.

204 McRay in Strobel, p. 103, quoting Ian Wilson, *Jesus: The Evidence* (San Francisco: HarperSanFrancisco, 1988), p. 67. Italics mine.

205 Bruce, *New Testament Documents*, pp. 82–83.

if he gets all the local titles and offices and right, if what he is trying to prove is that people in these locations healed the sick with their snot rags, survived the bites of poisonous serpents, brushed themselves off unhurt following fatal stonings, resurrected teenagers their sermons had bored to death, blinded some and killed others merely by a word of power?

I'm afraid that getting an 'A' on an ancient civics test is of no real help in vindicating these wonder-stories. Why would anyone think the one set of data would in any way corroborate the other? What has (the civil administration of) Athens to do with (a man ascending into heaven from) Jerusalem?

The same applies to the supposed accuracy of John's gospel of which John A.T. Robinson[206] and A.M. Hunter[207] made so much. Posing as cutting-edge radicals seeking to overthrow the moss-back opinion of John's gospel as a late and historically worthless tissue of theological allegory, these churchmen were just retrenching, seeking to recall New Testament scholarship to its comfortable, pre-critical stages. (In fact, that remains the disingenuous pose of apologists today.) Robinson, Hunter, and others ballyhooed the fact that John mentions the inscribed pavement called Gabbatha (19:13), and it has been found. John 5:5 mentions a healing shrine, the five-porched Pool of Bethsaida, and archaeologists have turned it up. John 9:7 mentions the Pool of Siloam, and they found that, too.

It might be more accurate to say that, just as Constantine's research department did, they found sites that might qualify as being these places and so christened them. Who knows? But I am willing to accept the identifications. What I am *not* willing to accept is the wild inference that, because a genuine location is mentioned, the events recounted as happening there must therefore really have occurred. The ancient world knew its share of historical novels, and they, too, set events at well-known locations (and had their characters interact with real kings, governors, *etc*).

But does it not at least attest that the fourth evangelist had genuine memories of Jerusalem as it was before the disaster of 70 CE? No, as numerous place names and such appearing in the Mishnah and Talmud imply. Traditions continued to percolate down the ages by all manner of lateral and circuitous routes. Babylonian rabbis who had never once

206 John A.T. Robinson, "The New Look on the Fourth Gospel," in Robinson, *Twelve New Testament Studies*. Studies in Biblical Theology No. 34 (London: SCM Press, 1962, pp. 94–106.

207 Archibald M. Hunter, *According to John: The New Look at the Fourth Gospel* (Philadelphia: Westminster Press, 1968).

visited Jerusalem knew of its major landmarks from the old tales of these things they had heard from their forbears, at whatever remove, and from younger contemporaries who had been there, they or their fathers.

For instance, the scribe who added John 5:3b–4 is an example of a later copyist who 'knew' of the Pool of Bethsaida and a healing legend associated with it because the story of the descent of Raphael the healing angel to stir up the waters had been passed down like a barnacle on the hull of the gospel, a gloss regularly told to explain the story of Jesus healing a man there. We need posit no eyewitness recollection of the Pool of Bethsaida.

In the analogous case of the Pool of Siloam, we have a genuine ancient location made the springboard for a patently unhistorical story. The tale of the congenitally blind man (a doublet of the congenitally lame man healed by Peter and John in Acts 3:1–10 *ff.*) occasions a story based on the gross anachronism of excommunication of Christ-confessing Jews from the synagogues (9:22), something which this very gospel elsewhere reserves as a *future* event (16:1–2)![208]

Taking Leave of Your Census

Strobel and McRay are retreating to the margins, and that is not where the action is. To evaluate the reliability of Luke-Acts, one must look closely at the narrative, the stories that compose the double work, not the window-dressing. That is just what I want to do here, though trying to do that in the course of a single chapter necessitates a flying survey.

Surely Luke's greatest historical embarrassment, and one from which his most ardent defenders have never been able to rescue him, is the matter of the Roman census coincident with Jesus' birth in Bethlehem. In chapter 3, Luke contrives to get the Nazarene couple Mary and Joseph down to Bethlehem in time for Jesus to be born there. He asks himself just what it would take to get the pair on the rough hilly roads this far into Mary's pregnancy. Surely no mere vacation. Perhaps his imagination was influenced by the well known story of Krishna's birth while his earthly father was away registering for taxation.

In any case, Luke has a Roman census require Joseph's (and Mary's?) presence elsewhere, in Bethlehem, where King David once lived—Joseph being a remote descendent of David. The absurdity of this is obvious. No taxation census ever required individuals to register, not where they themselves live but rather where their remote ancestors once lived! What, after all, is the *point* of a census in *any* century? The government wants to

[208] Maurice Casey, *Is John's Gospel True?* (NY: Routledge, 1996), pp.54–55.

know how much in taxes they can expect to collect and at what address. Imagine asking people to register where their forbears lived a thousand years previously! That is what Luke bids us imagine, but we cannot.

McRay thinks he has a solution: "Actually, the discovery of ancient census forms has shed quite a bit of light on this practice." He then quotes a Roman order from 104 CE:

> Gaius Vibius Maximus, Prefect of Egypt: Seeing that the time has come for the house to house census, it is necessary to compel all those who for any cause whatsoever are residing out of their provinces to return to their own homes, that they may both carry out the regular order of the census and may also attend diligently to the cultivation of their allotments.[209]

McRay is like the Hebrews enslaved by Pharaoh, only he is enslaved to the doctrine of biblical inerrancy. If the Hebrews had to make bricks without straw, McRay is grasping at straws without straw. This ancient decree is much too weak a reed to pull him out of the quicksand. Can he really not see the difference between what Gaius Vibius Maximus commands and what Luke describes? In the one case, tax-payers *who are currently staying elsewhere* must return to *their* homes, their official addresses, for enrollment; otherwise the IRS would have to go looking for them. But in the second case, Luke posits that the Roman government might, for some unguessable reason, direct its subjects to sign up for tax collection where they do *not* live, but where their remote ancestors lived a full millennium before!

Even if we felt we could swallow a camel of such volume, there are gnats aplenty at which to strain. For one thing, the census Luke posits (2:1), levied at the command of Caesar Augustus, is unknown to any historian of the period. This is exceedingly strange, given the meticulous documentation of the era. (Moses of Chorene says this census had been carried out in his homeland of Armenia, but he wrote in the sixth century CE and was a Christian, perhaps trying to harmonize the biblical account by reference to some local census, much as apologists for Noah's Flood try to connect it with geological 'evidence' of local flooding in the same region.)

Matthew and Luke both place Jesus' birth in the reign of Herod the Great, a client king of Rome. His was a satellite state of the Roman Empire, like Poland or Czechoslovakia before the break-up of the Soviet Bloc. At

---

209 Strobel, p. 101.

this time Palestine was not yet officially a Roman province, so it could not have been included in any taxation of the empire proper. After the inept Archelaus, son of Herod the Great, was deposed, Judea did become a part of Rome, ruled by the Roman governor of the province of Syria. The governor Quirinius *did* conduct a census as Luke says (Luke 2:2). But this census was carried out in 6 CE, a full decade later than Luke supposes here and no one had to return to ancestral homes. Neither Quirinius nor anyone else governed Judea as a Roman territory while Herod the Great still lived. But there *were* Roman governors of Syria, which did not yet include Judea.

The apologist Sir William Ramsey tried to get rid of this contradiction by gratuitously positing a previous term as governor of Syria for Quirinius on an earlier occasion. What led him to think this? Not much (other than a desire to vindicate Bible accuracy, that is). All Ramsey discovered was an inscription saying Quirinius had been honored for his aid in a military victory, and Ramsey gratuitously guessed that Quirinius' reward had been a previous tenure as governor of Syria. Besides, there is no room for it. We know who occupied the post in Herod's time, and it was not Quirinius. As Tertullian tells us, this post was occupied successively by two men, Sentius Saturninus (4–3 BCE) and Quinctillius Varus (2–1 BCE).

Luke also knew quite well (Acts 5:37) that when Quirinius did tax Jews, in 6 CE, it was an unprecedented outrage among Jews, who responded by rebellion at the instigation of Judas the Gaulonite, issuing in thousands of crucifixions all over the Galilean hills. This shows that Roman taxation of Jews could not have been taken for granted a decade earlier, no matter who we might imagine conducting it.

McRay makes the fantastic suggestion that "there were apparently two Quiriniuses,"[210] based on "micrographic" letters carved onto the thin edge of a coin naming Quirinius as proconsul of Syria and Cilicia from 11 BCE until past the demise of Herod the Great. Richard C. Carrier has completely exposed the hoax underlying McRay's bizarre claim. In a series of unrefereed papers, Jerry Vardaman claimed to have found, peering through a microscope, great clusters of letters on both the edges and the faces of Greek coins (Latin letters, mind you!) with all sorts of juicy historical notes, including tenure dates for Pilate and other familiar figures utterly out of sync with all other sources. Jesus is even commemorated as a reigning king of Galilee!

210 McRay in Strobel, pp. 101–102.

As Carrier notes, the porous and uneven faces of ancient coins (and stones, where Vardaman also claims to scry microletters) makes it impossible for such letters to have survived the typical weathering processes. Additionally, for them to be there in the first place, to inscribe such letters, would require the use of microscopy and diamond-tipped tools unavailable in the ancient world. Vardaman omits even the most elementary references and appears to have added the very elements in his drawn pictures of coins that he claims to have found there. There is something disturbingly pseudoscientific going on here, and it is no surprise that only apologists like McRay, Strobel, and Yamauchi have associated themselves with this hypothesis. Worst of all for the present case, Carrier points out:

> There is no Quirinius coin. McRay's reference is to an unpublished paper that no doubt comes up with more complete nonsense about Quirinius in the reading of random scratches on some coin or other. But Vardaman hasn't even published this claim. Instead, almost a decade later, when he did present a lecture on the matter, his paper on the dating of Quirinius, though over twenty pages in length, never mentions this coin that apparently McRay read about. Instead, a date of 12 B.C. is arrived at using nonexistent microletters on a stone inscription (the...*Lapis Venetus*). Hopefully this pseudohistory can be seen for what it is. Any claim based on this work must be held in the highest suspicion.[211]

Suppose Luke was mistaken in associating Jesus' birth with Herod the Great. Could we then salvage the census of Quirinius as the context of Jesus' birth, albeit at the cost of having Jesus born in 6 CE? No, because under Quirinius the region of Galilee had been split off from Judea and remained outside direct Roman control. It was instead (still) ruled by Herod's son Archelaus (Matthew 2:22). Thus Mary and Joseph, living

[211] Richard C. Carrier, "Pseudohistory in Jerry Vardaman's magic coins: the nonsense of micrographic letters," in *Skeptical Inquirer*, March, 2002 (http://findarticles.com/p/articles/mi_m

in Nazareth, as Luke supposes, would be unaffected by any census in Quirinius' domain.

Luke seems to have imagined Palestine united as it was under Herod the Great but all under the jurisdiction of a Roman governor. Luke falls victim to the same sort of confusion in Acts 9, where he has Saul sent by the Sanhedrin from Jerusalem to Damascus to arrest Christians, even though the Jerusalem authorities had no authority there and could not have imparted any to Paul. Luke just wanted to have Saul in Jerusalem for the death of Stephen and in Syria for his own conversion. He did his best to get him there, as he did to get Mary and Joseph to Bethlehem from Nazareth, but his skills as a travel agent were not up to the task.

Ascent of the Christ, Descent of the Dove

To jump to the opposite end of the supposed earthly life of Jesus, when did the ascension happen? Luke 24 makes it very explicit that Jesus departed the company of the disciples once and for all on the evening of Easter Day (Luke 24.1, 13, 29, 33, 36, 50). Acts 1:9–11 makes it equally clear that the ascension occurred forty days later. It is true, some manuscripts lack the words "and was carried up into heaven" in verse 51. Nevertheless, the story seems to be trying to narrate the final departure. And if he were not going up into heaven, where was he going? Why not stay with the disciples if, as in Acts 1, he was planning to eat with them and teach them for forty days as he had before the cross? It is not unreasonable to suggest that the author is simply rounding off his narrative in the first book, to finish the Jesus-episode before embarking on the Apostles-episode. But if that is true, it admits that the author did not mind telling stories as in fact they did not happen, for theological effect. And if you're willing to grant that, you need to quit Lee Strobel's team and come over to mine.

If we skip ahead to the birth of the Church, as it is usually considered, to the first Pentecost, we find another example of absent-minded story telling. It is not miracles that are the problem so much as bad narration. As Reimarus noted long ago,

> Luke here forgets that he has represented the apostles sitting in a room. He says at the beginning of his recital, "And suddenly a sound came from heaven like the rush of a mighty wind, and it filled all the house where they were sitting. It was the custom of the apostles to assemble in the upper chamber in the house εν τω υπερωω, immediately under

> the flat roof. My gracious! How could upward of three thousand people have found room there? For these three thousand do not constitute all the persons present. Three thousand were those who "received his word [and] were baptized" [Acts 2:41] so there must have been others who did not accept the word of Peter, and besides these the assembled company numbered a hundred and twenty [Acts 1:15]. So we may reckon that there were altogether about four thousand people. Such a number would require a large church. How does Luke contrive to cram them all into this one chamber of the apostles?[212]

All right, one might grant that the author of Acts lost track of the setting, that he had no details like that and had to fill them in as he went, and that he just forgot his initial setting. He just forgot to look back over the draft and change the setting to something that might accommodate such a huge audience and yet allow the audience to hear at a distance that a bunch of Galileans were speaking languages they couldn't be expected to have learned (though even this is beginning to sound cumbersome conceptually). We still are left to wonder if it is not more likely that our author has simply borrowed mythemes from prior literature.

For instance, in the *Bacchae* Euripides has the inspired Maenads graced by flickering fiery tongues that did not burn their hair. And then what have you got left? Peter's speech? I was afraid you'd say that, for it has been established beyond reasonable doubt (though not beyond the blind faith of apologists) that the speeches in Acts are every one of them Lukan compositions. A careful scrutiny of the vocabulary in both the speeches and the surrounding prose makes that clear, as does the manner in which each speech is a set piece for the surrounding scene.

> In order to let the speech end at this important point and so to emphasize the meaning of the final words [Acts 22:21], the author again employs a literary device, that of an intentional interruption of the speaker by the hearers. We can see from the frequency with which Luke uses it that this really is a literary device. The speeches of Stephen and Demetrius and Paul's speeches on the Areopagus and before Agrippa are concluded in a similar way. The fact that these interruptions each occur at a significant point suggests literary technique; the speech is always allowed to reach just that point which is significant to the author. We should certainly miss the

212 Reimarus, pp. 265–266.

> author's intention were we to suppose that each of these speeches did in fact lack a concluding section. (Martin Dibelius)[213]

Luke's creative hand is equally evident when the opposite happens, and a speech plods on to make its point come hell or high water, even though, in reality, the audience would never allow it.

> Zahn was quite right! — It is incomprehensible that the judges did not interrupt Stephen after the first few sentences and order him to keep to the point... But his suggestion for coming to terms with whatever he finds incomprehensible, namely that the judges "were held spellbound" and therefore listened in silence to "the lecture," might be credible of some lectures, but certainly not of *this* one. (Ernst Haenchen)[214]

Sanhedrin Sitcom

An adventure of Peter is full of the same conceptual holes. Peter and his wordless shadow John heal a man born blind and are hauled before the assembled Sanhedrin, apparently for disturbing the peace. They want at all costs to silence the preaching of the Apostles. Why? Because they believe it to be incorrect? It seems not, since they admit among themselves that a damaging (as we should say) miracle, an undeniably genuine one, has occurred (Acts 4:16). There is no question of it being a 'lying wonder,' not even a trick. It is simply 'one for their side,' as if we were privy to the back-room machinations of a cynical political party during an election campaign. It is all caricature, precisely as in Matthew 28, when the same body is said to understand perfectly well that the true Son of God has risen from thc dead but seek to suppress the knowledge of it. Why? Are they a gang of Satanists? In 4:21, the Sanhedrin gives

---

213 Martin Dibelius, "The Speeches in Acts and Ancient Historiography," in Dibelius, *Studies in the Acts of the Apostles* (London: SCM Press, 1956), p. 160. For vocabulary studies of the speeches and the rest of the book, see Earl Richard, *Acts 6:1-8:4*; Soards, *Speeches in Acts*. To be sure, some apologists, like W. Ward Gasque, *A History of the Criticism of the Acts of the Apostles* (Grand Rapids: Eerdmans, 1975), just hold their breath and stonewall, as oblivious of the data as Mormon apologists are to the obvious usage of the King James Bible by the author of the Book of Mormon.

214 Ernst Haenchen, *The Acts of the Apostles: A Commentary*. Trans. Bernard Noble and Gerald Shinn (Philadelphia: Westminster Press, 1971), p. 288.

up in futility, fearing the reprisals of the people who idolize Peter and his men. But, as F.C. Baur said,

> If the people had been so much to be feared, the rulers would never have dared to seize and imprison the Apostles (iv.3) in the midst of their discourse to the assembled crowd astonished by the miracle. All this can only be disregarded by taking a standpoint from which the Apostles are thought to be glorified the more the ill deeds of their enemies are brought forward to their humiliation and confusion.[215]

But it gets worse. An angel, surely a literary *deus ex machina*, breaks the apostles out of prison and tells them to get back to work, which only issues in their re-arrest. But once they come back before the Sanhedrin, it is as if we have picked up right where we left off! No one mentions the miraculous escape or its implications! So what on earth was the point? Edward Zeller comments:

> If the interposition of angels[216] in the course of the history is of itself a sure sign of the mythical, this interposition is, moreover, quite objectless in the present case, for those who were liberated by the angel are nevertheless arrested again. To this must be added that, in the later transactions before the Sanhedrim, not the slightest notion is taken of the miraculous liberation; that neither do the accused appeal to this conspicuous voucher of divine favour, nor do the judges investigate such a striking and suspicious circumstance – certainly an unexampled proceeding if the thing really happened.[217]

Rabban Gamaliel's intervention on the apostles' behalf (Acts 5:34–39) is clearly meant as an aside to the reader; it is he (if he is a Roman) who is to consider that a wait-and-see attitude might be the wise course of action. The advice goes right over the heads of the Sanhedrin, who still risk the wrath of God by flogging the apostles to within an inch of their lives (people frequently expired before the thirty-ninth lash was laid down) and ordering a moratorium on preaching, neither gesture exactly compatible with a hands off policy. And the speech of Gamaliel is, if anything, less historical than the tale in which it has been inserted.

---

215 Baur, *Paul the Apostle of Jesus Christ*, Vol. 1, p. 18.

216 Why not leprechauns?

217 Edward Zeller, *The Contents and Origins of the Acts of the Apostles Critically Investigated.* Trans. Joseph Dare (1875; rpt. Eugene: Wipf & Stock, 2007), Volume One, p. 222.

First, it is plainly based on the warning disregarded, to his peril, by Pentheus in *The Bacchae*:[218] "I warn you once again: do not take arms against a god" (788–789). And the rest of Gamaliel's lines come from Josephus. As everyone (except, of course, biblical inerrantists) now agrees, the Acts author has carelessly reproduced what he read in Josephus, who mentioned the rebel Theudas, active in 44–46 CE (a decade *after* Gamaliel!), then, in a flashback, Judas of Galilee, an earlier rebel who had fomented the uprising attendant upon Quirinius' census in 6 CE Luke remembered *the order in which they were mentioned*, not their historical order.

Acts 21:38 also mentions one unnamed Egyptian rabble-rouser also mentioned by Josephus. How odd that *both* writers should fail to remember the name of this notorious criminal! Come to think of it, how odd that, of the three such revolutionaries Josephus mentions, taking them as examples, he says, from a larger number he could have named, Luke mentions *the very same three and no others*![219] Well, you know what that means. McRay and Strobel, alas, do not.[220]

Three Deaths

The exciting episodes of Ananias and Sapphira and the martyrdom of Stephen (Acts 5:1–11; 6:8–15) make new sense when considered as a rewrite combining the story in 1 Kings 20:1–21:21 of Ahab and Jezebel cheating Naboth out of his vineyard and that in Joshua 7 of sticky-fingered Achan.[221]

Ahab covets Naboth's cozy vineyard, and Jezebel counsels him to take it by underhanded means. Luke has punned the innocent Naboth into the righteous Bar-*nab*as, and now it is the donation (rather than possession) of

---

218 I am using William Arrowsmith's translation in David Grene and Richard Lattimore (eds.), *Greek Tragedies*, Volumc 3 (Chicago: University of Chicago Press, Phoenix paperbound edition, 1972), pp. 189–260.

219 Steve Mason, *Josephus and the New Testament* (Peabody: Hendrickson, 1992), pp. 208–213.

220 Naturally, anyone who believes his eternal salvation depends on believing Gamaliel actually delivered this speech can find room to deny his better judgment to believe the Rabbi was referring to an otherwise unknown, *earlier* Theudas. There *must* have been one. But this is not historical criticism.

221 Thomas L. Brodie, "Luke the Literary Interpreter: Luke-Acts as a Systematic Rewriting and Updating of the Elijah-Elisha Narrative in 1 and 2 Kings." Ph.D. dissertation presented to Pontifical University of St. Thomas Aquinas, Rome. 1988, pp. 271–275.

a field that arouses a wicked couple's jealousy. Ananias is Ahab, Sapphira Jezebel. But they do not conspire to murder. That element is left over for the judicial murder of Stephen.

The couple's crime is borrowed instead from that of Achan, who appropriated for himself booty ear-marked for God. Ananias and Sapphira have sold a field but kept back some of the money, claiming to have donated the full price. They have no right to this remainder; it belongs to God since they dedicated it as "devoted to the Lord."

Peter confronts Ananias and Sapphira, just as Joshua did Achan (Joshua 7:25) and as Elijah confronted Ahab (1 Kings 20:17–18). Luke transforms Ahab's disturbance in spirit (20:4) into Ananias and Sapphira lying to the Spirit of God (Acts 5:3b–4, 9b). Elijah and Peter pronounce death sentences on the guilty. Ananias and Sapphira (like Achan's family) expire on the spot (Acts 5:5a, 10a), while Ahab and Jezebel linger for some time. Fear falls on all who hear of Ananias' and Sapphira's fate, just as Elijah's doom oracle (1 Kings 20:27–29) sparks the fear of God in the spineless Ahab. Shortly after Naboth's death, we read that the young men of Israel defeated the greedy Syrians (21:1–21), a tale which likely contributed the idea of having the young men (never in evidence elsewhere in Acts) carry out and bury the bodies of Ananias and Sapphira (Acts 5:6, 10b).

The hapless Naboth has become Stephen, the proto-martyr. Naboth was railroaded by the schemes of Jezebel. She orders the elders and *freemen* to frame Naboth through the testimonies of lying witnesses. Stephen suffers the same fate at the hands of the Synagogue of *Freedmen*. Stephen, like Naboth, gets accused of double blasphemy (Naboth: God and king; Stephen: Moses and God). Both men are carried outside the city limits and stoned to death. Upon hearing of the fruit of his desires, Ahab tears his garments in remorse. Luke has made this into young Saul of Tarsus checking the coats of the stoning mob.

Perils of Pauline Conversion

In telling the story of Paul's conversion Luke has borrowed freely from two well-known literary sources, Euripides' *Bacchae* and the 2 Maccabees tale of the miraculous conversion of Heliodorus. He derived from 2 Maccabees the basic story of a persecutor of the people of God being stopped in his tracks by a vision of heavenly beings (3:24–26), thrown to the ground in a faint, blinded (3:27), and nursed to health by righteous

Jews who pray for his recovery (3:31–33), whereupon the ex-persecutor converts to the faith he once persecuted (3:35) and begins testifying to its truth (3:36). Given Luke's propensity to rewrite the Septuagint, it seems special pleading to deny that he has done the same in this case, the most blatant of them all.

Luke must also have mined the *Bacchae*, which also features a persecutor being converted against his will by the decision of the deity whose followers he has been persecuting. Pentheus was hell-bent on driving the orgiastic Maenads, Dionysus's devotees, out of Thebes, rejecting the sage advice of Cadmus, Teiresias, and others who warn him he may find himself fighting against a god (Teiresias: "Even if this Dionysus is no god, as you assert, persuade yourself that he is. The fiction is a noble one." (333–335) "Reckless fool, you do not know the consequences of your words. You talked madness before, but this is raving lunacy!" (357–360) Dionysus later reiterates the warning: "I warn you once again: do not take arms against a god" (788–789). "A man, a man, and nothing more, yet he presumed to wage war with a god" (636-637; *cf*, Acts 5:33–39).

Best mark how the Maenads, who may seem to be filled with wine, are really filled with divine ecstasy ("not, as you think, drunk with wine," 686–687; *cf*, Acts 2:15), as witnessed by the old and young among them prophesying ("all as one, the old women and the young and the unmarried girls," 693–694; *cf*, Acts 2:17–18) and the harmless descent of fiery tongues upon their heads ("flames flickered in their curls and did not burn them," 757–758; "tongues of fire," 623–624; *cf*, Acts 2:3).

Stubborn Pentheus will not be moved, and he orders the arrest of the newly-arrived apostle of the cult, in reality Dionysus himself, the very son of god, disguised as a mortal. An earthquake frees him from Pentheus' prison (585–603; *cf*, Acts 16:25–34), and Dionysus walks into Pentheus' throne room and mocks him ("If I were you, I would... not rage and kick against necessity, a man defying god." 793–796; *cf*, Acts 26:14) yet offers Pentheus an opportunity to find the outlaw disciples in their secret hideaway. If he would spy on them at their sport, he must wear their distinctive doeskin outfit (912–916; *cf*, Acts 9:26–30). At his command, Pentheus, no longer in control of his own will, agrees to the plan (922–924; *cf*, Acts 9:17–18). By the time he has donned his costume and wig, he has become a true believer (929–930). And his new savior Dionysus sends him to his doom, knowing full well Pentheus will be found out and torn to pieces by the Maenads.

The poor fool could dish it out but not take it! Now let him see how it feels from the standpoint of the persecuted! He becomes a true believer, only to suffer the fate of one. And so does Paul. In light of the parallels with the *Bacchae*, we can detect the awful irony of Acts 9:16, "I will show him how much *he* must suffer for the sake of my name!"

Apples Don't Corroborate Oranges

Remarkably, Reverend Strobel quotes McRay on whether archaeology can prove the truth of the Christian faith, and he says it can't. "If we dig in Israel and find ancient sites that are consistent with where the Bible said we'd find them, that shows that its history and geography are accurate. However, it does not confirm that what Jesus said is right. Spiritual truths cannot be proved or disproved by archaeological discoveries."[222]

So what, pray tell, is the point of chapter five? Take a closer look at what McRay says: he seems to think archaeology can confirm the accuracy of the gospel, including securing our knowledge of what the historical Jesus said. That is highly doubtful. But beyond this, we might suspect there is a nuance implicit in Reverend Strobel's argument that he is not explicitly stating. For him, I suspect, the factual inerrancy of the gospels is not a *sufficient* condition for saving faith in Christ, but it is a *necessary* condition. Believing in inerrancy will not save you by itself, but you have to believe it as a prior condition or you will never get to the point of accepting the fundamentalist gospel.

Believing in inerrancy is just a fancy way of saying you have a childlike credulity when it comes to what this ancient book says, and that is just what apologetics seeks to restore: a second naïveté—or, more often, I suspect, it seeks to preserve an initial naïveté that fails to realize its time is long over.

222 McRay in Strobel, p. 95.

Chapter Six
A Butt Load of Evidence
The Jesus Seminar and Mainstream Biblical Research

Responding to Strobel's Chapter 6, "The Rebuttal Evidence," is a unique experience for me. On the one hand, I have for some fourteen years been a Fellow of the Jesus Seminar, the scholarly think tank vilified and burlesqued in this chapter. On the other hand, I am friends with Greg Boyd, whom I have debated publicly, by my count, seven times now. I think I am in a position to offer an interesting evaluation of both sides of this debate—of which, of course, we hear only one side in Reverend Strobel's presentation. Get a load of this:

> Now that I had heard powerfully convincing and well-reasoned evidence from the scholars I questioned for this book, I needed to turn my attention to the decidedly contrary opinions of a small group of academics who have been the subject of a whirlwind of news coverage... In recent years the news media have been saturated with uncritical reports about the Jesus Seminar, a self-selected group that represents a miniscule percentage of New Testament scholars but that generates coverage vastly out of proportion to the group's influence.[223]

First off, note the glowing terms in which Reverend Strobel speaks of the side he has already heard. Obviously, he has been convinced already. (Actually, it is obvious he settled the whole business by a sheer act of faith before the whole thing started, perhaps in order to make it easier to get along with his newly converted wife, and he went on his journey trying to quiet his doubts, understandable with so much at stake). Note just as well the dismissive terms in which Pastor Strobel minimizes the Jesus Seminar: it can't be good for much, being a bunch of cranks outside the mainstream (something he considers a virtue when it is true of evangelical Christians), self-appointed experts who owe what reputation they have to an obedient and compliant news media. In any case, wouldn't you think a reporter, a researcher, who knew there was another side to be heard from would have sought out a representative of that side? And this is exactly what Strobel, 'Mr. Objectivity,' does *not* do, nor even *thinks* of doing.

---

223 Strobel, p. 111.

> Were the Jesus Seminar's findings solidly based on unbiased scholarly research, or were they… well meaning but ultimately unsupported? For answers, I made the six-hour drive to St. Paul, Minnesota, to confer with Dr. Greg Boyd.[224]

He wants the inside story about the no-good Jesus Seminar, and so the first place he makes a beeline for is the office of a man he has chosen because of his published criticisms of the Seminar: Greg Boyd! It is really a farce. Not that I blame Greg for giving his opinion when asked. Why shouldn't he?

Strobel asks him, "People… read the conclusions of the Jesus Seminar, and assume this represents the mainstream of New Testament scholarship… But is that really the case?" Boyd replies, "No, no, that's *not* the case."[225] "The Jesus Seminar represents an extremely small number of radical-fringe scholars who are on the far, far left wing of New Testament thinking."[226] But I am afraid Greg is mistaken.

It is clear to anyone who has made it his business to keep up with "mainstream" critical scholarship that the Jesus Seminar does speak for it. That is not to say that every decision going into the two volumes *The Five Gospels* and *The Acts of Jesus* was unanimous. As Greg mentions, the Seminar Fellows, after lengthy deliberations, vote on the authenticity of sayings and stories in just the same fashion as the text critics under Bruce Metzger who meet periodically to update the United Bible Societies *Greek New Testament.* Metzger's team discusses each textual variant and votes to grade them at an A, B, C, or D rating. The Jesus Seminar simply used colored beads to vote. Red equals the A rating of the UBS Greek New Testament text, pink equaling B, and so on.

The very nature of the enterprise, yielding voting percentages and nuances of certainty, demonstrates that the scholars have different opinions. There is no single party line on single gospel passages, though the bottom line is a set of majority estimates that only eighteen percent of both the sayings and the stories go back to Jesus. And I don't believe any saying unique to the Gospel of Thomas has been accorded a red rating.

The question seems to be, how do you define 'mainstream New Testament scholarship'? I am referring to the majority of scholars who publish books and articles in refereed journals and who present papers at academic conferences such as the Society of Biblical Literature and the Society for New Testament Studies. I do not include those whose primary

224 *Ibid.*, p. 112.

225 Strobel and Boyd in Strobel, p. 113.

226 Boyd in Strobel, p. 114.

interest is in apologetics, which means they are subjecting New Testament scholarship to the demands of conservative theology.

That does not mean there are not conservative, genuine New Testament scholars, like Donald M. Guthrie, F.F. Bruce, I. Howard Marshall, R.T. France, Ralph P. Martin, and Gordon D. Fee, though even they, to use James Barr's helpful term, betray themselves as 'Maximal Conservatives,'[227] automatically gravitating toward the most traditional position they can get away with. Those whose books appear only from traditionally evangelical publishers like Baker Academic, Kregel, and Zondervan tend to be 'court prophets'— spin doctors. (Hendrickson and Eerdmans have escaped this ghetto, venturing out into genuine scholarship.)

The Jesus Seminar's membership is open to anyone with a Ph.D. degree or its equivalent, usually in New Testament, but sometimes in adjacent fields. One only need be nominated by a Fellow to become a Fellow. If any conservative wanted to join, he or she would be welcome, but I imagine none ever have because they would feel the disfavor from the church hierarchies sponsoring their institutions. And of course they would be foolish to do otherwise in such circumstances. I do not mean to criticize them. But it remains true that none of the evangelical critics of the Seminar has ever darkened our door even as an observer.

As for "uncritical press reports," I can only say that I have perused *Time* and *Newsweek* coverage of meetings at which I was present and have been amazed at the inaccurate reporting—making us sound like lunatics and heretics, which is of course the strategy of crusading reporter Lee Strobel. But this is no surprise to me.

Once I was a talking head on Reverend Strobel's TV show *Faith under Fire*, pitted against apologist Hank Hanegraaff. I had previously explained to the producer how I reject absurd, nit-picking pot-shots at the gospels such as the mustard seed not actually being the smallest of all seeds. Who cares? Let's get on to the real business. But then Dr. Hanegraaff took me to task for making a big deal over the mustard seed! It took me a few minutes to get across the fact that he had been misinformed, that he was refuting a view I myself scoff at. After the show, Hank sent me a kind apology, but it wasn't really his fault. No, it was the 'objective reporting' of Lee Strobel. Do you think I was surprised?

By the way, I think I know what it is like to be located on the fringe of radical New Testament scholarship in a recognized minority. If you have read my other books and articles you will know I am a latter-day exponent

---

227 Barr, *Fundamentalism*, pp. 85–89.

of the Dutch Radical Criticism. I think, for instance, that it is very likely there was no historical Jesus at all, and that the 'Pauline epistles' were one and all written in his name in the late first, early second centuries by various Marcionites and Gnostics (and subsequently doctored by Catholic editors).

I think the Jesus Seminar is way too conservative! I believe I am right, though in the nature of the case it is always a question of pursuing research paradigms, not pronouncing dogmatic certainties. I am in the minority. I do not mind. I figure, who cares about the consensus of scholars? After all, it was the consensus of scholars that Jesus ought to die as a blasphemer. Every person curious about these questions must scrutinize all the sources, as well as the opinions of all who have done so previously, and then decide—provisionally.

It is a tall order. It is a career. I have done it. I invite you to do the same. Until you do, I'm afraid your opinions are worthless. Parroting the writers who tell you what you want to hear doesn't cut it. But once you do your homework, wherever you come out will be your business. I do not "demand a verdict." No real scholar does. Pastor Strobel does, though.

Greg Boyd quite properly gets something specific on the table:

> "If you look at their book *The Five Gospels*, they give 'seven pillars of scholarly wisdom,' as if you must follow their methodology if you're going to be a true scholar. But a lot of scholars, from a wide spectrum of backgrounds, would have serious reservations about one or even most of these pillars."[228]

Now we're talking. First, let me note that I think the seven pillars are a description, up front, of the methodology the Seminar Fellows used, so the reader will understand their deliberations (summarized in the discussion of each gospel passage, like a gospel commentary). They know full well that there are many possible viewpoints.

1. *We must separate the Jesus of history from the Christ of faith.*

The Jesus Seminar does not start from square one here. All who know their deliberations and their writings know they are carrying on the tradition of scholarly research chronicled by Albert Schweitzer in *The*

---

228 Boyd in Strobel, p. 114.

Quest of the Historical Jesus.[229] Schweitzer shows how the eighteenth-century Rationalists and the nineteenth-century Liberal Protestants arrived at hard-won insights, some listed below, that led ineluctably to peeling away layers of theological embellishment from the original figure of Jesus—provided one could find a recognizable figure at the center of it all. Greg is opposed to the whole approach, it is clear to me, for entirely dogmatic reasons. He feels he needs the Sunday School Jesus to walk with him and talk with him and tell him he is his own. This is just as much a shameless exercise of recreating Jesus in one's own image as the Liberal scholars' attempts that he lampoons.

2. *The Synoptic Gospels are closer to the historical Jesus than the Gospel of John.*

Well, the Synoptic gospels might be closer or they might not be. But John certainly can't be closer than anyone else, and for one simple reason: it represents a total and systematic rewrite of the others. Everyone, whether Jesus, John the Baptist, the narrator, or Jesus' opponents, speaks the same way. They are like characters in a Woody Allen movie: he wrote the script and didn't bother giving each character his or her own style and vocabulary.

John's gospel is like Kahlil Gibran's masterpiece, *Jesus the Son of Man*,[230] in which, in an admitted fiction, he pretends to supply reminiscences about Jesus by all sorts of people, from relatives to disciples, from enemies to people who heard him speak just once, *etc.* It is very impressive, but, boy, do they all sound just like Gibran! Same with John's gospel. For theological reasons, John changes the Synoptic order of events. He places the cleansing of the temple at the start of the ministry so he can portray the whole gospel as a long reply by Jesus, from the witness stand, to his accusers.[231] He changes the very day of the crucifixion to make it

---

229 Albert Schweitzer, *The Quest of the Historical Jesus: From Reimarus to Wrede*. Trans. W. Montgomery (1906; rpt. NY: Macmillan, 1962).

230 Kahlil Gibran, *Jesus the Son of Man: His Words and Deeds as Told and Recorded by Those Who Knew Him* (NY: Knopf, 1976). I am quite certain that, if this book were to be inducted into the canon, Greg Boyd and all the other apologists would begin marshalling their arguments for why Gibran's accounts of Jesus' teachings are historically authentic, despite their stylistic and material differences from either John or the Synoptics. Seriously. And I wish that fact would make them stop and think.

231 J. Ramsey Michaels, *John*. A Good News Commentary (San Francisco:

coincide with the slaying of the Passover lamb. He puts the institution of the Eucharist in Galilee, in the Capernaum synagogue, back in Chapter 6 instead of at the Last Supper, since he wants to interpret it in light of the Passover there. All of this is quite impressive. But obviously such a reshuffling of the data cannot be called factual. Greg thinks it is because they told him it was in Sunday School.

3. *Mark was written before Matthew and Luke and was the basis for both.*

Yes, virtually all New Testament scholars make this an axiom. Some few believe Matthew used Mark, after which Luke used both Matthew and Mark, but the result is pretty much the same. Greg tries to chip away at the widespread theory of Markan priority because he realizes that, if he admitted it, he could no longer treat the gospels as independent witnesses, which he wants to do, for apologetics' sake.[232] Greg uses the same old apologist's boast that it is he and not the critics who is up on the latest scholarship: "They're failing to realize that an increasing number of scholars are expressing serious reservations about the theory that Matthew and Luke used Mark."[233] Well, that's ridiculous. The Seminar Fellows are fully aware of the diversity of opinion on this point. It's just that most of them, like James M. Robinson, have found the Markan Priority model very useful, which seems to prove it out as a research tool, so they use it. Others in the Seminar, like Richard J. Arthur and Bishop Spong, hold to some of the alternative source-critical models Greg is referring to. Again, the 'seven-pillars' list just describes the principles held by most of the Fellows. A confession, as it were, not a creed.

4. *The hypothetical source 'Q' explained Matthew's and Luke's common tradition not found in Mark.*

Greg has this to say about it.

> "As for Q, it's not a discovery but a theory that has been around for one and a half centuries, which tries to account for the material Luke and Matthew have in common [that they do not also share with Mark]. What's new is the highly questionable way that left-wing scholars are using their presuppositions to slice this

Harper & Row, 1984), pp. 32–33.

232 Boyd in Strobel, p. 118.

233 *Ibid.*, p. 118.

> hypothetical Q into various layers of legendary development to back up their preconceived theories."[234]

His rhetoric is so unremittingly hostile that it becomes plain he has no real interest in this or any source-critical paradigm, but just wants to go back to the pre-critical simplicity of proof-texting. For him, if the gospels say it, Jesus said it, and he doesn't care to bother with all these complications. Greg is a theologian, not a historical Jesus scholar. I just wish he would not pontificate as if he were. He wields a bludgeon when a scalpel is required. As for stratifying Q: of course it's "questionable"—it's a hypothesis inviting scholarly scrutiny, not a dogmatic pronouncement. Greg says it is the product of some nefarious leftist's "presuppositions." It's never that simple.

As R.G. Collingwood pointed out, all historians (just like scientists) develop hypothetical frameworks which they impose like a transparency over the data to see if patterns and connections emerge. If they do, the paradigm appears to have explanatory power, and the debate begins. All results are tentative, and historians adopt them provisionally in their work to see how helpful they are in clarifying things further and further. It is a way of carrying out the thought-experiment further. The Q hypothesis has proven itself so revealing, so fruitful, that many scholars feel the case is closed, and they have busied themselves compiling critical editions of Q, publishing a reconstructed Q as a gospel alongside other gospels.[235] I find Q very convincing, but I do not go quite that far.

The stratigraphical analysis of Q[236] does not yet have quite as many adherents, possibly because it is a newer idea and has not yet been as thoroughly tested. Or possibly because it is a weaker, less helpful hypothesis; I am not the one to say. But I can say it is based on "presuppositions" only in Collingwood's sense.[237] One begins with the educated hunch, "What if the explicitly Christological materials belonged to a secondary layer? If you bracketed that stuff, what would you get?" Then, when you do that, what do you know? You suddenly see the remainder fall neatly into seven topics, all with a decidedly Cynic flavor, no Christian dogma. That, it

---

234 *Ibid.*, p. 122

235 Robert J. Miller, *The Complete Gospels: Scholars Annotated Version* (Santa Rosa: Polebridge Press, 1995). I do not include it in my *The Pre-Nicene New Testament* (Salt Lake City: Signature Books, 2006).

236 John S. Kloppenborg, *The Formation of Q: Trajectories in Ancient Wisdom Collections*. Studies in Antiquity & Christianity (Philadelphia: Fortress Press, 1987

237 Collingwood, *Idea of History*, pp. 242–245.

seems to me, is worth exploring. It might turn out to be a way of taking depth soundings in the tradition, to distinguish earlier and later stages.

Why is Greg so hostile to such notions? It is because he doesn't like what might be done with them. He doesn't want to climb into the car with the beckoning likes of Burton L. Mack,[238] who argues for a pre-Christological Q-community that saw Jesus merely as a Cynic sage, that knew nothing about any saving death or resurrection.

No, such early communities, in Greg's simple picture of the early church, should not have existed at all. Whatever their differences, all early Jesus communities *must* have affirmed the death and resurrection of Jesus (not to mention biblical inerrancy!). Such theories have two things against them in evangelical eyes: they are speculative instead of dogmatic, and evangelicals much prefer the latter. And these theories threaten to muddy the baptismal water. Evangelicals want things to be simple and clear so they can continue to offer evangelistic invitations at the end of debates, as if they were only another kind of evangelistic rally. And, isn't it obvious? They are.

> 5. *The noneschatological Jesus who speaks in aphorisms and parables must be liberated from the eschatological Jesus, whom the Church constructed.*

Greg doesn't like this because he is a biblical inerrantist (that's really why he rejects all biblical criticism. All else is fancy spin, but he doesn't fool me.) and cannot bring himself to surrender any words that the Bible says "Jesus said." He ought to rethink his position, though, because if he could go along with this one, he'd be able to get rid of the brain-tumor headache from which all literalists suffer: Jesus is said to have predicted the end of the world in his own generation and it didn't happen. Sure would be nice if he hadn't actually said it, huh? But if Greg felt free to cut these lines, he fears he wouldn't know where to stop, and then Jesus would be as much of an enigma to him as he is to historical critics.

But critics don't dump the eschatological sayings of Jesus because they don't happen to like them. (Even if they did, we'd still have to evaluate their arguments one by one; whatever crazy thing may have motivated the theory is irrelevant. You have to do the hard work of evaluating any argument's strengths and weaknesses. Otherwise, you're committing the *ad hominem* fallacy.) And of course there are hard-hitting critics like Bart

---

[238] Burton L. Mack, *The Lost Gospel: The Book of Q and Christian Origins* (San Francisco: HarperSanFrancisco, 1993), pp. 107–110.

Ehrman, Paula Fredrikson, and Richard J. Arthur who do understand Jesus as an eschatological prophet. There are so many opinions on the historical Jesus, not because there is a paucity of evidence, but rather because there is *too much* and it points in too many different directions. Too many contradictory opinions are attributed to him.[239]

> 6. *The contrast between the oral culture of Jesus and the print culture of later times (Jesus only spoke in short, memorable, oft-repeated phrases, never longer discourse).*

Personally, I think recent orality studies are proving (despite themselves!) that the gospels are literary all the way through, though some oral materials may have factored into them. It is ironic that Greg Boyd and Paul Eddy exploit what they can of orality studies to argue for an accurate word-of-mouth transmission of gospel material, though I fear they misunderstand and/or misapply them. The work of Parry and Lord certainly gives no aid and comfort to the notion of specific wording getting memorized and successfully passed down unchanged. In fact, the big lesson the orality people have taught is that oral transmission is a process of evolution to such a degree that it is useless even to speak of an original version of a saying or story, since each performance variation, each new spontaneous, ephemeral version, must count as a *new work* in its own right. That is another way of saying what the critics Greg and company hate have been saying for generations: embellishment is not corruption; rather it is the oak growing from the acorn.

Bruce Metzger recognized this sixth scholarly pillar when he taught that Jesus didn't give the Sermon on the Mount at one sitting; rather some redactor must have compiled it from poetic aphorisms into which Jesus or others had distilled longer lessons he had taught on numerous occasions.[240] Metzger, I suppose, realized it is unreasonable to posit that any hearer of a long discourse could have possibly remembered it in such detail. Ditto the speeches of the apostles in Acts and, especially, the looping, spiraling monologues and dialogues of Jesus in John. These things could never

---

239 I hope you will forgive me if I refer you to my books *Deconstructing Jesus* (Amherst: Prometheus Books, 2000) and *The Incredible Shrinking Son of Man* (Amherst: Prometheus Books, 2003). I just cannot take the space to rehearse the necessary arguments again here.

240 Metzger in class, Summer 1977.

have survived in the process of oral tradition and did not pop up from that stream in one huge piece.

> 7. *The Gospels are now assumed to be narratives in which the memory of Jesus is embellished by mythic elements that express the Church's faith in him, and by plausible fictions that enhance the telling of the Gospel story for the first-century listeners who knew about divine men and miracle workers firsthand.*

Yes, that's the conclusion form-criticism seems to lead to, and it is such an insightful method that one feels bound to keep using it and to accept its implications. The more closely acquainted one becomes with the inter-gospel contradictions and the parallels with other contemporary myths, the more one feels grateful for a method that makes sense of them. Greg Boyd, by contrast, sees the danger in these data for the fundamentalist biblicism he wants to espouse and therefore fights them off every inch of the way.

Greg resents the implied pretension of the self-styled 'Scholars Version': "And the Jesus Seminar calls its translation of the Bible 'The Scholars Version' – well, what does that imply? That other versions aren't scholarly?"[241] Such a claim would be so patently absurd that I have to think they mean something else: what, exactly, I don't know. But Greg is right. It does sound like they mean previous Bibles were unscholarly. And that is hardly the worst thing about it. As I have tried to read it, the Scholars Version sounds like a Liberal version of the Living Bible. It is unnecessarily paraphrastic and irritatingly slangy. "Woe to you!" becomes "Damn you!" It is comically awful, and personally I can't stand it.

One of the oldest criticisms of the Jesus Seminar concerns its apparent theological agenda. "And what they have in mind is a totally new form of Christianity."[242] For a long time, the Seminar Fellows protested that they had no such goal, that they were just historians trying their best to excavate the historical Jesus. But it was always pretty apparent many of them were doing this for the same theological reason that had motivated the nineteenth-century Liberal Protestants: to find a Jesus who could be conscripted as an ally against repressive institutional Christianity.

---

241 Boyd in Strobel, p. 118.

242 *Ibid.*, p. 115.

I believe these two faces were not the result of hypocrisy, but rather reflected the different interests of different people in the group. Once we had finished the eleven-year examination of the gospels, we deliberated over where to go next. Two or three years before the sad passing of Bob Funk, the founder (with John Dominic Crossan) of the Jesus Seminar, it became quite overt that Bob wanted to use the Seminar to reinvent Christianity for the new millennium.

Accordingly we welcomed aboard well-known Liberal and radical theologians like Bishop Spong, Elaine Pagels, Don Cupitt, Lloyd Geering, and others. But as soon as the new direction became evident, a number of the oldest and most committed Fellows protested, insisting that we had always billed ourselves as historians without any theological axe to grind and ought to stay that way.

As a result, the Seminar has recently restored its historical focus, devoting papers to the origins of Christianity in various regions of the Roman Empire. The theological interest remains, fueled by the avid Associate members, many of whom are Unitarians, Unity members, or Liberal Protestants. They continue to regard the Seminar, and the educational materials it publishes, as a means of church renewal. To put it bluntly, they have had enough of the Christianity represented by Lee Strobel and his institutional allies, and they are delighted to find there is an alternative way of looking at Christianity. This is not my interest in the Jesus Seminar. I only wait on the sidelines to see if they will manage to reinvent Unitarianism, and I think we already have one too many of those.

Alien Assumptions

Now we come to Greg Boyd's mortal sin, one I hope he eventually repents of.

> "Here's what they do: they rule out the possibility of the supernatural from the beginning, and then they say, 'Now bring on the evidence about Jesus.' No wonder they get the results they do."[243] "For instance, they assume that the later church put these sayings into the mouth of Jesus, unless they have good evidence to think otherwise. That assumption is rooted in their suspicion of the gospels, and that comes from their assumption that the supernatural can't occur."[244]

---

243 *Ibid.*, p. 116.
244 *Ibid.*, p. 117.

I have to make two points here.

Firstly, what on earth does skepticism about the occurrence of miracles have to do with doubt that Jesus' sayings have been passed down accurately? There is no necessary, or even likely, connection as far as I can see.

Secondly, the shoe is not on the other foot that Greg thinks is wearing it. It is he who arbitrarily controls the data by bringing in an alien assumption. It is not historical critics who smuggle in philosophical naturalism, but apologists who smuggle in the belief in biblical inerrantism.

Ask yourself what principle it is that would account for the fact that apologists (who would like to be thought of simply as 'New Testament scholars') *never find a single biblical miracle to be problematical* while also rejecting *every single* non-Christian, non-canonical miracle as spurious. What principle would that be? Obviously, it is no mere openness to the theoretical possibility of miracles breaking into the cause-and-effect nexus. It is rather the will to believe that every biblical narrative is factually true. And it is the unwillingness of historical critics to abide by inerrantism that Greg and his buddies are really complaining about. They have just turned the tables, hoping no one will notice.

And where do the apologists derive the notion that historical critics are philosophical naturalists? They cannot seem to get straight the difference between 'methodological Atheism' and 'philosophical Atheism.' The former means simply that, like the meteorologist predicting the weather on a probabilistic basis, the historian can only say what probably did or didn't happen, based on observable trends. The historical critic makes no judgment that nothing ever superceded the "trend" of calculable regularities. He wasn't there; he doesn't know for certain and does not claim to.

It's just that you can't measure, detect, or reckon with miracles, even if they actually occurred. How would you know they did? Anyone can claim they did, but how could we verify it? Suppose someone asserted that the world had been created only ten hours ago, complete with fabricated memories, history books, fossils, *etc.* Even if perchance he was correct, we could never know it and would have to conclude he was probably wrong. The fact of a creation ten hours ago must remain invisible to us.

And here is where the principle of analogy comes in. This is why we cannot recognize even true reports of miracles (assuming for the moment there *are* any) as 'probably true.' Looking at claims of ancient events, which we are in no position to verify (as Joe Nickell investigates modern ones, in person), we have to ask what modern phenomena does the story resemble most closely?

The best we can do in rendering our verdict of 'probably true' or 'probably not true' is to make the best analogy match we can. It might be that the ancient story matches quite closely modern accounts of, *e.g.*, military conflicts, featuring reasonable estimates of troops, weapons, casualties, *etc.* But it might be that it matches ancient legends, recognized by all as legends, in which, *e.g.* Hercules routes a huge number of the enemy single-handedly. Which does Judges 15:14–17 look like, in which Samson dispatches a thousand Philistines with no more armament than a fresh bone? Did they obligingly line up to get brained one by one? I think it is a safe judgment that this story is probably a legend. And the verdict has nothing to do with a stubborn bias against the supernatural. It's just that the story makes no sense, whether or not God can empower a man with superhuman strength. Let's assume he can; our verdict on the story, probably a legend, does not change.

The plain fact is that biblical and gospel miracles have many, many parallels, and that their existence automatically renders the canonical miracles as probably legendary—even if they really did happen. It is an epistemological issue ("What knowledge could we have of ancient miracles?"), not a metaphysical one ("What can and cannot happen?"). Sometimes apologists seem almost to admit the point; hence their desperation in trying to discount the parallels. "If the virgin who bore the demigod was not named Mary, we don't have a real parallel!" "The differences are greater than the similarities!" They don't seem to grasp the point of an "ideal type," a synthesis of the features shared in common by the phenomena we seek to group together, ignoring their differences.

The surprise is not where phenomena differ but where they strikingly agree. The ideal type, cataloging common features, is like the skeleton. The various instantiations, the actual cases, will differ at many points. We want to explain both differences and similarities. And the way to start is by grouping the data by similarities, to get them into the same group. Then we can best understand why and where they also differ.

For instance, if we observe that religions generally have overarching explanations of what is wrong in the world, plus systems of salvation, plus divine entities who help us to be saved, we will not deny that Theravada Buddhism is a religion, even though belief in saving gods is not integral to it. No, we must recognize it as a religion because of the many features it shares in common with Christianity, Judaism, Islam, Hinduism, Santeria, Voodoo, Jainism, *etc.*, and then ask, "Wow! That's interesting! How did they come to differ at *this* point?" And there is an answer, found all the more easily when we spot the point of difference from the ideal type.

If the gospel tales can be plausibly placed alongside other ancient miracle tales as legends, and if the dying and rising god theme or the miraculous conception theme can be recognized among similar stories in other faiths, then why insist only the Jesus versions are true? Apologists for any of the traditions can only proceed by arguing, I think preposterously, that either the ideal type doesn't exist or that Christianity does not conform to it. The strategy is to deny the analogies.[245] Let's watch Greg try.

> The radical nature of his miracles distinguishes him [from ancient charismatic rabbis]. It didn't just rain when he prayed for it; we're talking about blindness, deafness, leprosy, and scoliosis being healed, storms being stopped, bread and fish being multiplied, sons and daughters being raised from the dead. This is beyond any parallels."[246]

It is unwise for Boyd to argue that the miracle stories attached to Jesus are *even more* extravagant than those told of the semi-legendary Hasidim. That seems to shove them even farther across the boundary into fanciful myth. In fact, it is the less dramatic miracles that have the greatest chance of qualifying for historical plausibility: deafness, blindness, bent spine and psoriasis (biblical 'leprosy') are notoriously psychogenic in origin and susceptible to faith-cure even today (which means they *pass* the test of analogy). I think Greg, along with many others, misunderstands the stories of Jairus' daughter and the widow of Nain's son as resurrections. I think, again, based on close analogies with ancient novels, legends, and ostensible medical cases, that we are supposed to understand Jesus rescuing the comatose from premature burial.

Jewish legend attributed the stilling of a storm on the Mediterranean to Hanina ben Dosa,[247] and both this and the gospel version are probably

---

245 One apologist actually confided in me after our debate that the analogy argument was devastating, but that did not stop him from continuing to deny it in public thereafter!

246 Boyd in Strobel, p. 118.

247 David L. Dungan and David R. Cartlidge, eds., *Sourcebook of Texts for the Comparative Study of the Gospels*. Society for Biblical Literature Sources for Biblical Study 1 (Missoula: Scholars Press, 4th ed., 1974), p. 69.

based on the Book of Jonah. And, as for the miraculous multiplication of food, how can Greg forget the literary prototype of 2 Kings 4:38–41, where Elijah performs practically the identical stunt. What is more probable, do you think: that one man miraculously multiplied food for hundreds of people? Or that another man copied out a well-known Old Testament story and changed the names? Get out your Occam's Razor and do the experiment.

Maybe somebody can explain this next one to me. It seems the lamest of arguments—if, that is, it is correctly represented. I tend not to trust press coverage, especially if the reporter is named Lee Strobel. I know that when I appeared on his show *Faith under Fire*, they chopped up my videotaped remarks to the point that even *I* couldn't tell what I was talking about! It even seemed to me they used my answer to one question as the reply to another one. So maybe Strobel is making a hash of Greg's words as well. At any rate, Strobel says Greg said:

> "Jesus' biggest distinctive is how he did miracles on his own authority. He is the one who says, 'If I, by the finger of God, cast out demons, then the kingdom of God is [upon] you' – he's referring to himself. He says, 'I have been anointed to set the captives free.' He does give God the Father credit for what he does, but you never find him asking God the Father to do it – he does it in the power of God the Father. And for that there is just no parallel."[248]

In the first sentence Greg has Jesus imperiously commanding miracles on his own authority, while in the second he correctly notes that Jesus appealed to divine authority above his own: "if I cast out demons by the finger of God." Which is it? Does he mean to say that Jesus meant it was his *own* finger, because he was the second person of the Trinity? I hope not. Surely he knows better than that. The second statement he attributes to Jesus is a shorthand quote from the Nazareth synagogue sermon (Luke 4:18–19) of Isaiah 61:1–2 and 58:6 (a lectionary conflation impossible on a single Sabbath) in which Jesus makes three references to his *delegated* authority: "The Spirit of the Lord is upon me," "he has anointed me," and "He has sent me." And do we never find Jesus asking God for a miracle? How about John 11:41–42: "I thank you Father, that you have heard me. I knew you always hear me, *etc.*" This implies Jesus prayed for both this miracle and others before this. Mark 9:29 surely implies Jesus had prayed before attempting exorcisms like that of the deaf-mute epileptic, just

---

[248] *Ibid.*, p. 119.

performed. I'm not even sure what Greg means to say here, but a miracle-worker who prays to God for his power does not sound so remarkable to me.

I Belong to Apollonius

The most astonishing set of parallels between the gospels and extra-Christian literature must be Philostratus' *Life of Apollonius of Tyana*. The Neo-Pythagorean sage's mother had a divine annunciation by the god Proteus who told her that he would soon be born as her son. As a lad, Apollonius distinguished himself serving at the temple of the healing god Asclepius by healing patients the god himself failed to heal (much like Jesus and the temple elders, or Jesus besting the poor performance of the Pool of Bethsaida). He casts out demons and heals illnesses, including the revival of a young bride being carried to her tomb. He does all this in the course of a peripatetic teaching career, accompanied by a few disciples, until he winds up arrested and jailed, awaiting an audience with the evil emperor Domitian, whom he tells off. He vanishes from the courtroom, teleports across the Mediterranean, and appears among his disciples whom he had sent on ahead. At first they imagine they are seeing a ghost come for a last goodbye, but he extends his hands and invites them to verify his corporeal reality. Later on, he ascends bodily into heaven and afterward appears to a doubting disciple in the presence of his colleagues to convince him of his immortality.

The stories do not give the appearance of being copied from the gospels to which they are so parallel, nor *vice-versa*. What *The Life of Apollonius* demonstrates is the currency of stories about "divine men," the θηειος ανερ. The point that gospel critics make is not that the gospel writers drew upon stories of Apollonius. That would be parallelomania. The stories are not *that* close. But the *types* of stories, and thus the type of hero biography, *are*. The point is the principle of analogy, not plagiarism.

Greg Boyd is completely unfair in his treatment of Apollonius.

> "[Apollonius'] biographer, Philostratus, was writing a century and a half after Apollonius lived, whereas the gospels were written within a generation of Jesus. The closer the proximity to the event, the less chance there is for legendary embellishment, for error, or for memories to get confused."[249]

[249] *Ibid.*, p. 119

By my reckoning, the gospels were all written nearly a century after the ostensible time of Jesus, but we could adopt more conservative dating. The key thing is how long it takes for legends to grow, and the answer is: *not very*. As I show in *Beyond Born Again*,[250] the case of Sabbatai Sevi, a charismatic messiah of the seventeenth century, of whom many contemporary records, rumors, and reports survive, make it absolutely clear that extravagant legends can crowd out the 'historical Sabbatai' (or Jesus or anyone else) in no time flat: weeks or days. Once we know that, it doesn't matter how much *more* time has passed between the historical figure and the documents containing the legends. And, as Greg neglects to note, Philostratus claims to have used not only extensive oral traditions, gathered locally at the various shrines and cities where Apollonius was said to have taught and worked miracles, but also the diary of Damis, the closest disciple of Apollonius. Now those claims may very well be part of the fiction, but guess what? The same question must be (and has long been) raised concerning the familiar claims that the Gospel of John was based on the recollections of the 'Beloved Disciple,' or that Mark's gospel was based on Peter's preaching.

> Philostratus was commissioned by an empress to write a biography in order to dedicate a temple to Apollonius. She was a follower of Apollonius, so Philostratus would have had a financial motive to embellish the story and give the empress what she wanted. On the other hand, the writers of the gospel[s] had nothing to gain – and much to lose – by writing Jesus' story, and they didn't have ulterior motives such as financial gain.[251]

Look, there is no reason to think any less of Philostratus than of Luke, whose writing of his gospel was apparently sponsored by his patron Theophilus, to whom he dedicated Luke-Acts, or at least that is what such book dedications usually denoted. Why suppose Philostratus did not try to stick to the facts to whatever extent Luke thought he was doing? And to charge poor Philostratus with trumping up false miracles as if he was a pulp writer being paid by the word is totally gratuitous. I assume Greg Boyd and Lee Strobel accept money for their literary labors. I hope they

---

250 Robert M. Price, *Beyond Born Again: Toward Evangelical Maturity* (Eugene: Hypatia Press, 1993), pp. 66–71; Gershom Scholem, *Sabbatai Sevi, the Mystical Messiah 1626-1676*. Trans. R.J. Zwi Werblowsky. Bollingen Series XCIII (Princeton: Princeton University Press, 1973), pp. 265–266, 274, 375, 390–391, 410*ff*, 417–418, 454, 456,535, 539, 592, 605, 920.

251 Boyd in Strobel, p. 120

do! It doesn't make them prostitutes or liars. And did the gospel writers really take any risks by writing their (anonymous) gospels? There is no reason to think so. It's not as if all early Christians had Nero, Decius, and Diocletian breathing down their necks, as in sword-and-sandal flicks like *Demetrius and the Gladiators*.

> "Also, the way Philostratus writes is very different than the gospels. The gospels have a very confident eyewitness perspective, as if they had a camera there. But Philostratus includes a lot of tentative statements, like 'It is reported that…' or 'Some say this young girl had died; others say she just was ill.' To his credit, he backs off and treats stories like stories."[252]

Then good for Philostratus! It would seem to be he, more than the Christian evangelists, who tried to maintain some reportorial objectivity. The you-are-there approach is the mark of story-telling, not of history. I'm afraid Greg is arguing against himself here.

> Philostratus was writing in the early third century in Cappadocia, where Christianity had already been present for quite a while. So any borrowing would have been done by him, not by Christians.[253]

But, once again, borrowing is not the point, not what anyone claims. It is simply the same *kind* of writing, and that is what is so important, so important that Greg dares not see the distinction.

History versus *Mystery*

Another major source of apologetics headaches is the Mystery Religions with their plethora of dying and rising god myths (and rituals). Once you learn of these, it becomes very tempting to think Christianity, first, simply was another one of these, and, second, received influence from converts from these faiths.[254] But you know what Greg is going to say to that. He will say just what Reverend Strobel wanted to hear. Strobel knew he would—that's why he picked him to ask in the first place!

> That was a very popular argument at the beginning of the century, but it generally died off because it was so discredited. For one thing, given

[252] *Ibid.*, p. 120.

[253] *Ibid.*, p. 120.

[254] Richard Reitzenstein, *The Hellenistic Mystery-Religions: Their Basic Ideas and Significance*. Trans. John E. Steely. Pittsburgh Theological Monograph Series Number 15 (Pittsburgh: Pickwick Press, 1978), p. 149.

> the timing involved, if you're going to argue for borrowing, it should be from the direction of Christianity to the mystery religions, not vice versa.[255]

I must turn Greg's own words against him. Given the timing involved, the influence must have been from the dying and rising god religions to Christianity for the simple reason that the myths and cults of Baal, Osiris, and Tammuz predated Christianity by many centuries. Their rituals are even mentioned in the Old Testament. Ezekiel 8:14 mentions the women of Jerusalem engaging in ritual mourning for Tammuz, raised for half of each year by his sister Ishtar taking his place (*cf.* Zechariah 12:11).

The worship of Aleyan Baal was popular for centuries among Israelites, to the chagrin of the prophets, as every attentive Sunday School child knows. Joseph, himself a Hebrew version of Osiris, is actually said to have married into the royal priestly house of Osiris (Genesis 41:45). The Song of Solomon is almost certainly based on the liturgies of Ishtar and Tammuz.[256] Ancient Israelites did not even understand themselves to be worshipping borrowed gods in any of these cases. It only looked that way once the Deuteronomic Reform imposed a hitherto-unknown monotheism on Judah, along with the revisionist premise that Israel must always have been ostensibly monotheistic, hence their polytheism *must* have been an alien import.[257]

But there was also some actual syncretism. For instance, the Epistle of Aristaeus, verse 15, gladly identifies the Jewish Yahweh with Zeus. The Sabazius religion of Asia Minor appears to be a combination of the faiths of Yahweh and Dionysus. Various Greek scholars equated the two anyway, and when Antiochus Epiphanes tried to Hellenize Judea, he persuaded many to embrace Dionysus worship (2 Maccabees). My guess is that he convinced them of the identity of their ancestral deity with Dionysus. Greg protests: "[T]he Jews carefully guarded their beliefs from outside influences. They saw themselves as a separate people and strongly resisted pagan ideas and rituals."[258]

---

255 Boyd in Strobel., pp. 120–121.

256 Marvin H. Pope, *The Song of Songs*. Anchor Bible Vol. 7c (Garden City: Doubleday, 1977).

257 Margaret Barker, *The Older Testament: The Survival of Themes from the Ancient Royal Cult in Sectarian Judaism and Early Christianity* (Sheffield: University of Sheffield / Phoenix Press, 2005).

258 Boyd in Strobel, p. 121.

But this is only half the picture. Zealous "old time religion" Jews like Mattathias and his sons, the Hasmoneans, undertook revitalization movements to keep traditional ways pure only when others in the same community were enthusiastically borrowing the seemingly more successful ways of outsiders. When Judah Maccabee 'resisted' pagan influences, it was only because many other Jews were welcoming them. This is why we even find second-century synagogues depicting Hercules, Yahweh driving a chariot through the wheel of the Zodiac, and caskets ornamented with both the Jewish menorah and the wheel of Attis.[259]

But the decisive consideration against the Mysteries borrowing the dying and rising god theme from Christianity is that *early Christian apologists themselves admitted* their rivals had it first. This is why they resorted to the incredible argument that Satan had counterfeited the death and resurrection of Jesus among the pagans—*in advance*! Greg continues with an oft-heard argument.

> While it's true that some mystery religions had stories of gods dying and rising, these stories always revolved around the natural life cycle of death and rebirth… Crops die in the fall and come to life in the spring. People express the wonder of this ongoing phenomenon through mythological stories about gods dying and rising. These stories were always cast in a legendary form. They depicted events that happened 'once upon a time.' And Christianity has nothing to do with life cycles or the harvest. It has to do with a very Jewish belief – which is absent from the mystery religions – about the resurrection from the dead and about life eternal and reconciliation with God.[260]

But this misses the point: Christ-Myth theorists know good and well that the myth must have originated as a cyclical myth unconnected with historical events. Their point is that at some point people began to historicize these myths. For instance, the Cretans claimed that Dionysus (Young Zeus) had been slain once and for all, and they showed tourists his grave! As Arthur Drews[261] suggested, later institutional demands led to one proto-Christian faction claiming an historical Jesus as their founder so they could claim their leaders (the bishops) had been taught

259 Reitzenstein, pp. 125, 176–192.

260 Boyd in Strobel, p. 121.

261 Arthur Drews, *The Christ Myth*. Westminster College–Oxford: Classics in the Study of Religion (Amherst: Prometheus Books, 1998), pp. 271–273, 288–289

by his immediate successors. This gave them the advantage over others (Gnostics, *etc.*) who welcomed new and contradictory revelations (as Irenaeus[262] bemoaned). Only with an orthodoxy of belief reinforced by claims of succession from an objective, historical founder could institutional authority prevail over chaotic charismatic 'authority.'

But was Christianity unique among the Mysteries in offering resurrection and fellowship with God? Hardly: Mithraism offered the heavenly ascent of the saved soul, while Isis and Osiris promised resurrection. But it seems Christianity inherited resurrection belief from Second Temple Judaism, where the belief had been inherited, during the Exile, from Persian Zoroastrianism.[263] They believed that, at the end of the age, the Saoshyant ('Benefactor'), a virgin-born descendant of the Prophet Zoroaster (and sometimes identified with Mithras) would arrive to defeat the evil entity Ahriman and raise all the dead for a final judgment. Those Jews who embraced these doctrines were called, sneeringly, 'Parsees' (*Pharisees*) by those skeptical of such new-fangled, foreign ideas.[264]

You tell me; is this an example of straight reporting? Strobel pontificates: "the Jesus Seminar [*offers*] a symbolic Jesus, but one who's impotent to offer the world anything except the illusion of hope."[265] Suffice it to say that the prospect of a purely symbolic Jesus Christ is a beacon of hope for many, like the Jesus Seminar Associate members, who know enough about historical Jesus scholarship to believe it is Strobel's Jesus who is the illusion, the weak reed for one's hopes. I guess hope is in the eye of the beholder.

---

262 Irenaeus, *Against Heresies*, Book 1:21:5..

263 Cohn, *Cosmos, Chaos and the World to Come*, Chapter 13, "Jews, Zoroastrians and Christians," pp. 220–226; Alan F. Segal, *Life after Death: A History of the Afterlife in Western Religion* (NY: Doubleday, 2004), pp. 174–175, 179–180, 181, 183–184, 190–192, 195, 197–198.

264 Manson, *Servant Messiah*, pp. 18–20.

265 Strobel, p. 125. Strobel's theological boorishness inevitably reminds me of the words of Paul Tillich: "Only a symbol? He who asks this question shows that he has not understood... the power of symbolic language, which surpasses in quality and strength the power of any nonsymbolic language. One should never say 'only a symbol,' but one should say, 'not less than a symbol'" (*Dynamics of Faith*. World Perspectives Series Volume X (NY: Harper Torchbooks / Cloister Library, 1958), p. 45.

Out of the Prayer Closet

As apologists always do at the close of supposedly scholarly debates, Greg Boyd—invited to do so by Lee Strobel—gives an evangelistic testimony essentially amounting to the old Billy Graham line: "You may know *about* Christ, but do you *know* him? Don't miss heaven by eighteen inches!" That is the distance between the head and the heart. Even so, Greg admits that receiving Christ as one's personal savior goes considerably beyond historical evidence into existential encounter. Boy, does it! I should say there is no evidence in the New Testament that any early Christians articulated their faith in terms of an imaginary "personal relationship with Christ" such as dominates Christianity in our day, having begun as late as the Pietist Movement[266] within Lutheranism. Where in the Bible does it describe or prescribe such a thing? I'm still looking. 'Having faith in Christ' certainly does not imply some sort of sticky 'personal relationship' as evangelicals claim to have. Boyd speaks from experience.

> So it is with falling in love with Jesus. To have a relationship with Jesus Christ goes beyond just knowing the historical facts about him. I believe in Jesus on the basis of the historical evidence, but my relationship with Jesus goes way beyond the evidence. I have to put my trust in him and walk with him on a daily basis.[267]

Once I was teaching a course on "Great Devotional Classics." Among books like Miles Sanford's *The Green Letters*, Dietrich Bonhoeffer's *The Cost of Discipleship*, and C.S. Lewis's *The Screwtape Letters*, I assigned Malcolm Boyd's *Are You Running with Me, Jesus?* I recall how one student remarked that he loved Boyd's book; he had never before read such a powerful display of a moment-by-moment personal relationship with Jesus. I then told him that Malcolm Boyd was a homosexual. I couldn't wait to see the result of the experiment. It was not long in coming: I could see the portcullis slamming down behind the student's eyes. From being the perfect poster boy for the personal relationship with Christ, Boyd had now sunk to where he was and could be no genuine Christian at all!

The irony of the thing is the combination of homophobia with a devotional style that must be described as homoerotic. "Falling in love with Jesus"? Nor is such language at all uncommon in pietistic circles. Here is a devotional style that demands its adherents cultivate feelings

---

266 Peter C. Erb, (ed.), *Pietists: Selected Writings*. Classics of Western Spirituality (Ramsey, NJ: Paulist Press, 1981).

267 Boyd in Strobel, p. 126.

of emotional adoration and tender cherishing for a fellow male figure.[268] It makes a kind of symbolic sense for nuns to imagine themselves as being engaged to Christ—but for men? How absolutely fascinating that the muscular Christianity of the Promise Keepers and of fundamentalist men everywhere creates and shapes romantic feelings in men for a man.[269] It might even help account for fundamentalist homophobia as a reaction formation against the implicit homoeroticism to which their 'personal relationship with Christ' commits them.

If you decide to take the apologist's advice, will you be starting with Greg Boyd and ending up with Malcolm Boyd? Not that there's anything wrong with that.

---

268 "He must be an ardent lover of Christ... [learn] to love the Lord Jesus." "Let every minister look to his own heart, and see to it that he himself loves Christ fervently... You must learn to be a zealous lover of Christ" (August Hermann Francke, "On Christian Perfection," in Erbe, pp. 123–124). "If we wish thus to come to following the Lord Jesus we must first learn to know the heart of Jesus properly and his fervid love for us. .. Look upon this, and in your soul, and the dear Jesus will become loving and sweet; it will warm your heart" (Francke, "Following Christ," in Erbe, p. 144). "These words are to be applied to the marriage and union with Christ and in the bride chamber itself where one learns to know one's bridegroom, Christ Jesus, in true inwardness and in proper joy and pleasure of the heart" (Francke, "The Foretaste of Eternal Life," in Erbe, p. 156).

269 See also Philip M. Helfaer, *The Psychology of Religious Doubt* (Boston: Beacon Press, 1972): "Generally, homosexual feelings and fantasies, and feminine submissive longings, can be channeled into the relationship with God. Various forms of 'witnessing' and evangelizing... are also common channels for homosexual libido. The man's intense love for Jesus may be a homosexual, narcissistic object choice, sometimes overriding any other object choice in the individual's life" (p. 132).

PART TWO
USING JESUS AS A VENTRILOQUIST'S DUMMY

Chapter Seven
The Identity Crisis
Did Jesus Memorize the Nicene Creed?

Our intrepid reporter next drives off to Kentucky to have his opinions endorsed by Ben Witherington III. He was a classmate of mine at Gordon-Conwell Theological Seminary back in the days when Fleetwood Mac's *Rumors* album was ubiquitous on the radio. In fact, I've just gotten up to put that album on the CD player. Now I'm back at my desk and reminiscing—but not about Witherington. I didn't really know him. We didn't travel in the same circles. I hung out with co-conspirators who used to issue fake spiritual retreat schedules with designated times for snake-handling and fire-walking, followed by recreation at Paddy's Disco Pub. We'd circulate phony memos from faculty members speaking in tongues. Stuff like that. He went on to prestigious Cambridge University to study with the esteemed C.F.D. Moule.

Ben Witherington III (or as a form letter from *TIME* magazine, based on his subscriber's label, addressed him, "Mr. III") has written a Talmud's worth of tomes since then. For all his erudition, though, the ones I've read always sound like Campus Crusade for Christ with footnotes. Even if he's ostensibly writing about something else, say, the role of women in the New Testament, the whole damn thing's about apologetics: why this passage really does go back to Jesus, why that one's genuine, too.

Well, now you know why Strobel wanted to talk to him for *The Case for Christ*. And in this chapter, the topic is basically this: how Jesus already believed in the Nicene Creed, even though he never exactly *said* as much. But remember, these guys are both fundamentalists. They don't want theology that rests on inference and remains provisional, like adults. No, they have to have it down in black and white—or better, in red, since they believe Jesus said everything a Red Letter Bible depicts him saying.

Witherington says, "If he had simply announced, 'Hi, folks; I'm God,' that would have been heard as 'I'm Yahweh,' because the Jews of his day didn't have any concept of the Trinity."[270] But Jesus *did*? Is that it?

I have never seen a more blatant case of circular argumentation. Jesus does not make overt claims to divinity. Okay. Now, one might suppose (and one certainly has no right to do any more than suppose) that he made no such claims to be God[271] because he had no such notion about himself.

---

270 Witherington in Strobel, p. 133.

271 It is surprising that, to his credit, Witherington knows better than to take all

That is why most of us don't claim to be gods, after all. But Witherington is sure that Jesus was being tactfully coy. Because, you see, being a member in good standing of the Blessed Trinity, he already knew about the doctrine of the Trinity. And how does Witherington know Jesus knew this? Well, he had to, because Witherington believes in it as an orthodox Protestant, and Jesus must have been at least as smart as Witherington! Can anyone doubt that evangelical apologists approach scriptural interpretation deductively, as their prior theology dictates?

> If the Twelve represent a renewed Israel, where does Jesus fit in? ... He's not just part of Israel, not merely part of the redeemed group, he's forming the group – just as God in the Old Testament formed his people and set up the twelve tribes of Israel. That's a clue about what Jesus thought of himself.[272]

Uh, that would mean Jesus saw himself as… the new *Jacob*, right? The father of the twelve tribes? Surely that's more likely than implying he was *Yahweh*. But if that is what Jesus meant, that he was Yahweh, then what happens to the fancy distinctions between members of the Trinity that Witherington claims Jesus secretly drew?

The Dead Sea Scrolls sect was organized with the Teacher of Righteousness at the head, and below him twelve men. Does Witherington imagine that the Teacher was supposed to be Jehovah God, too? The ascension itself pales in comparison to Witherington's leaps of logic.

> Jesus says, 'Of all people born of woman, John is the greatest man on earth.' Having said that, he then goes even further in his ministry than John did – by doing miracles, for example. What does that say about what he thinks of himself?[273]

We have no right, as Witherington seems to think he does, to cram the whole gospel narrative into that one passage, to make it look as if Jesus was asserting or implying an unfavorable contrast between himself and John. "Look at my track record compared to his!" We have to take each passage by itself first. And if you do that,

---

the lines given the Jesus character in the Gospel of John at face value. His fellow apologists have no qualms about grossly overstating the evidence, as if "Jesus claimed to be God," as they say over and over again.

272 Witherington in Strobel, p. 134.

273 *Ibid*, p. 134.

why, it's obvious that Jesus thinks *less* of himself than of John! Just as the fourth gospel has John humbly defer to Jesus (John 3:30, "He must increase, and I must decrease."), it should not be surprising that Jesus should exalt the venerable John above himself. Of course, Jesus might just be engaging in flattering hyperbole as people often do in such situations, as when the pope bent down to wash the feet of Francis of Assisi. But there's no way you can take Bill saying Sam is the greatest man in history as implying Bill thinks he is greater than Sam! Here is what Albert Schweitzer called "the twisted and fragile thinking of Christian apologetics."[274] Another example:

> Jesus makes the truly radical statement that it's not what enters a person that defiles him, but what comes out of his heart. Frankly, this sets aside huge portions of the Old Testament book of Leviticus, with its meticulous rules concerning purity… We have to ask, What kind of person thinks he has the authority to set aside the divinely inspired Jewish Scriptures and supplant them with his own teaching?[275]

First, the passage cannot go back to Jesus, since Mark 7:7 quotes Isaiah 29:13 (on which Mark's Jesus character predicates his critique of the scribes) not from the Hebrew, which would not have established the desired point,[276] but from the Greek Septuagint translation, which Palestinian scribes loathed, but which does apply to the point at issue.

Second, even at that, the very passage cited condemns those who set aside the Torah commandments to replace them with their own! Jesus is shown here condemning the scribes for doing what Witherington thinks Jesus was bragging about doing! On Witherington's logic, Jesus should have recognized that the scribes were claiming divine nature and authority for themselves!

Third, what can Witherington do with the Jesus of Matthew 5:17–19 and Luke 16:17, who says the cosmos itself will perish before the least bit of the Torah will be set aside?[277]

---

274 Albert Schweitzer, *Out of my Life and Thought*. Trans. C.T. Campion (NY: New American Library / Mentor Books, 1953), p. 186.

275 Witherington in Strobel, pp. 134–135.

276 "This people draw near with their mouth and honor me with their lips, while their hearts are far from me, and their fear of me is a commandment of men learned by rote."

277 Oh, I know the drill: "until all is fulfilled!" Until Jesus fulfils prophecy by dying as a sacrifice, and then it will be open season on ham sandwiches. Non-

Fourth, you will look in vain for these sentiments about the law-smashing Jesus in Witherington's other books where he argues fashionably for the thorough "Jewishness of Jesus." Witherington, like all slippery apologists, is an exegetical opportunist.

Fifth, if Jesus really had founded a sect teaching that kosher laws were defunct, he would have invited swift and merciless elimination that would have made the treatment he receives in the gospel Passion narratives look like a chorus of "For He's a Jolly Good Fellow!" To get an idea of what must have happened, look at the secrecy of the seventeenth-century messianic sect of Jakob Frank who knew eschatological freedom from clean and unclean strictures must be practiced behind closed doors in the dark of night.[278]

I find it ironic that conservatives repudiate the 'criterion of dissimilarity' which says we cannot confidently trace a saying back to the historical Jesus if it matches either contemporary Jewish practice (from which Christians may have borrowed it) or early Christian practice (which may have been retroactively fathered onto Jesus). It is ironic because they love to boast that Jesus' teaching or practice was a "radical departure" from this or a "radical negation" of that, and they do this by exaggerating the differences.

For instance, they want to make Jesus an egalitarian proto-feminist for PR purposes, so they rummage through the ocean of rabbinical materials and take a few statements out of context to create a misogynist stereotype of Judaism against which Jesus starts looking like Gloria Steinem. Without this cosmetic make-over, you really can't say much more than "Jesus was not a fanatical misogynist."

Norman Perrin's and Rudolf Bultmann's version of the criterion of dissimilarity was "If it's radically new, Jesus must have said it." Witherington's version is, "If Jesus is supposed to have said it, then it must have been radically new." And why? That makes him appear a man out of time, a divine insertion into the time stream with a perspective not conditioned by his place in ancient history and culture. But this is an illusion, a sleight-of-hand trick, because the anachronistic perspective is *their own*, the result of the apologists looking back at the text from their own historically conditioned slot in the timeline.

---

sense. In that case, why condemn anyone who henceforth teaches that we are free to set aside the commandments (Matthew 5:19)?

278 Gershom G. Scholem, "Redemption through Sin," in Scholem, *The Messianic Idea in Judaism and other Essays on Jewish Spirituality*. Trans. Hillel Halkin (NY: Schocken Books, 1971), pp. 78–141.

> Jesus taught in a radical new way. He begins his teachings with the phrase 'Amen I say to you,' which is to say, 'I swear in advance to the truthfulness of what I'm about to say.' This was absolutely revolutionary… In Judaism you needed the testimony of two witnesses.[279]

Again the circular reasoning. Again the absurd proof-texting. The requirement of two or three witnesses (Deuteronomy 17:6; 19:15) is to secure reliable testimony *in court*, obviously, so people couldn't be done in by the groundless allegations of some enemy. It has not a thing to do with making assertions of one's opinions, as Jesus is shown doing. And what a way to read Jesus' assertions! He says, "*I* say unto you," without appealing to authority. So wouldn't that naturally seem to mean he was daring to assert his own ideas, anticipating the spirit of the Renaissance or the Enlightenment? That he didn't need the saved-up capital of the past but could speak on his own authority, for the hearer to accept or reject? Like the Buddha is said to have done? But, no, Witherington thinks it must mean Jesus thought he was a god, or at least possessed "the power of direct divine utterance." That's a heck of a leap.

Strobel "asks": "Jesus used the term 'Abba' when he was relating to God. What does that tell us about what he thought about himself?"[280] Witherington gives him the answer he was fishing for, demonstrating what a charade the whole 'investigation' really is:

> 'Abba' connotes intimacy in a relationship between a child and a father… But Jesus used it of God – and as far as I can tell, he and his followers were the only ones praying to God that way… It's the term of endearment in which a child would say to a parent, 'Father Dearest, what would you have me do?'[281]

This is all wrong, all gratuitous. The notion that *Abba* meant 'Papa' or 'Daddy' is a speculation of Lutheran Pietist Joachim Jeremias,[282] based on pre-New Testament Aramaic linguistic evidence. The idea is cherished by evangelicals because it seems to feed their sticky religious sentimentalism. But Raymond E. Brown[283] rightly points out that the word

279 Witherington in Strobel, p. 136.

280 Strobel, p. 136.

281 Witherington in Strobel, p. 136. *This* is supposed to be informal intimacy? Does Witherington live in a Victorian novel?

282 Joachim Jeremias, "Abba" in Jeremias, *The Central Message of the New Testament* (NY: Scribner's, 1965), pp. 9–30.

283 Raymond E. Brown, "The Pater Noster as an Eschatological Prayer," in Brown, *New Testament Essays* (Garden City: Doubleday Image Books, 1968), p. 284.

by no means implies such coziness. It might have, originally, but by the time of the New Testament it had come to mean, simply 'father.' In fact, we have the word of Paul himself in Galatians 4:6 that *Abba* meant simply 'Father,' since that's how he translates it. Ironically, Witherington himself [284]mentions that Jewish rabbis were called *Abba* by their students. But then the word cannot mean what Witherington says it means; were rabbi and disciple on such intimate terms? Were Hart and Kingsfield?[285] And were Jesus and his disciples the only Jews who dared address their god this way? Hardly. Geza Vermes cites instances of Galilean *Hasidim* who were known to "beseech Abba" in prayer.[286]

But how do we even know whether Jesus addressed the deity this way? *Abba* occurs three times in the New Testament. "You did not receive the spirit of slavery to fall back into fear, but you have received the spirit of sonship. When we cry, 'Abba! Father!', *etc.*" (Romans 8:15–16). In Galatians, Paul says, "because you are sons, God has sent the spirit of his son into our hearts, crying 'Abba! Father!'" So from these verses we can surmise Christians called on God as *Abba*, but not that it meant anything all that intimate, since it is made the equivalent of the generic Greek word πατηρ. Because we are sons to God, we may address him as father. No news there. But neither Pauline passage says *Jesus* used to pray that way. For that we have to refer to Mark 14:36, "And he said, 'Abba, Father, all things are possible for you,' *etc.*" Once again, "Abba" is translated from Aramaic into Greek by the biblical writer himself, and there is nothing of the daring familiarity Jeremias and Witherington want to see there.

In any case, is this evidence that the historical Jesus used to address the deity as *Abba*? I'm afraid not, since the scene is clearly the dramatic invention of the evangelist Mark. Notice, if you will, that Mark has carefully eliminated all possible witnesses from the scene. He has Jesus leave most of his men at a far remove, taking with him only the inner circle. But then he leaves them far enough away that he only realizes they are asleep once he rejoins them. So who heard Jesus' prayer? Who knew what he said to God? Mark 'knew' only because it was he who made it up. He is the omniscient narrator. Or are we to imagine Jesus hastily

284 Witherington in Strobel, p. 136.

285 "You call him Donny, your analyst? I call mine Dr. Chomsky… or – uh, he hits me with the ruler." Woody Allen, "Manhattan," in *Four Films of Woody Allen: Annie Hall, Interiors, Manhattan, Stardust Memories* (NY: Random House, 1982), pp. 209–210.

286 Geza Vermes, *Jesus the Jew: A Historian's Reading of the Gospels* (London: Fontana / Collins, 1976), pp. 210–211.

whispering to the disciples as Judas was leading the mob his way, "In case one of you fellows wants to record it in a gospel one day, here's what I was just saying to my Father…"?

So to me the evidence reads that early Christians simply took for granted that Jesus would have prayed as they themselves did. Mark took it from there, having Jesus use the familiar term 'Abba' in his darkest hour because it seemed appropriate. But that would be pretty much worthless for evangelical devotionalism, so Witherington sees it differently:

> Actually, … the significance of 'Abba' is that Jesus is the initiator of an intimate relationship that was previously unavailable. The question is, What kind of person can change the terms of relating to God? ... Jesus is saying that only through having a relationship with him does this kind of prayer language – this kind of 'Abba' relationship with God become possible.[287]

And wait a second—who is the saving relationship supposed to be *with*? The heavenly Daddums or with Jesus himself? Witherington just cannot keep his persons of the Trinity straight, so aflutter is he by this time with pious fervor.

Reverend Strobel notes that already within twenty years of the crucifixion Christians were thinking of and praying to Jesus as a god. "Do you see any possible way this could have developed – especially so soon – if Jesus had never made transcendent and messianic claims about himself?" Mr. Bones leans on his cane and replies,

> "Not unless you're prepared to argue that the disciples completely forgot what the historical Jesus was like and that they had nothing to do with the traditions that start showing up twenty years after his death… Frankly, as a historian, [*really*?] this would not make any sense at all."[288]

Oops! I think that must be a typo! Because what Witherington must have meant was that *as an apologist* the notion wouldn't pass muster for him. As a historian, on the other hand, he really shouldn't have a problem with it. We know of other characters, some much nearer to us in history, of whom we can be quite sure that deification was accorded them in two decades or less, and without their say-so. Usually it wouldn't take nearly *that* long.

---

[287] Witherington in Strobel, p. 137.

[288] Strobel, pp. 139–140.

First, think of Ali, cousin and adopted son of the Prophet Muhammad. We read that already in his lifetime he was embarrassed by devotees who proclaimed him the very Incarnation of God, Allah, in the flesh.[289] He had some executed for the blasphemy, but the rest only admired that as an exercise of divine fiat!

Invariably apologists deny that Jews could have thought to deify Jesus alongside the Father because of their strictly monotheistic Jewish background.[290] That is, unless they were forced to. Uh, by *what*? Jesus' resurrection? Even if that happened, there is no obvious connection. Or maybe that Jesus must have taught it. But here's Ali, heir to an equally strict monotheism, elevated to godhood by his followers against his will ("Only the true Messiah denies his divinity!").[291]

So, could it happen that a prophet was shortly deified, and that against his intent? I love the anecdote where noted preacher Charles Haddon Spurgeon was on a train and the guy next to him recognized him and started pestering him: "Dr. Spurgeon, do you believe in infant baptism?" Spurgeon replied, "*Believe* in it? Why, man, I've *seen* it!"

Similarly, twentieth-century Congolese prophet and evangelist Simon Kimbangu was widely hailed by his admirers, the Ngunzists ('Prophetists') as "the God of the Blacks" and "the Christ of the Blacks." Once this news got back to him in prison, he was chagrinned and anguished, as he held no such exalted views of himself. He tried to clamp the lid on this false propaganda, but he could not. Even some subsequent scholarly studies took the divinity claims as his own teaching.[292]

Subsequent scrutiny, however, managed to pare away the praise of his followers from his own, more modest claims,[293] precisely as in the case of New Testament scholars, trying to distill the true historical Jesus from the encompassing myths and magnifications of him, have done. But one can be sure that, if Witherington was a Kimbanguist, he would be a Ngunzist with plenty of arguments at hand proving that Kimbangu *must*

---

289 Matti Moosa, *Extremist Shi'ites: The Ghulat Sects* (Syracuse: Syracuse University, 1988), pp. xvi–xvii.

290 C.S. Lewis, *Mere Christianity* (NY: Macmillan, 1960), p. 56.

291 Graham Chapman, John Cleese, Terry Gilliam, Eric Idle, Terry Jones, Michael Palin, *Monty Python's The Life of Bryan (of Nazareth)* (NY: Ace Books, 1979), p. 111.

292 Vittorio Lanternari, *The Religions of the Oppressed: A Study of Modern Messianic Cults* (NY: New American Library / Mentor Books,1965), pp, 25–28; G.C. Oosthuizen, *Post-Christianity in Africa* (Grand Rapids: Eerdmans, 1968), p. 40.

293 Marie-Louise Martin, *Kimbangu: An African Prophet and his Church* (Grand Rapids: Eerdmans, 1976), pp. 73–75.

have claimed his own divinity; otherwise such a belief could never have gotten off the ground and spread so quickly!

Another famous case is that of Rabbi Menachem Mendel Schneerson, a charismatic Rebbe of the Brooklyn-based (and before that, Lithuanian) Lubavitcher sect of Jewish Hasidism. In the 1990s he preached to avid throngs the imminent advent of King Messiah. His devoted followers were persuaded of the same, and many or most believed the Rebbe himself would be manifested as Messiah. When he lapsed into a coma and soon expired (1994), their faith did not fail. Soon, they believed, he would rise from the dead, heralding the general resurrection. Even before his death, some had begun describing him as "the essence of the Infinite in physical garb."[294] *Only two years later*, one publication calls the Rebbe "our Creator."[295] In the same year, another says, "In him the Holy One Blessed be He rests in all His force just as he is… so that this becomes his entire essence."[296] And "his entire essence is divinity alone."[297] *That* sure didn't take very long! And with no help from the Rebbe, who had never said any such thing.

Of Jesus, Witherington deduces the following:

> "Now, God, in his divine nature, doesn't die. Now how was God going to get this [the work of salvation] done? How was God going to be the Savior of the human race? He had to come as a human being to accomplish that task. And Jesus believed he was the one to do it."[298]

So Jesus understood not only the doctrine of the Trinity three centuries before it was promulgated (though he didn't save us all a lot of time by explaining it); he was also aware of Greek essentialist metaphysics and the soteriologies of Athanasius and Anselm of Canterbury! The gospel snippets Witherington quotes are like leaves floating on a stream of dogmatic theology running through his mind. He just does not know the difference between theology and inductive exegesis.

> Jesus said in Mark 10:45, 'I did not come to be served but to serve and give my life as a ransom in place of the many.'[299] This is either the

---

294 David Berger, *The Rebbe, the Messiah and the Scandal of Orthodox Indifference*. (Portland, OR: Littman Library of Jewish Civilization, 2001), p. 30.

295 Berger, p. 81.

296 Berger, pp. 82, 92.

297 Berger, p. 92.

298 Witherington in Strobel, p. 141.

299 Actually, Witherington has substituted the first-person 'I' reference from

> highest form of megalomania or it's the example of somebody who really believes, as he said, 'I and the Father are one.' In other words, 'I have the authority to speak for the Father; I have the power to act for the Father; if you reject me, you've rejected the Father.'[300]

Where does he see this link between godhood and saving people? And who says "for many" means the whole human race? The "ransoming/redemption" language denotes martyrdom, as in 2 Maccabees 7:37–38 and 4 Maccabees 6:27–29. Likewise, in times of persecution, "some Rabbis would, on certain occasions, exclaim, 'Behold, I am the atonement of Israel.'"[301] The idea is that, if God allows Jews to be persecuted as a way of settling up for their sins, a few righteous, not guilty like the run of the population, may stand in the gap, dedicating their suffering and death at the persecutors' hands as an expiatory sacrifice to avert Yahweh's wrath from their countrymen whose sins brought the persecution in the first place. The fact that Witherington crams this one verse like a Thanksgiving turkey full of theological stuffing shows, once again, where he is coming from. He is merely a theologian proof-texting the Bible on behalf of the party line. When a perfectly good Jewish context of meaning is ready to hand, he leapfrogs it on the way to later Christian theology.

It also bothers me that he starts quoting the Gospel of John as an unproblematic source of sayings of the historical Jesus. He knows better. Witherington admits: "When you're dealing with the gospel of John, you're dealing with a somewhat interpreted picture of Jesus, but I also believe it's a logical drawing out of what was implicit in the historical Jesus."[302] But here he lapses into InterVarsity default mode, substituting bunk apologetics for whatever C.F.D. Moule may have taught him at Cambridge: Jesus said all that self-aggrandizing stuff in John after all!

Witherington finishes the chapter with a final blaze of glory in which he signals once and for all that he knows not the difference between dogmatic belief and historical judgment.

Luke's version (Luke 22:27) for Mark's third-person "the son man came not to be served but to serve, and to give his life as a ransom for many." So why didn't Witherington simply use Luke's version instead? Because Luke's version lacks "and give his life as a ransom for many." In Mark, Jesus doesn't *quite say* it is *he* who will redeem many, while in Luke it's Jesus serving, all right, but not necessarily giving his life as a ransom.

300 Witherington in Strobel, p. 141.

301 Solomon Schechter, *Some Aspects of Rabbinic Theology* (NY: Macmillan, 1910), p. 311. See *Mechilta* 2a; *Mishna Negaim* 21.

302 Witherington in Strobel, p. 138.

> We have to ask, Why is there no other first-century Jew who has millions of followers today? Why isn't there a John the Baptist movement? Why, of all first-century figures, including the Roman emperors, is Jesus still worshipped today, while the others have crumbled into the dust of history? It's because this Jesus – the historical Jesus – is also the living Lord. That's why. It's because he's still around, while the others are long gone.[303]

Well, Mister Third, let me tell you why there are no first-century Jews worshipping a fellow Jew today. For all your exploitation of Jewish sources, mainly out of context, to domesticate Jesus, it has apparently not occurred to you that, as Jacob Neusner explains,[304] there are no gospels in Rabbinic Judaism because the rabbis preferred anonymity, fading into the larger collective. To them, attaching some truth to any individual's name was to imply he had invented it, that he was greater than it. By contrast, the rabbis felt they were simply disclosing the implicit meaning of the oral Torah (as innovative as we may recognize their efforts to have been). They associated a stand-out name, like Eliezer ben-Hyrkanus, with certain halakhic opinions because, even though they were deemed not without merit, they stemmed from a heretic and thus might be tainted. Even today millions of Jews do live by the teachings of these humble teachers, even without knowing their names. It was a conscious choice; it is not as if they might have had a messianic rival but Jesus knocked him out and took the title.

Why isn't there a continuing John the Baptist movement? Uh, there *is*. That would be the Mandaeans (see my brief remarks on them in Chapter 4).

Why are other would-be religious founders mere museum relics today, unavailable for personal-savior appearances to their fans? It's because my savior can beat up your savior. Here Witherington shows his true colors. Here historical reasoning gives way with a crash (though not much of one, as it is only a flimsy stage-set that is collapsing) to dogmatic belief. But this is the rabbit that has been barely hidden in Witherington's hat all along, even though most of the time you could pretty easily catch a glimpse of a pink ear or a cotton-ball tail peaking out.

---

303 Witherington in Strobel, p. 141

304 Jacob Neusner, *Why No Gospels in Rabbinic Judaism?* Brown Judaic Studies 135 (Atlanta: Scholars Press, 1988), p. 70–72.

Chapter Eight
The Psychology of Heresy
Must Apologists Be Crazy When They Say Jesus Believed He Was God?

In this chapter I want to pass over most of the argument of Strobel's Chapter 8: whether there really are demons, whether Jesus was a mesmerist, *etc.* I want to concentrate directly on the two major issues: Did Jesus think he was the Son of God? And would he have to be insane if he thought so but was wrong?

Did Jesus call himself God's son? Did he accept the honorific from others? Again, we must dismiss John's gospel as a piece of dramatized theology pure and simple (which is no criticism!). As D.F. Strauss put it, the self-revelation statements of Jesus in John, so totally unparalleled in the Synoptics, surely represent the devotion of Jesus' worshipers, put back into the mouth of Jesus.

> He made his Christ speak as the Christ spoke within himself; he made him move and act as he lived in his own imagination.[305]
>
> The speeches of Jesus about himself in this Gospel are an uninterrupted Doxology, only translated out of the second person into the first, from the form of address to another, into the utterance about a self.[306]

What they predicate of him by way of praise and adoration is transferred to his own lips. This is the spirit in which we read John's gospel, so we notice nothing untoward about it. We are stricken and intrigued with numinous awe when we read Jesus saying, "I am the light of the world; whoever follows me will not walk in darkness but will have the light of life." We do not pause to think of how such words must sound coming from a historical contemporary. When some guru says such things of himself today, we think, "What a megalomaniac!" and we question his motives. And if we insist that the historical Jesus really did say these things, the sort of thing we read in John, we start imagining a megalomaniacal Jesus. This is the sort of Jesus who makes people recoil and ask if this man were not insane after all.

---

305 David Friedrich Strauss, *The Life of Jesus for the People* (London: Williams and Norgate, 1879), p. 209.

306 Strauss, pp. 272–273.

But, as Albert Schweitzer[307] said, those who seek to psychoanalyze Jesus on the basis of the Johannine sayings are like one who might seek to analyze Isis from the Isis aretalogies inscribed on Egyptian monuments. Martin Kähler,[308] too, denounced all attempts, friendly or hostile, to 'psyche out' Jesus, to see what made him tick. The Christ of Christian faith, of the New Testament gospels, is not simply a great historical figure who might be, *must* be, the result of early influences and good upbringing, *etc.* He is more than mortal. He is a living *Symbol.* This is the distance between the historical Jesus and the Christ of faith. Conservatives who mix the two invite suspicions, on the part of outsiders who take them seriously, that their Jesus was crazy.

There are three main passages to consider. First comes a Q text (Matthew 11:27/Luke 10:22), usually called "the Johannine thunderbolt" because it erupts into the peaceful Synoptic sky. "All things have been delivered to me by my Father; and no one knows the Son except the Father, and no one knows the Father except the Son and anyone to whom the Son deigns to reveal him." It parallels John 1:18, "No man has ever seen God; the only begotten son, he who rests in the bosom of the Father, has made him known." It does not fit its present context; such a saying is impossible for the ministry of the historical Jesus, as it presupposes the resurrection and exaltation, like Matthew 28:18, "All authority in heaven and on earth has been given to me." See also Ephesians 1:20–23; Philippians 2:6–11.

Second, the parable of the Wicked Tenants (Mark 12:1–9) is a transparent allegory of salvation history as viewed by Christians: God has sent his stubborn people prophet after prophet, despite their track record of rejection and martyrdom. Finally, in one last effort to persuade them to render him his due honor as their creator and redeemer, God sent his son, but he fared worse than the rest, being cast out of the city (to Golgotha) and killed, prompting God to wash his hands of the people and to deal with the Gentiles instead. There is a bit of confusion over whether the wicked sharecroppers are supposed to stand for stubborn Israel as a nation or for the corrupt temple elders (Mark 12:12). In the former case, the new tenants must be the Gentile Christians, as Matthew makes explicit (21:44, "the kingdom of God will be taken away from you and given to *a nation*

---

307 Albert Schweitzer, *The Psychiatric Study of Jesus: Exposition and Criticism.* Trans, Charles R. Joy (Boston: Beacon Press, 1948), pp. 40, 45.

308 Martin Kähler, *The So-called Historical Jesus and the Historic Biblical Christ.* Trans. Carl E. Braaten. Seminar Editions (Philadelphia: Fortress Press, 1964), pp. 52–53.

producing the fruits of it."). In the latter case, presumably the new tenants are the conquering Romans. Either way, the story is an anachronism looking back on the career of Jesus.

Jeremias tries to make the 'son/servants' element an integral part of the political/economic color of the parable, and so to secure it for the historical Jesus. Thus Jesus wasn't necessarily thinking of himself as a son distinct from the prophets in some Christological sense. No, Jeremias says, the story requires the appearance of an heir so the tenants can mistakenly infer his father is dead and assume that, if they kill the heir, they will inherit the land by squatter's rights.[309]

But this does nothing to mitigate the problem: it only explains why the sharecropper business was an attractive basis for a parable about the murder of the Son of God! If that is not the point, why is the arrival of a son even in the story? Why does not the absentee landlord simply send in men to kill the wicked tenants and replace them (as in Matthew's version of the Great Supper, Matthew 22:6–7, "the rest seized his servants, treated them shamefully, and killed them. The king was angry, and he sent his troops and destroyed those murderers and burned their city.")? We don't need to get as far as the son's murder unless we want the parable to describe the murder of God's son.

Plus, there is the matter of the parable's sympathies. Is it really likely that Jesus, a popular Palestinian preacher, would have symbolized his god as a rapacious absentee landlord and made the poor sharecroppers the villains? At any rate, if this parable went back to Jesus himself, we would indeed have a statement, only minimally veiled, that he deemed himself the Son of God. But we don't.

But does not Jesus refer habitually to his god as "my Father," implying a singular relationship? There are no such statements in Mark, one in Q (the Johannine Thunderbolt), two in Lukan redaction (22:29, added to Q as preserved in Matthew 19:28; 24:49), *fifteen* in Matthew, and *thirty-two* in John. Obviously, the tradition grew more Christological as it went along, with a rapid acceleration once it passed from oral to written form. It is almost a function of the written gospels. I would say this progression, if you follow it back to the source, arrives at the doorstep of the oral tradition *and does not cross the threshold*. It does not go back to Jesus.

Now I am fully aware that no evangelical scholar, no apologist, will grant the force of a single one of these arguments, though they seem to me decisive. Furthermore, there is no argument anyone could offer for

---

309 Joachim Jeremias, *The Parables of Jesus*. Trans. S.H. Hooke (NY: Scribner's, rev. ed., 1972) , pp. 70–73.

the inauthenticity of any gospel saying that an apologist would not hasten to rebut. Why is this? Is it because the gospels happen, simply as ancient writings, to be one hundred percent accurate, unlike many or most similar documents from antiquity? Or put it this way: if you *do* think the gospels are uniquely and completely accurate, this is to say you are an inerrantist. Your belief is derived from dogma, not from an inductive scrutiny of the evidence.

Anyone can see that the reflexive mode of these conservatives is to defend the authenticity of the sayings. "Innocent until proven guilty,"[310] they often say. And of course no such proof will ever satisfy them. Having been able to offer harmonizations for most errors and contradictions (satisfactory to *them*, seeming "plausible" because they comport with what apologists are committed to believe), they trust that someday some solution even to the most outstanding, stubborn problems will come along.

This is no different from B.B. Warfield taking last refuge in the unavailable autograph manuscripts. Any error that can otherwise be proven *must not have been contained in the original*. This is stubborn stonewalling and nothing else. Apologists are inerrantists by force of will. Supposed New Testament scholars like Boyd, Witherington, Blomberg, *et. al.*, are simply not interested in digging into the text. They want to defend the inerrancy of the Bible as it is.

In R.G. Collingwood's terms, the apologists are "scissors-and-paste historians"[311] who regard the ancient writings not as 'sources' (as a critical historian does) but as *authorities*, the chronicler's sacred information about the past that must be harmonized so he can use as much of it as possible.[312] The last thing the pre-critical historian wants is gaps in his story, so he is unwilling to part with any pieces of the puzzle. The critical historian asks if some of the pieces belong to a different puzzle, or if there

---

310 I. Howard Marshall, *Eschatology and the Parables* (Leicester: Theological Students Fellowship, n.d.), p. 5.

311 Collingwood, *Idea of History*, pp. 258–259, 274–275.

312 Collingwood, p.p. 258–259: "As soon as it became understood that a given statement, made by a given author, must never be accepted for historical truth until the credibility of the author in general and this statement in particular had been systematically inquired into, the word 'authority' disappeared from the vocabulary of historical method… The document hitherto called an authority now acquired a new status, properly described by calling it a 'source', a word implying that it contains the statement, without any implications as to its value. That is *sub judice*; and it is the historian who judges. That is 'critical history.'" And this is why apologists are not and cannot be true historians.

are finally enough surviving pieces to assemble to yield any real portrait of the past, knowing full well there may not be. And it is that uncertainty the apologist cannot abide. "Get it settled tonight!"

As long as we're on the subject of whether Jesus Christ was a lunatic, I want to propose that the shocking suggestion is implicit in one of the most valued weapons in the apologist's arsenal, the famous Trilemma argument. Here it is in its classic form, that of C.S. Lewis:

> A man who was merely a man and said the sort of things Jesus said would not be a great moral teacher. He would either be a lunatic – on the level with the man who says he is a poached egg – or else he would be the Devil of Hell. You must make your choice. Either this man was, and is, the Son of God: or else a madman or something worse.[313]

There's a lot wrong with this. For one thing, it's a classic case of the 'Bifurcation Fallacy'—oversimplifying the options in order to manipulate the audience into choosing the option you favor: "My friends, our only choices today are fascism or anarchy! Which is it to be?" For another, as we have seen, it is by no means clear whether the gospel passages in which Jesus affirms (or accepts acclamations of) his Godhood/divine Sonship really go back to Jesus or reflect the church's Christology. I think the latter is the case, but at least it is an issue in debate, and one therefore cannot simply cite those verses and "demand a verdict," ignoring the fact that the jury's still out on most of the evidence the plaintiff introduced! For yet another, we are not without examples of gurus who viewed themselves as divine avatars and who did not seem to be either madmen or conniving charlatans, though of course they may have been mistaken.

Some have sought to deflect this counterpoint by saying that claiming deity in a Nondualist context is a different matter altogether, but I do not think it is. If a guru claims to be a god embodied on this level of particularity, we have the same scenario we would if Jesus made the claim. Everyone is a god on the ultimate level of reality/perception in Nondualism, but so what? If a man is walking around among men and claims to be an avatar *in this world of Samsara*, he is claiming to be *God here* and not in the sense he also predicates of ordinary mortals.

Allow me just a glance at Dr. Gary R. Collins's argument in Strobel's interview that Jesus gives all the signs of psychological soundness. No one says they saw him defecating on the sidewalk, muttering to himself

313 Lewis, *Mere Christianity*, p. 56.

in the bus station, dressing like Abe Lincoln. True, but then again, what do they always say about serial killers before they go on their shooting sprees? They were the nicest guys, cared about people, never gave a hint of what they finally proved themselves capable of doing.

Or think of the Reverend Jim Jones—he of the raspberry Fla-Vor-Aid. As far as the public knew (and any gospels would have recorded), he was an upstanding preacher and social reformer. You had to be pretty far into the church, which turned out to be a cult, to get a whiff of what was really going on. Everyone else had to wait till the Guyana massacre to find out. My point is, of course, that a Jesus who went around claiming to be God would not necessarily have 'acted out' his insanity in any other way.

But I have said that the Trilemma argument itself gives grounds for positing the madness of Jesus. How does it do this? It is a great irony, to be sure, an unintended consequence. It only reveals what a bad argument it is. Here goes. The premise of the argument is that a healthy, normal human mind cannot hold the belief in its own godhood. It means to say that Jesus would be an exception because it would be true in his case. Just like in *Miracle on 34th Street*: "If you or I said we were Santa Claus, we would be insane, because we're not Santa Claus…But Mr. Kringle *is* Santa Claus." If Old Kris is right, then he's sane. If it can be shown he is not Santa, but only thinks he is, then off to Bellevue he goes.

Likewise, says C.S. Lewis, Jesus escapes messianic insanity if he turns out actually to be the Son of God (or God, period). But there is something missing. And that is the prosecution's rejoinder: "*Any*-one who believes himself to be Santa Claus is insane." There is something about the belief that renders it so extraordinary, so outrageous, that no sane mind may entertain it. If you did, it would drive you mad. I'm not sure this is true. Yes, there are men in lunatic asylums who believe they are Jesus (Maybe they got tired of being merely Napoleon), but their insanity does not consist simply in their erroneous belief. Rather, their schizophrenic delusion leads them to believe mistaken things. Such sad individuals also often believe they are persecuted ('delusions of grandeur'), but they believe so without any evidence. It is not that it is inherently insane to believe you are being persecuted. Thus insane people believe they are Jesus Christ, but that hardly means anyone who believes he is Jesus is *ipso facto* crazy.

But let's assume it is true: "No normal, human brain may hold a belief in its own deity." Don't you see what this has to imply? It means that

Jesus must have been out of his mind even if he were correct about being God. Such a belief would have exploded any merely mortal mind. If the belief did not drive him mad, he must have had a qualitatively superhuman mind, and that, if I am not mistaken, amounts to the Apollinarian heresy.

Apollinaris of Laodicea, a disciple of Athanasius, held fast to his master's teaching that the Son was of one and the same nature as the Father. But Athanasius had focused only on the divinity, not the humanity, of Christ and did not teach Jesus' *full* humanity. He left that for others to work out, and Apollinaris did, or tried. His theory was that the incarnate Logos possessed a genuine human body of flesh, as well as a genuine human soul, but that instead of a human spirit, he had the divine Logos.

The three Cappadocian Fathers, Gregory of Nyssa, Gregory of Nazianzen, and Basil of Caesarea, eventually prevailed against him with the reasoning that "whatever has not been assumed cannot be redeemed." That is, the incarnation saves believers by virtue of the Logos taking on their humanity and divinizing it. If there were any portion of the human being that the Logos declined to assume, the incarnation would have been only partial, and so would salvation. A fat lot of good it would do you to have your body saved without your soul, or your soul without your body. You'd wake up in the afterlife like Ronald Reagan in that movie, exclaiming, "Where's the rest of me?"

It seems to me that the Trilemma argument, in positing a Jesus who is God incarnate but with a qualitatively superhuman mind able to harbor the conviction of its own godhood, is the Apollinarian Christ; he has a god's mind instead of a human one, and that makes him a mythical demigod, like Hercules who was half god and half man, or like Gilgamesh who was somehow two-thirds god and one third man. The Apollinarian Jesus was two-thirds man and one-third God. Of course this conception would be superceded by the two-natures, one-person Christology, but the Trilemma takes us back to Apollinarianism. Welcome to it, if you want it. If you don't, your next move might be to deny that it would take a qualitatively superhuman mind to embrace the belief in one's own godhood. Then Jesus could have had a fully human mind and believed in his own godhood, and there would be no recourse to the Apollinarian heresy.

True. But then the Trilemma's sunk, because there is suddenly a fourth option: a man might sincerely believe himself to be a god and be wrong but not insane. Jesus could have believed he was God, taught many good things, but been wrong about his self-conception. That's not too hard to imagine. But again, I don't think it ever gets that far. It is absurd to go throwing around statements like "Jesus claimed he was God." You sound like the obtuse opponents of Jesus in the Gospel of John.[314]

[314] Once more: I'm not necessarily saying the Gospel of John does not portray Jesus teaching his own divinity, at least in some nuanced manner, though it is inconsistent, as the document has passed through many hands, belonging to rival theological camps, before it reached us. But my *Pre-Nicene New Testament* is, as I believe, the only version to translate "I came from God" as "I emerged from the Godhead." I just don't think these are sayings of a historical Jesus. I'm with Strauss on this one.

Chapter Nine
The Piffle Evidence
Could a Finite Jesus Correspond in any Way to an Infinite God?

Ladies and Gentlemen… He—re's DAV-ey!

And it's off to Trinity Evangelical Divinity School, where budding theologians are trained in spirit and spin, where the intrepid Lee Strobel has come to call upon David A. Carson. The question on his mind? He wants "to determine whether Jesus has 'the right stuff' to be God."[315] The question seems so absolutely wrong-headed in its enormity that I cannot help thinking of Kierkegaard saying that there is an infinite qualitative distinction between God and humanity such that we must either shudder at the blasphemy of making a human being God or dare to believe it as a scandalous paradox of faith.

But as soon as I read a few paragraphs I find myself astonished anew at a paradox almost as great: how can someone with Carson's erudition and training (Cambridge credentials again, together with expertise in Greek grammar and historical Jesus studies) still spew out the twaddle we expect from campus ministry workers? How can he just quote John's gospel glibly as the words of the historical Jesus? It is no surprise that everything Carson says is controlled by a dogmatic agenda, simply a function of intra-Christian theological discourse.

Goofy Gospel Exegesis

I never cease to be amazed at the perversity of the Jesus-idolaters who seem to prefer the false inferences Jesus' enemies drew from his words and start building Christology on that litter-box sand. Here's an example: "So along comes Jesus and says to sinners, 'I forgive you.' The Jews immediately recognize the blasphemy of this. They react by saying, 'Who can forgive sins but God alone?' To my mind, that is one of the most striking things Jesus did."[316]

First off, it makes more than a little difference that the mighty exegete Carson misquotes Mark 2:9, where Jesus most assuredly does *not* say, "I forgive you," but rather "Your sins are forgiven," implying the 'divine

315 Strobel, p. 157.

316 Carson in Strobel, p. 158.

passive,'[317] *i.e.*, *God* has forgiven the man's sin. Jesus claims but the right to pronounce absolution, as Catholic priests do today, just as evangelicals feel justified in assuring those who pray the magic formula of "the sinner's prayer" that they are freed from death and Hell and are alive for ever more.

Note further that Jesus argues, not that he, the Messianic Son of Man (no hint of this in the passage), has the unique prerogative of forgiving sins, but rather that *as a human being* he has the privilege of doing on earth (where pastoral assurances are audible to fleshly ears) what God does in heaven: remitting sins. His point is explicitly *not* that Jesus violates the divine/human barrier, but that absolution pronounced on one level is ratified on the other, precisely as in Matthew 16:19: "Whatever you bind on earth shall be bound in heaven, and whatever you loose on earth shall be loosed in heaven."

Matthew surely interpreted the Markan story of the forgiven/healed paralytic this way, since he interprets the amazement of the crowd thus: "they glorified God, who had given such authority to *men*" (Matthew 9:8). Carson must think Matthew as well as the crowd misunderstood Jesus but that the carping critics of Jesus were half right: Jesus *was* aggrandizing himself with insane boasts, but that that was all right since he did mean to "oppose and exalt himself against every so-called god or object of worship, so that he takes his seat in the temple of God, proclaiming himself to be God" (2 Thessalonians 2:4). Does Carson think that, when Jesus delegates authority to the disciples to forgive sins (or not, as they see fit!) in John 20:23, he is making them 'God,' too? Obviously Jesus is delegating the authority to them that had previously been delegated by God to him. He need be a god no more than them.

We meet with more of the same Cambridge-certified nonsense when Carson agrees with Reverend Strobel that Jesus boasted of never having sinned, as if such a claim would not automatically spoil one's record. "But along comes Jesus, who can say with a straight face, 'Which of you can convict me of sin?'"[318] For the sake of argument, let's wink at Carson's uncritical proof-texting and pretend Jesus really said this, and in these circumstances. Is he claiming, like Norman Greenbaum, "I'm not a sinner and I've never sinned"?

---

317 Jeremias, *New Testament Theology,* pp. 9–14.

318 Carson in Strobel, p. 158.

Carson doesn't give a damn about the context, despite his boast to do just this,[319] or he might notice how the text he quotes is Jesus' rejoinder to the threats of the mob to lynch him: "you seek to kill me, because my word finds no place in you" (John 8:37). "Now you seek to kill me, a man who has told you the truth which I heard from God" (John 8:49). Then, in verse 46, he says, "Which of you convicts me of sin?" The point is precisely that of John 18:38, "I find no crime in him." In other words, the issue is not whether Jesus may once have mocked an ugly girl in his town when he was a child, whether he had ever lusted, or swiped a pomegranate from a market stall, or made a cruel joke about Peter behind his back. The issue is that he has committed no crime worthy of death.

As for personal shortcomings, whatever they may have been, we need only look to Mark's baptismal story, the earliest in the gospels. Mark feels no embarrassment over Jesus getting in line to confess his sins, as inconsequential as you and I might have regarded them, and to receive John's watery absolution. It is Matthew, Luke, John, and the Gospel according to the Ebionites who have trouble with this simple scene in subsequent years, and each tries his hand at rewriting it to eliminate what, in light of more abstract Christology, had become a stumbling-block for the Jesus-idolizing reader.

Carson shows himself to be in fine gymnastic form again when Reverend Strobel asks him to soothe his 'doubts' about Jesus and the Rich Young Ruler of Mark 10:17–22. The zealous young inquirer approaches Jesus as young Gurdjieff approached "a Persian dervish, supposedly a performer of extraordinary miracles" for spiritual counsel, saying, "Be so kind, Father, and... explain to me what you think of what is called artificial breathing [Hatha Yoga]."[320] The suppliant asks Jesus, "Good master, what shall I do to inherit eternal life?" Jesus appears to react as if stung, recoiling from what the youth intends as honorific address, polite flattery, as when Catholics today address the pope as "Holy Father." Jesus is so sensitive to his obligation to render all glory to God that he recoils as if he is being tempted to pride: "Why do you call me 'good'? God alone is good."

But Carson will not have it! With an ear fine-tuned, not to what the text likely meant in its ancient context, but rather to how it must fit into modern evangelical dogmatics, he caricatures the text as follows: "He's saying, 'Do you really understand what you're saying when you say that?

319 Carson in Strobel, p. 163.

320 G.I. Gurdjieff, *Meetings with Remarkable Men*. Trans. A.R. Orage. All and Everything, Second Series (NY: E.P. Dutton, 1969), pp. 183, 187.

Are you really ascribing to me what should only be ascribed to God?' That could be teased out to mean, 'I really am what you say.'"[321]

Indeed, Carson's exegetical method sometimes seems to be simply to rewrite the text as he wishes it read even though it doesn't. He knows what Jesus or Paul *meant* to say! Colossians 1:15 poses a major problem for Nicene Christology, namely the notion that the Logos was co-eternal with the Father (which opponents said made the Logos the *brother* of God, not the son of God).

Colossians, in a hymn fragment praising Jesus Christ in terms of personified Wisdom, says he is the "firstborn of all creation," which Carson mistranslates as "firstborn *over* all creation" in order to smuggle his harmonization in ahead of time. The Greek has a simple genitive, no preposition υπηρ, no 'over.' By itself, and especially in view of the hymnic parallel in 1:18, "he is the firstborn from the dead," the point simply has to be that Jesus is first in temporal, sequential order, both of the old and of the new creation: first to be created, first to be resurrected. But this would play hell with Trinitarianism, so it can't be so!

Carson irrelevantly notes how sometimes 'firstborn' could be used of a person who had the same priority over an estate, even though he did not attain that position by virtue of being the former lord's firstborn son (primogeniture). Sure, there could be exceptions, but what would make us posit the Logos as one of them if not simply the trouble it gives Trinitarianism?

Interestingly, the Christadelphian sect employs the very same dodge, but for the opposite reason. They believe in the simple humanity and subsequent adoption of Jesus as God's son—no pre-existence in heaven. This last they dismiss as either metaphor or as denoting God's pre-existent plan to have Jesus perform his mission. So their problem with Colossians 1:15 is that it seems to make the Logos a real entity before his earthly appearance.

For Trinitarians Colossians threatens the eternal preexistence of the Word; for Christadelphians, it endangers the adoption of the mortal Jesus as the son of God. Not enough pre-existence in the one case, too much in the other! So both have to resort to the "as if a first-born" dodge. In fact, Carson goes so far as to say, "the very expression 'firstborn' is slightly misleading... I think 'supreme heir' would be more appropriate."[322] I'll *bet* he does.

---

321 Carson in Strobel, p. 162.

322 Carson in Strobel, p. 161.

Does not even the Johannine Jesus disclaim equality with God? "The Father is greater than I" (John 14:28). Not according to Carson:

> "The disciples are mourning because Jesus has said he's going away. Jesus says, 'If you loved me, you'd be glad for my sake when I say I'm going away, because the Father is greater than I.' That is to say, Jesus is returning to the glory that is properly his… the realm where he really is greater. "you ought to be glad because I'm going home.' It's in that sense that 'the Father is greater than I.'"[323]

But "I'm going home" is in no sense the equivalent to "The Father is greater than I"! (And this man is an accomplished Greek grammarian?) Plus, Carson pretends that for Jesus to be returning to a god greater than he is, is somehow the same as Jesus returning to a place where he, *Jesus*, is greater. This is a sleight-of-hand trick. Carson is just rewriting a difficult text to make it say what, because of his theology, he *wishes* it had said.

A Hell of a Thing

You can tell that Reverend Strobel is looking for a pro to give him a good PR trick for dealing with a particularly bad sticking point with the fundamentalist line. A real sales-killer. "The Bible says the Father is loving. The New Testament affirms the same about Jesus. But can they really be loving while at the same time sending people to hell?"[324]

You can tell Strobel doesn't give a damn about the real issue. He just wants a pointer for evading customer sales-resistance. How can we be sure of this? Simply because he too easily accepts the pat answers Carson feeds him.

"How could a loving Heavenly Father create an endless hell and, over the centuries, consign millions of people to it because they do not or cannot or will not accept certain beliefs?" Here he quotes ex-evangelist Charles Templeton.[325] Carson parries: "I'm not sure that God casts people into hell because they don't accept certain beliefs." [326] But he's being disingenuous in precisely the way that a political spin-doctor or an O.J. Simpson attorney is. It is an intellectual posture that corrupts Christian faith and has caused many of us to recoil from the whole damned thing in disgust. *Of course* Carson, with all evangelicals, believes God is going to

---

323 Carson, in Strobel, p. 163.

324 Strobel, p. 164.

325 Charles Templeton, *Farewell to God* (Toronto: McClelland & Stewart, 1996), p. 230, quoted in Strobel, p. 164.

326 Carson in Strobel, p. 164.

consign to endless torment all the poor hapless schlemiels who flunk their theology finals. It is just pathetic how they try to perfume their bigotry and make their odious views look innocent.

Once InterVarsity evangelist/apologist Paul Little was asked if Gandhi, one of the most Christlike individuals who ever lived, went to heaven when he died. His answer: Yes, if at the last minute, on his deathbed, he accepted Jesus Christ as his personal savior. Who does this man think he's fooling? Yes, if pigs can fly! Wherein lay poor Gandhi's damnation? Why did he end up on the barbeque spit next to Adolf Hitler? Was it that he lived for himself and not God? No, he just made the mistake of calling 'God' by the wrong name. Sure, he actually lived the Sermon on the Mount that most Christians only parrot. No, he might as well have been a serial child rapist. He loved and revered Jesus Christ, but that was worth a pile of dung. His crime was that he did not find the Christian doctrine of the atonement credible. If he wasn't damned because of his failure to accept this belief, what was it? That's what it always boils down to.

Evangelicals claim one is saved by the grace of God, but as Tillich and Bultmann cogently noted, evangelicals regard certain beliefs non-negotiable for salvation, and this amounts to *salvation by cognitive works*. They are at least necessary conditions if not sufficient ones. Do you love Jesus, but, alas, you are a Mormon with a heretical god-concept? You will fry, poor bastard. You're a Jew? You were *already* fried in the Concentration Camps? That's nothing compared to what *Reichsführer Jesu* has in store for you down below because you wouldn't accept him as the true Messiah. I mean, if this is not a matter of salvation by cognitive works, what is?

Let's suppose Jesus' death is really necessary, somehow, in the scheme of things, in order for the God to deal with sin. Why does one have to know about it? To believe in it? If Jesus died to save everybody, didn't it work? Is he the savior, or did his death merely prepare the ground for salvation? Is it still up to you to do the crucial thing: to believe in certain creedal articles? Ask any evangelical if you have to believe in the Trinity, the godhood of Jesus, his resurrection and atonement. You know what the answer will be. If you don't believe these things, you are no true Christian no matter what moral renewal you may have experienced, no matter how you may love the God. What makes the difference between being a true Christian and a fake? Why, the only way you can tell is which theological opinions one possesses. So, in the end, what does it come down to? Precisely as Templeton said: not believing in certain items in the creed. The Christian god is a merciless theology professor. If this is what you believe, have the guts to admit it. But evangelicals feel compelled to spin it. Why? They are ashamed of it. But they fear they dare not question it, or they themselves may wind up fake Christians—and damned.

So how does Carson spin it? "But in principle, if he's the sort of God who has moral judgments on those matters [*e.g.*, *the Holocaust*], he's got to have moral judgments on this huge matter of all these divine image bearers shaking their puny fists at his face and singing with Frank Sinatra, 'I did it my way.' That's the real nature of sin."[327]

Er, ah, *that's* the nature of sin? Carson's god creates individuals whose very divine image consists, presumably, in venturesome autonomy, just like him, and he damns people for wanting to do things as they think best? What is the image of this god? Is he a servile yes-man, gazing in slack-jawed subservience at Someone Higher? The very notion is absurd—even disgusting. You see, here is the real problem with the Christian message as many of us see it: it is not so much whether Jesus looks god-like, but whether we as human beings do!

That is, are we, as God's creations, supposed to be fawning lackeys, "needing him every hour"? Is wanting to go your own way tantamount to shaking your fist in that god's big face? Only if this deity is a pathological control freak! And is this god so petty and spiteful that, even if we were to shake our puny fists at him, he would take offense? It is all a cartoon, and Carson, Strobel, and their ilk are the most damnably pathetic of the type: they are poor submissive butt-kissers who have succumbed to Stockholm Syndrome and now identify with their tyrannical captors.

"Ohhh! What I wouldn't give to be spat at in the face! I sometimes hang awake at nights dreaming of being spat at in the face." "Crucifixion? Best thing the Romans ever did for us!"[328] And who are their captors? Not a paranoid deity, but his puppet-masters, the Grand Inquisitors who have taught the human race it was a sin to think for themselves, to gain too much knowledge. Strobel and Carson are doing just what Ivan Karamazov had the integrity *not* to do: accepting the ticket to heaven at the price of swallowing one's integrity. They have to spew sickeningly spurious excuses for their god's enormities; they have to cover for him and spin for him. It's part of the package, or you don't get that ticket. That's what's so sickening about apologetics.

---

327 Carson in Strobel, p 165.

328 *Life of Brian*, pp. 61, 62, 63.

"They're consigned there, first and foremost, because they defy their Maker and want to be at the center of the universe."[329] This has got to be the cruelest case of blaming the victim anyone has ever heard of. "Oh, God didn't *impose* hell on them; they *asked* for it by rebelling against God!" How? By a natural yearning for simple autonomy? Who in his right mind (not counting theologians!) would think to connect creative initiative with—rebelling against God? I should think I was *obeying* God's will!

Anyone who has ever known a self-abnegating, pious, humble member of another faith, a devout Jew, a Buddhist whose greatest goal is to extinguish egotistical striving and clinging, knows what an insult, what a slander it is to charge these poor souls with shaking their fists in the face of Jehovah, just because they practice a different religion. Isn't it after all a matter of failing that exam?

Insofar, however, as someone really does act self-centered and cannot see beyond his narcissism, isn't he or she simply immature? Why damn such a one to eternal punishment? Ultimately I just cannot understand why the Christian god does not simply *sanctify* everyone once they die. If he's planning on sticking you with a fate against your will anyway, why torture you? Why not sanctify you? Father, all things are possible for you; take this cup away from your poor creatures.

The Inconvenience of Slavery

"To be God, Jesus must be ethically perfect. But some critics of Christianity have charged that he fell short because, they say, he tacitly approved of the morally abhorrent practice of slavery."[330] Here comes the spin: "But you have to keep your eye on Jesus' mission. Essentially, he did not come to overturn the Roman economic system, which included slavery. He came to free men and women from their sins... Naturally, that has an impact on the idea of slavery."[331] How can these Christian apologists live with themselves? They love to take credit for Wilberforce doing what Jesus should have done but didn't do, as if the one was the same as the other. Jesus left his church to put two and two together; soon enough they'd realize they had to do something about slavery—and they did! A mere *eighteen centuries* later, Hallelujah!

Why couldn't Jesus have denounced slavery? The Stoics denounced it as against nature. Even the pre-Socratics had said the same. Compared

---

329 Carson in Strobel, p. 165.

330 Strobel, p. 166.

331 Carson in Strobel, p. 167.

with them, Jesus is badly retrograde. Christians love to get choked up and whisper about Jesus' call for "radical discipleship," but all they turn out to mean is "When Christ calls a man, he bids him come and have daily devotions and make a nuisance of himself witnessing to others." If anybody's endorsement might have meant something, you'd think that of Jesus Christ might have been of some help in getting slavery outlawed.

But at least Jesus does not, like the authors (or redactors) of the Petrine and Pauline epistles, command slaves to obey their masters in all matters, not even resenting the fact they have fellow Christians as masters! Carson, comically, points to Paul's Letter to Philemon as implying some Christian scruples about the incompatibility between the gospel and slavery. But here's a golden opportunity to condemn slavery among Christians – and he doesn't! At a time when others did. There is just no way out from under this one. Jesus and Paul are not depicted as transcending the moral horizon of their time. They do not even condemn the horrors of infanticide, so widely practiced, though the Qur'an did as soon as its author got the chance.

The whole thing is like the Watergate break-in: the original burglary was bad enough, but the cover-up was worse. Same thing with the Catholic child-abuse scandal. It was enough of a horror in its own right (even Jack Chick had never painted so damning an anti-Catholic portrait!). It was somehow worse that the bishops just didn't care and kept reassigning known molesters to new parishes. Doing what is bad is bad enough; making it sound good is even worse.

Chapter Ten
The Finger-Paint Evidence
A Mess of Messianic Prophecy

This chapter fakes you out. You think it's going to be still another tired review of supposed Messianic predictions from the Old Testament and how they were miraculously fulfilled by Jesus. But mostly it takes all that for granted and spends most of its time recounting the spiritual biography of Pastor Louis S. Lapides, a Jewish convert to Christian fundamentalism. Personally, I don't think it proves anything about Jesus' messiahship if a man goes into the Mojave Desert and asks Yahweh to give him a subjective feeling of certitude about Jesus being the Jewish Messiah. "'God, I have to know beyond the shadow of a doubt that Jesus is the Messiah. I need to know that you, as the God of Israel, want me to believe this.'" "God objectively spoke to my heart. He convinced me, experientially, that he exists. At that point, out in the desert, in my heart I said, 'God, I accept Jesus into my life'"[332]

Witness this poor man's utter confusion: he imagines a god spoke "objectively" through the medium of desperate emotions. Does he even know what "objective" means? His experience means nothing whatever. Sure, it meant a lot to Mr. Lapides, but it's beside the point for anybody else—lacking any and all probative value. It means no more than when some pimply-faced Mormon bike rider tells you that you can prove the Book of Mormon is an ancient document by asking God to give you a swelling feeling in your chest if it's true. Lapides might as well have just flipped a frackin' coin. Why is Strobel wasting time with this? Is he trying to prove that Jesus is the Messiah, or that Lapides is?

Strobel does eventually get to summarizing what Christians deem messianic prophecy—and it must qualify as the skimpiest attempt on record: one lousy paragraph, lacking even chapter-and-verse citations. One exception is Isaiah 53: "As Lapides progressed through the Scriptures, he was stopped cold by Isaiah 53. With clarity and specificity, in a haunting prediction wrapped in exquisite poetry, here was the picture of a Messiah who would suffer and die for the sins of Israel and the world – all written more than seven hundred years before Jesus walked the earth."[333]

---

[332] Lapides in Strobel, p. 180

[333] Strobel, pp. 177–178.

If you want to be convinced by messianic prophecy, it helps to be as ignorant as possible, and to be sure to read the passages with no reference to historical or literary context. None of what Strobel and Lapides find in this text (look it up, if you aren't already familiar with it.) is true at all. For one thing, it occurs in the *Second* Isaiah, a prophetic writing from just before the eve of the end of the Exile, still plenty of time before Jesus, but not from the pen of Isaiah of Jerusalem. Second, it never even mentions the Messiah, *i.e.*, the anointed king from David's dynasty who would one day appear to reestablish Jewish independence. I refer you to my book *The Paperback Apocalypse* for a discussion of the probable original context.[334]

Suffice it to say that the Servant was probably originally the pre-Exilic king of Judah in an annual penitence ritual, preceding his re-investiture with divine charisma. The vicarious suffering has nothing to do with some imaginary taint of Original Sin inherited from Adam, but speaks instead of national misfortunes. No reference at all is made to atonement for Gentiles. To make this a prediction of Jesus Christ is like Muslim apologists pretending (which they do) that John 16:7 is a prediction of the Prophet Muhammad. Or that, as Mormon evangelists claim, Ezekiel 37:19–20 predicts the joining of the Book of Mormon to the Bible. Can't you see that?

"Isaiah [7:14] revealed the manner of the Messiah's birth (of a virgin)."[335] Nonsense! Isaiah 7:14 plainly refers to the near-future birth of a child to a pregnant woman contemporary with Isaiah and the king whom he is addressing. As the context makes absolutely clear, little Immanuel is to be born to an *almah*, a 'young woman,' not necessarily a virgin at all (as any Hebrew scholar will tell you: 'virgin' would have been *bethulah*). And the 'sign' is no one's supernatural conception, but rather the fact that the named child (surely a son of Isaiah—see Isaiah 8:1–4 for another birth and another prophecy to the same effect) will grow only so old (old enough to turn up his nose at baby food he does not like) before the Syrian-Samaritan alliance threatening Judah has been obliterated by mighty Assyria. The prophecy cannot possibly refer to anything or anyone over seven centuries in the future from Isaiah's time. It has nothing to do with any Messiah, whether Jesus or anybody else. Can you find, can *Lapides* find, the word 'Messiah' anywhere?

---

[334] Robert M. Price, *The Paperback Apocalypse: How the Christian Church Was Left Behind* (Amherst: Prometheus Books, 2007), Chapter 2, "Messianic Prophecy," pp. 41–8.

[335] Strobel, p. 179.

"Micah pinpointed the place of his birth (Bethlehem)."[336] The text of Micah 5:2 reads: "But you, Bethlehem Ephrathah, though you are little among the thousands of Judah, yet out of you shall come forth to Me the One to be Ruler in Israel, whose goings forth are from of old, from everlasting." Does the Messiah even come in for mention here? The text does, however, make reference to a ruler and his awaited appearance, so maybe it's close enough.

Is the Messiah scheduled to be born in Bethlehem? The passage could bear that reading, no doubt, as some Jews apparently did read it (though we have no pre-Christian evidence for such a belief held by Jews). But one certainly need not read it that way. I consider the reference to Bethlehem, where David grew up, a bit of metonymy for the Davidic dynasty, like the frequent references to "the root of Jesse," David's father. The point would seem to be simply that the future king continues the unbroken dynasty stretching back to Jesse and/or to Bethlehem, *i.e.*, to David. King Messiah didn't have to be born in Bethlehem any more than he had to be Jesse's immediate offspring.

But even if Micah did mean to place a future king's birth in the very town of Bethlehem rather than indicating his dynastic origins, can we be so sure that Jesus was actually born there? The gospel accounts of the birth of Jesus in Bethlehem notoriously contradict each other. And there will never be any way of proving that early Christians did not simply begin from the *assumption* that, being the Messiah, Jesus *must* have been born in Bethlehem.

But let's suppose Jesus *was* born in Bethlehem. The seventeenth-century messianic claimant Sabbatai Sevi was born on the 9th of Av (or so our sources tell us), the date that rabbinical speculation had stipulated for Messiah's nativity. Does that mean Sabbatai Sevi was the Messiah?

"Daniel 9:24–26… foretells that the Messiah would appear a certain length of time after King Artaxerxes I issued a decree for the Jewish people to go from Persia to rebuild the walls in Jerusalem… That puts the anticipated appearance of the Messiah at the exact moment in history when Jesus showed up."[337] In fact, no one knows exactly which one of a few possible Persian decrees Daniel means.

And Lapides has the wrong 'anointed one' anyway. The text refers in minute detail to the persecution by Antiochus IV Epiphanes and of the ensuing Hasmonean revolt. (The actual writer of Daniel was a witness to these events, which is how he is able to describe them so minutely,

336 Strobel, p. 179.

337 Lapides in Strobel, pp. 184–185.

whereas his descriptions of life in ancient Babylon, centuries before, are vague and confused.) The phrase "an anointed one shall be cut off" refers to the high priest Onias III, killed during the persecutions of Antiochus.

"Psalms foretold his betrayal," Strobel tells us. I gather he is referring to Psalms 41:9, "Even my bosom friend in whom I trusted, who ate of my bread, has lifted his heel against me." But this is not even a prophecy, much less a messianic one! It is rather a typical Lament Psalm,[338] where one takes refuge in his god when all have abandoned him. Lament Psalms include Psalms 3, 4, 5, 6, 7, 10, 11, 12, 13, 14, 17, 25, 26, 28, 31, 35. These were complaints of suffering and prayers for vindication, pledging to return to the temple to provide a sacrificial feast to which the poor should be invited, to celebrate Yahweh's deliverance. On that occasion, "a new song," one of the Thank-offering Psalms (*e.g.*, 9, 30, 32, 33, 34), would be sung instead of the present gloomy plaint. The Everyman character of the Lament Psalm is evident from the vagueness and symbolism with which the envisioned trials and tribulations are described: wild dogs nipping at one's heels, strong bulls and lions, waters rising up to one's neck. Fill in the blanks as appropriate. Strobel imagines Psalms 41:9 is a messianic prediction, not because any Jewish scholarship or tradition has ever read it that way, but only because it is proof-texted shamelessly out of context by a *New* Testament writer, in John 13:18.

The Psalms, Strobel avers, also predicted "his accusation by false witnesses," and I am guessing he has in mind some other, similar Lament Psalm where Everyman seeks vindication against those who slander him and plot against him, like Psalms 31:11–18. But there certainly is no messianic prophecy with such a feature.

Strobel misinforms us that Psalm 22 predicts Messiah's "manner of death (pierced in the hands and feet, although crucifixion hadn't been invented yet)."[339] Psalm 22 belongs, again, to the large category of Laments. Strobel, like all apologists, cites "They have pierced my hands and feet" (22:16b) as a prediction of the nail-wounds of crucifixion, but the reference makes more sense in context as bite- and claw-wounds incurred by the sufferer as he tries to fend off the wild animals snapping at him (22:16a), the symbols of his real-life dilemmas. What/who were

---

338 Hermann Gunkel, *An Introduction to the Psalms: The Genres of the Religious Lyrics of Israel*. Ed. Joachim Begrich. Trans. James D. Nogalski. Mercer Library of Biblical Studies (Macon: Mercer University Press, 1998), pp. 121–198; Sigmund Mowinckel, *The Psalms in Israel's Worship*. Trans. D.R. Ap-Thomas (NY: Abingdon Press, 1962), Vol. II, pp. 1–25.

339 Strobel, p. 179.

these? Creditors? Political enemies? Romantic rivals? Vendetta avengers? Legal plaintiffs? Fill in the blank; that's the whole idea.

The business about dividing up the sufferer's garments just means, "They've given me up for dead." It could apply to anybody in the same straights. That was the whole idea. Psalm 22, any more than any other Lament Psalm, is no prophecy at all, no prediction of anything, much less of the crucifixion of Jesus. One can, on the other hand, easily imagine Jesus taking such a psalm as a fitting prayer in his hour of desperation, as Mark seems to imply he is doing, by having him quote the first lines of it, "My God, my God, why hast thou forsaken me?"

Strobel says, "the prophecies say the Messiah's bones would remain unbroken,"[340] a notion he derives from John 19:36, "For these things took place that the scripture might be fulfilled, 'Not a bone of him shall be broken.'" Uh, just which scripture would that be? Well, there are matching words in Exodus 12:46 and Numbers 9:12, instructions for cooking the Passover lamb, and in Psalms 34:21, a promise of Yahweh's protection of the righteous man. Either could have been taken as an appropriate allusion for Jesus, the Passover sacrifice and Lamb of God, but none of these references can be taken in context as a prediction of anything.

Poor clueless Lapides imagines fiendish skeptics trying to evade the "force" of these "prophecies," thinking "so maybe John invented the story about the Romans breaking the legs of the two thieves being crucified with Jesus, and not breaking his legs."[341] Lapides does not seem to realize that the ball is in his court: it is he who must account for how on earth anyone came to view any of these three texts as a messianic prediction in the first place. It is much more natural to picture Jesus' legs remaining unbroken for the reason the Fourth Evangelist gives us (Jesus was known already to be dead, so why bother with this hastening blow?) and then to imagine the evangelist looking for a proof-text to make even such a detail a matter of scriptural urgency.

Similarly, the hopelessly naïve Lapides tries to read the mind of a skeptic reading the mind of the First Evangelist. "And the prophecies talk about betrayal for thirty pieces of silver, so maybe Matthew played fast and loose with the facts and said, yeah, Judas sold out Jesus for that same amount."[342] This is no doubt, minus the pejorative tone, just what Matthew did, only he, rather like Lapides and Hal Lindsey, does not mind ripping texts from their proper contexts to fill in the blanks in the Christian story.

---

340 Strobel, p. 183.

341 Strobel, p. 183.

342 Strobel, p. 183.

Mark had neglected to inform his reader how much blood money Judas received from the Sanhedrin, so, pegging Zechariah as a series of predictions of Jesus, Matthew took the liberty of reading chapter 11, verse 12, as a prediction of Judas' fee. Lapides is wrong only insofar as he regards such embellishment as corrupted history rather than enriched story-telling. In any case, though, Zechariah 11:12 makes no reference to the Messiah. It speaks only of the prophet's own rejection, his firing from a shepherd's job with measly severance pay. It is only Matthew (26:15), in the New Testament, who rips the verse out of context to supply the figure for Judas Iscariot's bounty.

But Lapides isn't having any: "When the gospels were being circulated, there were people living who had been around when all these things happened. Someone would have said to Matthew, 'You know it didn't happen that way.'"[343] How does Lapides know anyone knew any better? Judas was dead, and Matthew was written so late, I doubt any surviving Sanhedrinists could have lived to see his gospel. And why would one suppose that if they *did* live so long they would be in the same geographic position as the author of Matthew's gospel and be able to see it?

"Besides… why would Matthew have fabricated fulfilled prophecies and then willingly allowed himself to be put to death for following someone who he secretly knew was not the Messiah? That wouldn't make any sense."[344] Uh, how does Lapides know how Matthew died? Whether he means the apostle or the evangelist (and he probably thinks they are the same, judging by the schools where he was indoctrinated)[345] we have no information about the manner or date of their deaths. For all we know, some Roman torturer offered to let him off the hook if he would admit he made up the gospel out of whole cloth—and he recanted the whole thing! We just don't know.

"What's more, the Jewish community would have jumped on any opportunity to discredit the gospels by pointing out falsehoods."[346] "They would have said, 'I was there, and Jesus' legs *were* broken by the Romans during the Crucifixion.'"[347] Yeah, like any of the small audience at Golgotha that day were scrutinizing the gospels decades later, looking for inconsistencies. Lapides just has no grasp of mundane historical realities. For him the ancient Jews are just characters in a Sunday School Easter

343 Lapides in Strobel, p. 184.

344 Lapides in Strobel, p. 184.

345 Dallas Baptist University and Talbot Theological Seminary, Strobel, p. 173.

346 Strobel, p. 184.

347 Lapides in Strobel, p. 184.

play. As if the witnesses to one more crucifixion would have come out of the woodwork decades later to debunk Christian texts they would not likely ever have heard of.

"But even though the Jewish Talmud refers to Jesus in derogatory ways, it never once makes the claim that the fulfillment of prophecies was falsified. Not one time."[348] So, let's get this straight: the anti-Christian Jews *accepted* that Jesus really did fulfill prophecy? *That*'s why we find no such charge in the Talmud? Perhaps Lapides does not know that one can easily see how medieval copies of the Talmud that escaped Christian incineration have self-censored various sensitive passages that might occasion persecution if Christians ever laid eyes on them. We are in no position to know exactly *what* criticisms Jews made and dared not make in the early years.

Strobel says the Psalms predicted "his resurrection (he would not decay but would ascend on high)."[349] He is thinking of the sermon ascribed to Peter in Acts 2:22–32:

> Men of Israel, hear these words: Jesus of Nazareth, a man attested to you by God with mighty works and wonders and signs which God did through him in your midst, as you yourselves know—this Jesus, delivered up according to the definite plan and foreknowledge of God, you crucified and killed by the hands of lawless men. But God raised him up, having loosed thc pangs of death, because it was not possible for him to be held by it. For David says concerning him, "I saw the Lord always before me, for he is at my right hand that I may not be shaken; therefore my heart was glad, and my tongue rejoiced; moreover my flesh will dwell in hope. For you will not abandon my soul to Hades, nor let your Holy One see corruption. You have made known to me the ways of life; you will make me full of gladness with thy presence." Brethren, I may say to you confidently of the patriarch David that he both died and was buried, and his tomb is with us to this day. Being therefore a prophet, and knowing that God had sworn with an oath to him that he would set one of his descendants upon his throne, he foresaw and spoke of the resurrection of the Christ, that he was not abandoned to Hades, nor did his flesh see corruption. This Jesus God raised up, and of that we all are witnesses."

---

348 Lapides in Strobel, p. 184.

349 Strobel, p. 179.

If one cares as much for the literal sense of Psalms 16:8–11 as for that of Acts 2, one will discern that the former speaks of Yahweh's favorite (the generic righteous man, perhaps the current Judean king, you fill in the blank) *evading* death, being *delivered from it* rather than dying and being resurrected. The whole thing is a prayer not to be left to die. Go ahead: show me the Messiah in this text.

Dim Intimations of the Obvious

"One other objection needed to be addressed: were the passages that Christians identify as messianic prophecies really intended to point to the coming of the Anointed One, or do Christians rip them out of context and misinterpret them?"[350] By now, or let's say, as soon as you study these passages in their Old Testament context, setting aside for the moment what fundamentalists tell you they mean, you can see the truth of the matter. In fact, after even a simple survey, the apologists' line is seen to be so flimsy, so utterly bankrupt, that one must call into question the basic sincerity of Lee Strobel and others like him. It is just like the faith healers. Once you read the exposés of their tricks and fraudulent stunts, there remains no room, no reason at all, to grant them the benefit of the doubt. They have to know better.

As for poor Lapide, one can at the most optimistic conclude that he is simply a victim of hopelessly obsolete, parochial exegesis. He clearly knows and appreciates not one thing about the Old Testament criticism of the last three centuries. He is living in an Amish Paradise. The poor fool thinks he is defending the Bible when in fact he is stationed stubbornly at the border of Kadesh-Barnea warning Joshua and Caleb not to lead Israel into scary old Canaan. There are gigantic advances, momentous discoveries to be made there, but he is too timid. Best stick with the desert in its arid familiarity.

> You know, I go through the books that people write to try to tear down what we believe. That's not fun to do, but I spend the time to look at each objection individually and then to research the context and the wording in the original language… and every single time, the prophecies have stood up and shown themselves to be true.[351]

---

350 Strobel, p. 185.

351 Lapides in Srobel, p. 185.

It's just infuriating to read this. Lapides can only see books of biblical criticism as "written to tear down what we believe." If only he could see how the Higher Criticism is the champion of advanced understanding of the text. The one who realizes, for instance, that the Pentateuch (the first five books of the Hebrew Bible) is a conflation of four earlier source documents, J, E, D, and P, is thereby enabled to study the texts at infinitely greater depth than the poor fundamentalist who feels obliged to hold at all costs that Moses wrote the whole thing.

To put it in the Sunday School terms that Strobel and Lapides can appreciate, imagine Lapides one day up in heaven, called to account for what he did with the talent entrusted to him. "You mean, you buried in the ground the tools I gave you to study the Bible in real depth? Take his talent away and give it to Wellhausen or Gunkel over there!"

PART THREE
RATIONALIZING THE RESURRECTION

Chapter Eleven
Dead Man Walking
The Swoon Theory

Black Sheep of Apologetics

How amazing that the Swoon Theory of the Crucifixion and Resurrection—which is all but universally reviled and ridiculed by apologists today—began precisely as a piece of apologetics *for* the resurrection narratives back in the eighteenth century! I will explain this odd paradox momentarily. But first just let me note that the shadow of eighteenth-century apologetics falls over the resurrection defenses of which we read in the next three chapters of *The Case for Christ*—as well as virtually all evangelical apologetics for Jesus and the gospels.

All alike presuppose (and will not work without) the assumption of eighteenth-century Protestant Rationalism and are thus hopelessly out of date. And that has nothing to do with trendiness or "what the latest scholarship is saying." No, it means that the unexamined assumptions that once made sense as functions of a particular system of thought make no sense at all outside of that system, and today's apologists are trying to bring those old apologetics to bear way out of the confines of the original system. The amazing thing is that neither side in the debate seems to notice the trick. Which means that, though they are all quite sincere, the joke is on everybody alike.

The Protestant Rationalists of the eighteenth century had an agenda none of the parties to the resurrection debate subscribes to today. They were caught in a transitional stage between pre-critical biblicism and genuine Modernism. They had embraced the modern science of the day, which meant a mechanistic universe, *à la* Isaac Newton, on the one hand, and the pious instinct to take the biblical narrative at face value on the other. They existed on the cusp of genuine Modernism, not yet having realized the implications of historical criticism.

They had moved but a single step in the direction of historical thinking *vis-à-vis* the Bible: they understood that it was no historical opinion to presuppose the Bible had been kept from error by divine inspiration or divine providence. That would smack of divine intervention into otherwise natural processes of causation, and that they could not brook. So, instead, they understood the biblical narratives as the products of direct eyewitness testimony. They figured it had to be in order to be accurate.

So even this was no historical judgment but rather a dogmatic deduction. It was not as if no genuinely critical alternative existed, as witness the scathing treatment accorded the Bible by Ethan Allen, Thomas Paine, and other Deists. The Protestant Rationalists held a compromise position, seeking to maintain a theology as close to the traditional as they might. The result was one of the most peculiar hybrids ever misbegotten in theology: naturalistic inerrantism.

Protestant Rationalists had their hands full trying to refute the rank unbelief of the Deists and of secular Freethinkers (also called Rationalists, but without the 'Protestant' prefix). The events told of in the Bible *did too* happen! Even the ones that seemed to the ancient writers miraculous in nature. Just as fundamentalist prophecy-mongers like Hal Lindsay still argue that Daniel was prophetically glimpsing speeding automobiles and John of Patmos was seeing Soviet helicopter gun ships ("locusts") but perforce described them in terms of the primitive technology of their own day, so did the old Protestant Rationalists imagine that the writers of Exodus or Mark saw what they recorded but just didn't understand the causation involved.

This meant they were unaware how close they were to shore when Jesus approached them walking on the inch-thick surf. Not being in the front row, Mark did not and could not know that Jesus was not miraculously multiplying food but only receiving it from assistants posted in the cave behind him, who handed him food from a hidden pantry. Had Jesus miraculously shriveled a fig tree? Or had he not rather merely noticed its sickliness from the absence of due figs, and his disciples took a closer look only subsequently, noticing the bad shape the tree was actually in (and had been in before they noticed).

Finally, the Protestant Rationalists had their toughest challenge when it came to Jesus' death and reappearance. If there are no literal (physics-defying) miracles, how does one get from Good Friday to Easter Morning? The answer was the Swoon Theory. Jesus was crucified, which nobody can deny; Jesus was seen alive a few days later. How can we get from point A to point B? Simply by positing that Jesus was crucified but did not die on the cross. He must have survived it if he were to be seen alive again. It was a way of saving the appearances. All the stories could be maintained as historically true this way, even if the traditional dots had to be connected in a new way.

With Newtonian naturalism (not Atheism) in mind, Protestant Rationalists proceeded, on the basis of belief in an inerrant Bible, to argue that no other event of ancient history was so well attested as the resurrection of Jesus, that no rival attempt to make sense of all the data of the gospel Easter narratives made any sense. The resurrection, albeit naturally accounted for, made much better sense than theories such as the disposal of Jesus' body in a common grave, that the disciples stole the body, that the women disciples visited the wrong tomb, *etc.*

What they were trying to show, and what evangelical apologists are still trying to show three centuries later, is that their version of the resurrection (back then, the Swoon Theory, today the supernatural resurrection) was the most compatible with *accepting all the details of the gospel Easter narratives as true and non-negotiable*. It is a very strange argument when you realize just what is actually going on: it is implicitly *an argument among biblical inerrantists* in which defenders of the resurrection assume (for the sake of argument?) that their opponents agree with them that all the details are true, that only the punch line is in question. But not in very serious question, for the resurrection fits the data as if tailor-made to do so.

In reality, it is just the other way around: the other details of the narrative have been designed to lead ineluctably to the resurrection. This is why, if apologists like William Lane Craig can get an opponent as far as admitting that Joseph of Arimathea probably did have Jesus interred in his own tomb, and if the women did probably visit the tomb, and that the tomb was probably found to be empty, he can then press on to the conclusion that, *Bingo!* Jesus must have risen from the dead!

What they somehow do not see is that to argue thus is like arguing that the Emerald City of Oz must actually exist since, otherwise, where would the Yellow Brick Road lead? (The analogy comes from an on-line "Jesus and Mo" cartoon.) Apologists are quite happy to live and breathe and exist within the confines of their favorite storybook, like Star Trek geeks who adopt Klingon or Federation names, ranks, and uniforms. You can see this in Reverend Strobel's interview with Bill Craig in the next chapter (if you'll forgive me for jumping ahead). He reasons that when Mark said that the women fled and did not give the report to Peter the young man had told them to give, this must have been a temporary silence, because, otherwise, how could Mark himself have known of it?[352]

Simple: he made up the story. He is the omniscient narrator. This is also how Mark 'knows' what Jesus prayed, *in private*, to the Father (Mark 14:32–37), how he knows what Jesus said to the Sanhedrin (Mark 14:62), *etc.*

---

352 Craig in Strobel, p. 217.

Straw Man Theory

Reverend Strobel and his source, Dr. Alexander Metherell, try to show us that, if we take every detail of the gospel Passion narratives literally (there's that unassimilated Protestant Rationalism again!) and if we then assume that everything we know about ancient crucifixion applies to the case of Jesus, then the Swoon Theory may be eliminated. This is doubly circular, I submit. We simply have no reason to *assume* that anything an ancient narrative tells us is true.

Reverend Strobel may not like it, but, as historian R.G. Collingwood[353] explains quite nicely, the critical historian (whether dealing with the Bible or the newspaper) demands that assertions in ancient or modern sources be corroborated. The historian does not simply take the ancient or modern writer at his word until he happens to find out different. I have been more than once astounded in debate to hear someone object that, if one approached everything with the "skepticism" I use on the gospels, we could never believe what we read in the newspaper! I replied that the newspapers provided the best example of what I was talking about! I have found myself quoted, or more often *mis*-quoted, in the paper several times, and I am far from likely to accept blithely whatever I read there.

I called the thinking of the apologists *doubly* circular. Besides inerrantism, the other circularity lies in the blanket application onto Jesus' case of what regularly happened in Roman crucifixions. The executioners were deadly accurate and well-trained. They wouldn't have missed a trick, because they always did A and B and C, and by the time they were finished, so were you.

But this is just what we do *not* know. If it is true, then of course Jesus must have died at their hands. But the very essence of the Swoon Theory is that maybe things did not go as they usually did.[354] You hardly have to be a "conspiracy theorist" (as Reverend Strobel[355] tars any advocates of this theory) to notice the oddity to which Mark expressly calls attention (was he, too, a conspiracy nut?), that Jesus was given a palliative—or perhaps soporific—drug (Mark 15:36) and then expired way ahead of schedule, to Pilate's astonishment (Mark 15:44).

---

353 Collingwood, pp. 236–239.

354 *Cf.* Craig on a different question: "If all you looked at was contemporary practice, yes, I'd agree… But that would ignore specific evidence in this case" (in Strobel, p. 208).

355 Strobel, p. 192.

I have just suggested that there is simply no reason to give apologists the benefit of the doubt by blithely assuming the historical accuracy of all details in the stories. So I am not arguing for a reading of the 'facts' that makes it look plausible that Jesus did not expire on the cross. No, what I will briefly argue (as I have elsewhere) is that one may very naturally read many striking gospel features as implying a slightly earlier version of the *story* in which its tellers *did* picture Jesus cheating death, not overcoming it. I realize it is impossible for apologists even to entertain such theorizing seriously, without trying to turn it back with automatic ridicule, because they hold it as a dogma, not a historical axiom, that the gospels are factual eyewitness accounts. But maybe the rest of you will give me a listen.

Go back to the prayer of Jesus in Gethsemane (remember: it provides one of the chief clues that we are dealing with a fictional account, since Mark carefully excludes the presence of possible witnesses, even among the disciples): Jesus affirms that it is always possible for God, the weaver of all circumstances, to open a new way for him, one that would render his impending crucifixion unnecessary. He is willing to go the hard way, however, devoted to the will of God above all.

Is it odd to read this prayer as a clue that Jesus is going to be freed from the cross, even from most of the suffering of it (*i.e.*, his early release)? It is common for Christian readers to read the Jesus story as a typological fulfillment of Abraham's near sacrifice of Isaac: Abraham's willingness to do the deed turned out to be all that Yahweh required. Jewish theology said something similar: Isaac's willingness to be sacrificed made the deed (albeit not carried to completion) a source of saving grace for all Israel to follow. It entails no great stretch to imagine the original tellers of the Jesus story as meaning to depict a Jesus whose self-sacrificing abasement to Yahweh's will was salvific in its own right, without his actual death.

Think of the mockery of the onlookers: "He saved others, but he can't seem to save himself! Hey! Come down from the cross right now, and we'll believe!" What choice irony if that is exactly what is about to happen, unbeknownst to them! If Jesus, thanks to the soporific fed him from the uplifted sponge, seemed to die but was taken down by sympathizers before death could take him—why not?

We know of a case in which this actually happened. Josephus, having just allied himself with Vespasian, caught sight of three men being crucified, his former companions in the fight against Rome, and he besought Titus to extend his compassion to them, too. Accordingly, the three were taken down and given into the care of physicians. Two were too far gone, but one survived. It has even been suggested, and by no means implausibly (unless of course one is a dogmatic inerrantist) that the Markan character Joseph of Arimathea is a fictional version of the Jewish historian himself, *Joseph* b-*ar-Matthia*-s, and that the whole story is based on Josephus' account of his rescuing his compatriot from the cross *alive*.

> I saw many captives crucified, and remembered three of them as my former acquaintance[s]. I was very sorry at this in my mind, and went with tears in my eyes to Titus, and told him of them; so he immediately commanded them to be taken down, and to have the greatest care taken of them, in order to their recovery; yet two of them died under the physician's hands, while the third recovered.[356]

This theory, obviously, is speculative. But all historical reconstruction is. Only dogmatists are impatient with such, because they want certainty, whether rationally justified or not. After all, one might perish in a bus crash going home from the crusade tonight, and then one would pass into a Christless eternity for failure to have adopted a particular 'historical hypothesis' by force of will. That's not history. That's evangelism. Too bad Reverend Strobel does not know the difference.

Follow the Yellow Brick Road

When Pilate is surprised to learn that Jesus is (seems) already dead, are we not to take this as the first shoe falling? Surely there was meant to be some sort of follow-up! It makes perfect sense if this is another mounting clue that Jesus will turn out to have cheated death. On the usual, orthodox reading, the detail makes no sense at all. *Why tell it*? Nothing is made of it if the denouement is a miraculous return of a dead man. Dead is dead, no matter how long it took to kill him. But if the quick 'death' was a hint that he was *not* actually dead, we have a story that makes sense.

But was not poor Jesus too beaten up, too bloodied, too mutilated, his entrails hanging out and his spine catching on the rough wood behind him?[357] Just as in Mel Gibson's gore-fest *The Passion of the Christ*?[358] The gospels do not suggest that Jesus was that badly damaged. It is interesting to see how the Strobel/Metherell exegesis bypasses the gospel texts to use pious folk tradition as the basis of their apologetic.

---

356 *Life of Flavius Josephus* 75, William Whiston trans., p. 25.

357 Metherell in Strobel, p. 195.

358 Is it true the working title was "Golgotha Chainsaw Massacre"?

Metherell describes the utter, enervating abuse that all criminals condemned to the cross suffered from preliminary flogging. How does he know Jesus suffered all that? He points to the gospel picture of Jesus stumbling under the weight of his crossbeam, dropping it, and having to have Simon take his place carrying it the rest of the way.[359] Only no gospel says this. According to John 19:17, Jesus himself hoisted it and carried it the whole way. Matthew 27:32; Mark 15:21; and Luke 23:26 have Simon carry it, with nothing about an initial attempt by Jesus. And there is nothing about him being too weak to carry it. That is sheer supposition. The notion of Jesus struggling with the weight of the cross for a brief distance and then dropping it is nothing but an inerrantist harmonization, as if one might harmonize blatant contradictions by just splitting the difference!

Plus, if the suffering was regularly so terrible as to prevent the condemned from carrying the weight of the cross beam, do we not have to suppose that *no one ever* managed to carry his own cross? By contrast, the gospels imply it was extraordinary with Jesus, since the Romans had to grab some bystander for the job. Metherell is also sure that a nail in the wrist would have induced blinding, unspeakable, and unendurable agony; how then were Jesus' co-crucifees able to aim snide cracks and jocular blasphemies at him, almost like the people on the crosses in *Monty Python's Life of Brian*? Maybe Metherell is being influenced just a little bit by the masochistic piety of "Jesus suffered *this much* for me! Sniff!"

Those who debunk the Swoon Theory like to produce John 19:34–35 as their trump card: "See? Jesus must have been stabbed in the heart! And John 20:25 says he had been nailed to the cross, just like Metherell says!" But these texts look like those rare birds, the exceptions that prove the rule, for what are they doing there?

It appears that both snippets are subsequent additions to the text, aimed precisely at squashing a current theory much like I have been describing. Note that the first one, John 19:34–35, first agrees with the Markan story that Jesus was dead before the others, dead surprisingly soon. The other two criminals required the special treatment (clubbing of the legs) to hasten their death, while Jesus, it was plain to see, was already dead. Or was he? Verse 35 has them verify what they already knew in the previous verse. Which was it? Was his death plain to them or not?

No, the confusion arises from a *redactor* trying to make the *reader* certain that Jesus was truly dead. It is he who affirms, a bit too stridently if you ask me, that blood and water emerged from Jesus' side. The redactor

---

359 Metherell in Strobel, p. 196.

wants to prevent people reading the Passion narrative as one in which the hero Jesus "escape[s] in the final reel."[360]

Likewise, notice that the crucifixion scene in John, as in all the gospels, does not say (despite some bad translations) that Jesus was "nailed to the cross" as we are used to saying. They merely say he was crucified, which allowed (as Metherell admits)[361] for either nails or ropes around the wrists, or nailing through the palms with tied wrists. Metherell extrapolates a great deal of frenzied suffering from the nail wounds, but we only 'know' Jesus was nailed to the cross from the single verse John 20:25, not from John's crucifixion account, where one might have expected it had it been intended.

Furthermore, the resurrection episode that mentions nail wounds appears to be another secondary addition. It has been tacked onto a prior one, also represented in (if not borrowed from) Luke 24:36–43, in which the Twelve (minus Judas) are plainly supposed to be present since Jesus imparts his spirit to them so they can continue his work, remitting sins, *etc*, the so-called Johannine Pentecost.

In the nature of the case, the eleven have to be present for this epochal scene. But then, suddenly, we find Thomas was out picking up the pizza when Jesus dropped by! And why has a Johannine redactor added the scene? I am guessing it is once again to make sure the reader knows Jesus was really dead. He wanted to counteract the Lukan version (the original?), in which the reappeared Jesus showed his hands and feet, presumably because the rest of him was swathed in robes, to demonstrate his corporeality. This scene is so much like that in Philostratus' *Life of Apollonius of Tyana* in which Apollonius teleports across the sea into the midst of his own disciples that it seems quite natural to read both the same way.

> Damis groaned out loud, and said something like, "Gods above, will we ever see our good, noble comrade?"
>
> Apollonius, who was now standing at the entrance of the grotto, heard this and said, "You will, in fact you already have."
>
> "Alive?" asked Demetrius, "But if dead, we have never stopped weeping for you."
>
> Apollonius stretched out his hand, and said, "Take hold of me. If I elude you, I am a ghost come back from Persephone's domain, like the ghosts which the gods below reveal to men when mourning makes them

---

360 *Jesus Christ Superstar*.

361 Metherell in Strobel, p. 200.

> too despondent. But if I stay when you grasp me, persuade Damis, too, that I am alive and have not lost my body." (8:12)[362]

The point of the Apollonius reunion episode is that, amazingly, the hero has escaped what seemed sure death. His disciples had held out no hope he might still be alive, and here he is! It is the same in Acts 12:12–17 when Peter, written off for dead by his flock (despite their prayers for his safety!), nonetheless appears to them, leaving them completely flabbergasted. They, too, first think he is a shade temporarily returned from the dead (v.15), but his physicality puts an end to that.

I suggest that if one tries to bracket the familiar reading of Luke 24:24–36 for a moment, the story will look quite different: just like the Apollonius episode. Jesus had not returned from death but rather cheated it. And this ought to make us reconsider the apologists' refrain that the twelve, as typical Jews, could not have expected a pre-eschatological resurrection of an individual. That factor does not even come into play if they thought they were seeing a ghost come, for a moment, to comfort them in their hour of loss.

The Johannine redactor did not like the sound of this: on the basis of it some must have been saying Jesus, like other heroes of antiquity (and especially of contemporary novels), had escaped death, even death on the cross. So he rewrote the scene: in his version, Jesus reveals, Lyndon Johnson style, not his hands and *feet*, as in Luke, but his hands and *side*. And this because John has already added references to the side having been harpooned, the hands having been nailed. He wants to correct Swoon Theory belief and make sure the story is henceforth read as one of genuine death and resurrection.

Nor is even this the end. Why does Matthew specify that Joseph of Arimathea was a rich man? Probably not to make his role a fulfillment of Isaiah 53:9a ("They made his grave with the wicked and with a rich man in his death"), as the parallelism would make "rich man" equivalent to "wicked man," which Matthew certainly did not think Joseph of Arimathea was (Matthew 27: 57).

This detail is hardly required for the logic of the gospel story as traditionally understood. John lacks it, having Joseph and Nicodemus merely stash Jesus' corpse in a nearby tomb because the descending Sabbath allowed time for no permanent arrangements. So what is it doing there?

---

362 Philostratus, *The Life of Apollonius of Tyana*. Trans. C.P. Jones (Baltimore: Penguin Books, 1970), p. 232.

I suggest it is there for the same reason it occurs in contemporary Hellenistic novels.[363] In, *e.g.*, Chariton's *Chaereas and Callirhoe* and Xenophon's *Ephesian Tale* (or *Habrocomes and Anthia*) the comatose heroine, believed dead, is prematurely interred in an opulent tomb. Once it is sealed, covetous tomb robbers notice and decide to seize the rich funerary tokens they assume must lie stacked within, alongside the corpse. They do break in, only to find the heroine emerging from her stupor. They want neither to kill her nor to leave a witness, so they kidnap her. It would fit this pattern quite nicely if Matthew intended Jesus' burial in Joseph's rich tomb to provide the narrative motivation for grave robbers to come and fortuitously release the waking Jesus. Indeed, I would not be surprised if Matthew's story of the fainting guards was rewritten from this feature of the story, retaining the shock of the robbers opening the tomb and finding a living man inside. But who knows?

I hope you can tell that I am not suggesting that the historical Jesus actually remained alive through his crucifixion and appeared later, mistakenly thought to be resurrected, like the eighteenth-century Protestant Rationalists did. I am presenting no theory of what happened to him; I do not think, given the present state of our sources, that we will ever know.

I am instead pointing out an astonishing paradox: today's apologists, taking for granted the eyewitness accuracy of the resurrection stories, and subtly manipulating their opponents into doing the same, are using the same strategy to reject the Swoon Theory (and other, more recent, alternatives) that their Rationalist Protestant forbears employed to *defend* it! This is because, if one approaches the data of the Easter narratives as integral details of a piece of fiction (with some of them attempted redactions/corrections), the Swoon Theory is a better, more comprehensive reading of the data. As a defense of the Easter story as an historical account, it is of no use at all, since it presupposes the very accuracy it seems to be trying to prove. It seems convincing to conclude the reality of Oz if you can get your dialogue partner to believe he is already standing on the Yellow Brick Road.

---

[363] Read them for yourself in B.P. Reardon, ed., *Collected Ancient Greek Novels* (Berkeley: University of California Press, 1989.

Chapter Twelve
The Evidence of the Empty Argument
Was Jesus' Body Ever Even in a Tomb?

Holy Ghost Evangelist

Reverend Strobel thinks to give his next infomercialist, William Lane Craig, a big compliment when he says of him, "he isn't out to pummel opponents with his arguments; he's sincerely seeking to win over people who he believes matter to God."[364] Well, of course, that's just the problem.

When I debate Dr. Craig or any of his colleagues, I am only trying to expose what I consider bad arguments. I am trying to correct gratuitous misunderstandings and misuse of the New Testament. I am not trying to convert anybody to or from any particular religious faith. Their personal beliefs are none of my business. People are people to me. But the desire to convert people to a religious posture that requires belief in certain ancient stories, lest those who withhold belief in them get damned to hellfire, is hardly the ideal posture from which to expect scholarly objectivity.

Thus it is no surprise that we are very far from getting it from pulpiteer Craig, who concludes every 'scholarly debate' with an evangelistic invitation. For him it is just a lucky coincidence that the 'best' evidence just happens to match up with what the Holy Spirit tells him is true. And that includes six-day Creationism—anti-evolutionism.

Craig, in short, is a theological snake-oil salesman. That his articles are published in mainstream theological periodicals (along with the same sort of stuff from N.T. Wright, Ben Witherington III, *et al.*) is a sad commentary on the level to which 'professional' New Testament scholarship has sunk. It is professional, all right, but not the profession one would expect. This 'scholarship' begins and ends with a profession of faith.

Craig rehearses his usual drill, beginning with the empty tomb story, which his infra-red glasses are somehow able to detect in the quoted formula of resurrection preaching in 1 Corinthians 15:3–8: "he died for sins in accordance with the scriptures, ... he was buried."

So what? The point would seem to be to cap the death, to eliminate any notion that Jesus had not really died (see previous chapter): "dead and buried." There is nothing here about Joseph of Arimathea or the rest

[364] Strobel, p. 207.

of the gospel story. This brief note is not inconsistent with the Joseph story; it is just that it provides no independent evidence for it. And though "and was buried" is certainly part of the build-up to the assertion of the resurrection, it implies nothing about the discovery of an empty tomb. *It is the death not the burial, that the resurrection reverses.*

We have here an exact analogy to Matthew's note (1:18, 24–25) that Mary and Joseph did not come together sexually before Jesus was born. Roman Catholics are certainly correct in maintaining against Protestants that the sole implication is that Jesus is therefore not Joseph's son, since Joseph's penis had not made an appearance during the whole pregnancy or beforehand. It is downright grotesque to suggest that Matthew meant to imply they *did* begin doing the dirty deed *after* Jesus was born. He just doesn't mention the issue. As we should say, he doesn't go there. Nor does 1 Corinthians 15:4 imply a darn thing about the tomb having a further role in the story—such as being discovered empty.

"The creed definitely implies the empty tomb… You see, the Jews had a physical concept of resurrection. For them, the primary object of the resurrection was the bones of the deceased – not even the flesh, which was thought to be perishable… In light of this, it would have been simply a contradiction [in] terms for an early Jew to say that someone was raised from the dead but his body was left in the tomb. So when this early Christian creed says Jesus was buried and then raised on the third day, it's saying implicitly but quite clearly: an empty tomb was left behind."[365] To this one must say that Craig, like Wright and their multitude, are oversimplifying the evidence of ancient Jewish resurrection belief,[366] but that, even if they weren't, they are ignoring evidence much closer to hand: the assertion in 1 Corinthians 15: 35–38 and following that the expected resurrection body, like the paradigm case of Christ, will be a *spiritual* body, *not* a physical body, an entity that leaves its defunct fleshly containment behind like an exhausted cocoon.[367]

---

365 Craig in Strobel, p. 211.

366 George Eldon Ladd, dean of evangelical New Testament scholars, has a more nuanced review of the disparate evidence in his *I Believe in the Resurrection of Jesus*. I Believe Series No. 2 (Grand Rapids: Eerdmans, 1975), Chapter 5, "The Resurrection in Judaism," pp. 51–59, esp. pp. 56–57.

367 Richard C. Carrier, "The Spiritual Body of Christ and the Legend of the Empty Tomb," in Robert M. Price and Jeffrey Jay Lowder, eds., *The Empty Tomb: Jesus Beyond the Grave* (Amherst: Prometheus Books, 2005), Section 5, "Paul on the Resurrection Body," pp. 118–155.

The Man from Best Disciple Town

Remember what I said in the previous chapter about apologists arguing against everyone as if they were the eighteenth-century Protestant Rationalists resurrected. They assume the Easter stories of the gospels are inerrant, seamless textures of eye-witness testimony, a strategy which seeks to manipulate their opponents into agreeing that the set-up to the punch line is historically true, making it seem that the natural next step is to accept the historical truth of the punch line, too.

"The Emerald City must be real, because where else would the Yellow Brick Road lead to?" I got news for you, Bill: there ain't no Yellow Brick Road, either! It's just a story. Craig senses the danger here and tries to head it off at the pass by arguing first for the historicity of Auntie Em..., er, I mean, Joseph of Arimathea.

> Joseph of Arimathea... would not be the sort of person who would have been invented by Christian legend or Christian authors... Given the early Christian anger and bitterness toward the Jewish leaders who had instigated the crucifixion of Jesus... it's highly improbable that they would have invented one who did the right thing by giving Jesus an honorable burial – especially when all of Jesus' disciples deserted him! Besides, they wouldn't make up a specific member of a specific group, whom people could check out for themselves and ask about this. So Joseph is undoubtedly a historical figure."[368]

Listen to this man pontificate! As though he knows the literary predilections of early Christian authors, as if he's talking about his buddies in the Evangelical Theological Society! And on such exceedingly lame arguments does the faith once for all delivered to the saints rest! First, Craig is once again begging the inerrancy question. Ever since S.G.F. Brandon,[369] it has been a very strong historical hypothesis that Markan-era Christians, after the fall of Jerusalem, shifted the blame for the execution of Jesus from the Romans, whose favor they now sought to cultivate, onto the Jews who were now *personae non gratae* with Rome. If this is so, as it may well be, then the depiction of Joseph of Arimathea as friendly to Jesus may be a surviving vestige from the earlier understanding of things, whether a historical one or a fictive one. There would have been no more of a problem inventing him than, well, inventing Nicodemus.

---

368 Craig in Strobel, p. 210.

369 S.G.F. Brandon, *The Fall of Jerusalem and the Christian Church: A Study of the Effects of the Jewish Overthrow of A.D. 70 on Christianity* (London: SPCK, 1951), pp. 192–195.

In fact, the very contrast Craig correctly notes between Joseph and the fled disciples[370] points up the possibility that 'of Arimathea' is meant to function as an equivalent to 'the Beloved Disciple' since *Arimathea* (only doubtfully identified with any known location) may be broken down into syllables denoting 'Best [*ari*] Disciple [*mathetes*] place.'[371] This would imply he is an ideal or symbolic figure such as we not infrequently find in the gospels, their names reflecting their narrative role.

Nicodemus means 'ruler of the people,' and he is what? "A ruler of the Jews" (John 3:1). *Martha* means 'lady of the house,' and so she is (Luke 10:38, "*her* house," 40–41). *Jairus* means 'he awakens,' and guess what happens to his daughter (Mark 5:41–42)? *Zacchaeus* is a pun on *zakkat*, 'almsgiving,' and what does he do (Luke 19:8)? *Bar-Timaeus,* 'son of Timaeus,' seems dependent upon *timyah*, 'beggar,' which is what he is (Mark 10:46). *Stephen* perishes, stoned for his gospel preaching, thus winning the martyr's *crown*, which just happens to be what his name means ('crown'). *Joseph of Arimathea* might be another of these, the 'best disciple' precisely in that he hung in there and saw to the burial of Jesus when no one else did. We will never know for sure, but neither will Craig, and he is the one pretending to be proving things.

Again, Dennis Ronald MacDonald[372] makes a good case for Joseph of Arimathea as a Markan rewrite of King Priam in Homer's *Iliad*, who courageously appears before his enemy Achilles to plead for the corpse of his son Hector. Why the name *Joseph*? Because the name 'Joseph' had already taken root as the name of the father of Jesus (as in Matthew and Luke), and Mark thought it a good hint to name this Priam-like father-figure after the name others gave to Jesus' father. In connection with this, note that the evolving Joseph of Arimathea character eventually becomes depicted as Jesus' uncle.[373] As with James the Just and Simeon bar-Cleophas both being shifted over to the position of Jesus' 'cousins,' having originally been his brothers (Mark 6:3), this might imply an earlier tradition in which Joseph of Arimathea was actually supposed to have been the same as Joseph the father of Jesus.

---

370 Though let's be fair—what *could* they have done with the body? Abandoned it in a hotel room?

371 Richard C. Carrier , private correspondence.

372 Dennis Ronald MacDonald, *The Homeric Epics and the Gospel of Mark* (New Haven: Yale University Press, 2000), pp. 154–161.

373 C.C. Dobson, *Did Our Lord Visit Britain as They Say in Cornwall and Somerset?* (Merrimac, MA: Destiny Publishers, 1944), pp. 8–12.

I have already mentioned the possibility that Joseph of Arimathea is a fictive doublet of the Jewish historian Josephus, or Joseph b-***ar-Matthia***-s. Josephus, newly in favor with Vespasian, prevailed upon his Roman master's son Titus to release three friends Josephus recognized on their crosses, two of whom soon expired anyway, but the third of whom recovered. This explanation would have the added benefit of accounting for why Joseph would have sought custody only of Jesus' body, not the other two: the gospel version would be a slightly streamlined and oversimplified version of the Josephan original in which we also move from three crucified men to one coming down alive. Since the other two did not survive, the gospel tradition loses sight of them, omitting them from Joseph's request.

Would Mark not have dared fabricate a character like Joseph of Arimathea lest opponents of Christianity hasten to get out their copies of the *Congressional Record* to verify whether such a person was in fact a member of the Sanhedrin? The whole notion is absurd. *Mark wrote after the Fall of Jerusalem,* when any access to such information would have been unavailable—destroyed. And what would Mark or any other evangelist have cared what their opponents said? They'd just call them liars and tools of Satan.

Craig does not take seriously the evolution of the Joseph character from one gospel to another. We have to wonder whether Mark understood Joseph to have voted against Jesus; as he says "they all condemned him as deserving death" (Mark 14:64) and that Joseph was "a prominent member of the council" (15:43). His membership in the Sanhedrin is apparently mentioned in order to account for his having entrée to the Roman governor. Mark also characterizes him as "looking for the kingdom of God" (15:43; *cf.* Luke 2:25, 38; 24:21).

Did it even occur to Mark that he was thus introducing an element of tension into his narrative? I doubt it, though the tension is real: you mean Joseph was a pious Jew yearning for eschatological fulfillment—and yet dismissed Jesus as a dangerous lunatic? I doubt Mark connected the two narratives; he never noticed the contradiction he himself had created.

As Craig notes, Luke seems to have noticed the difficulty: Luke's Joseph "had not consented to their purpose and deed, and he was looking for the kingdom of God" (Luke 23:51). The contradiction still occurs in Luke, since he has the whole Sanhedrin condemn Jesus and bring him to Pilate (22:70–71; 23:1–2) yet later has Joseph refusing to join in the decision (23:51). Craig tries to harmonize the contradiction by rewriting what Luke says: "he added one important detail – Joseph of Arimathea wasn't present when the official vote was taken."[374]

That is what Craig would have written, but it is not what Luke actually did write. What Luke wrote was that Joseph wouldn't go along with the plan, not that he had a conflicting appointment of some sort. But that would do inerrantist Craig no good. That would point up the freedom with which Luke, like Mark before him, felt free to embellish the story.

Matthew implies a unanimous verdict ("They answered, 'He deserves death.'" Matthew 26:66) but solves the problem neatly by no longer having Joseph belong to the Sanhedrin! He is merely "a rich man from Arimathea" and "a *disciple* of Jesus" (Matthew 27:57). John 19:38 has the same: no Sanhedrin seat and "a disciple of Jesus but secretly for fear of the Jews" or Jewish authorities, from whom he is here distinguished.

Where does Joseph bury the body? Again, there is no one unanimous tradition as Craig seems to think.

Mark has Joseph inter the body in some unspecified tomb cut from rock (15:46), while Matthew 27:60 makes it Joseph's own tomb, newly finished.

Luke 23:53 knows nothing of it being Joseph's own tomb, adding instead to Mark the notice that no one had previously been buried there, just as Jesus must ride a donkey never before ridden (Luke 19:30; Mark 11:2; *cf.* 1 Samuel 6:7).

In John, Joseph is accompanied by his double, Nicodemus, and he buries Jesus only temporarily, in a handy nearby tomb (not Joseph's) because it is too close to the descending Sabbath to make permanent arrangements (John 19:41–42). And yet the body is given extravagant preparation suggesting a permanent resting place (John 19:39–40).

I know the apologists' tactic of reducing contradictory accounts to their lowest common denominator and pretending the contradictions don't mean anything.[375] I doubt that works in this case, for it is far more than a circumstantial detail whether Jesus' corpse was stashed momentarily with a view toward permanent reburial elsewhere, since this option opens up the possibility (made explicit in John 20:2; 13–15) that the tomb was empty for altogether natural reasons, and that it was henceforth too late to locate it.

Beyond that, the very involvement of Joseph becomes one of the negotiable 'details' once one realizes that—despite Craig's wishful

---

374 Craig in Strobel, p. 210.

375 Craig in Strobel, p. 215.

thinking—there exist variant traditions of Jesus' burial which have no role for him.[376] For instance, the *Apocryphon of James* has Jesus accorded a disrespectful burial in a shallow sand pit (5:17). The *Toledoth Jeschu* 5:7 has the Sanhedrin bury the body. *Book of the Resurrection / Questions of Bartholomew* has the Sanhedrin take charge of the body, wondering where to bury it. Philogenes, a gardener whose son Jesus had cured, offers his tomb for the burial, and he then removes and hides it to keep it out of their control. Acts 13:27–29 has the same people who had Jesus executed then entomb him.

Multiple Attestation?

Craig throws source criticism (which he relies on when it comes in handy) out the window when it comes to the empty tomb narrative:

> The differences between the empty tomb narratives suggest that we have multiple, independent attestation of the empty tomb story. Sometimes people say, "Matthew and Luke just plagiarized from Mark," but when you look at the narratives closely, you see divergences that suggest that even if Matthew and Luke did know Mark's account, nevertheless they also had separate, independent sources for the empty tomb story.[377]

Craig's summing up of genuine New Testament scholarship, with which he holds no truck, is sloppy to the point of misrepresentation. The "plagiarism" nonsense refers only to the manifest fact that Matthew and Luke have followed Mark, tweaking and editing as they went, all through the Passion narrative and up through the empty tomb, going their separate ways only once they ran out of Markan track at his abrupt ending. Mark 16 has the empty tomb discovered by puzzled female disciples who are then informed by a young man (an angel?) that the absence of the body means Jesus has risen. He predicts a Galilean appearance of Jesus, but none is narrated because the terrified women are pointedly said not to have relayed this message to the male disciples.

Matthew and Luke both jump off the diving board of Mark 16:1–8, but in different directions. Given that each evangelist's continuation bears clear signs of his distinctive style and vocabulary, the natural inference would be that each is making it up as he goes along. They do have other

---

376 If "this burial by Joseph were a legend that developed later, you'd expect to find other competing burial traditions about what happened to Jesus' body. However, you don't find these at all."

377 Craig in Strobel, p. 216.

sources to supplement Mark, but, as we will see, these sources are Greek translations of the Book of Daniel and various borrowed Hellenistic miracle stories. And, of course, their own imaginations, something I am far from blaming them for.

Matthew has altered Mark's unseemly ending so that the fleeing women now *obey* the orders of the angel at the tomb. And he adds a sudden appearance of the Risen Jesus to the same women. But this Jesus only repeats the angel's command—how anticlimactic! Why such an alteration? I think it most likely that in this way Matthew sought to clear up Mark's ambiguous mention of the "young man"—who was he? An angel? Or Jesus himself?

Matthew decided to cover both bases, dividing the scene between an angel and Jesus, both bearing the identical tidings. Nor is this Matthew's most extravagant embellishment. He has added the posting of guards in order to raise the stakes and so add to the glory of Jesus' triumph, deriving the idea from Daniel 3:20, where Nebuchadnezzar "ordered certain mighty men of his army to bind Shadrach, Meschach, and Abednego, and to throw them into the fiery furnace." Matthew makes this into a committee of priests and Pharisees requesting Pilate to supply a cordon of guards to stop Jesus' disciples from body-snatching the remains and floating a resurrection hoax.

Pilate agrees. They seal the tomb (27:62–66), just as in Daniel 6:17, "And a stone was brought and laid upon the mouth of the [lion's] den, and the king sealed it with his own signet and with the signet of his lords, that nothing might be changed concerning Daniel." Matthew has the angel descend from the sky right on camera, and the poor guards faint dead away (Matthew 28:4), as in Daniel 3:22, "Because... the furnace was very hot, the flame of the fire slew those men who took up Shadrach, Meschach, and Abednego."

Matthew decides to supply the missing Galilee reunion Mark had the young man mention. "And when they saw him, they bowed before him, though they doubted" (Matthew 28:17). The doubt business ought to be, as it is in Luke's and John's resurrection appearance stories, preliminary to a convincing demonstration of the resurrection, but it is not. The words of the resurrected Jesus are redolent of favorite Matthean vocabulary: "to disciple," "unto the consummation of the age." But most of it comes from two Greek versions of Daniel 7:14. "Behold, all authority in heaven and on earth has been given to me" comes from the Septuagint ("to him was given the rule... and his authority is an everlasting authority," while Theodotion's version supplies "authority to hold all in the heaven and on the earth." The scope of the evangelistic mission is "all nations," and this comes from the same verse: "all peoples, nations, and languages should serve him." At any rate, we must regard every bit of the forgoing as pure Matthean invention.

What has Luke done, faced with Mark's seemingly washed-out bridge? He, too, has the women obey the angel—or rather the two men. Mark and Matthew had only one each. Let's be honest with the text. There weren't 'actually' two, with Matthew and Mark choosing only one to mention. No, the truth is that Luke decided the story would read better if there were *two* heavenly spokesmen, just like the two men he has talking with Jesus at the Transfiguration and again with the Twelve at the ascension.

Why does Luke's speech of the two men at the tomb differ from that in Mark? Mark had the man say, "Go to Galilee; there you will see him, as he told you." Luke has changed this to "Remember how *when he was in Galilee* he told you the Son of Man must be delivered into the hands of men," *etc.*

Luke wants salvation history to proceed from Jerusalem; thus his appearances happen in and around Jerusalem. He has simply lopped off the Galilean appearance Mark implied but neglected to narrate. He has the men at the tomb say what he knows no one actually said on that morning. It is not a question of lying or hoaxing. This is a writer creatively rewriting a story. He has decided, for the sake of his story's flow, to exclude Galilean appearances, and it is to obscure Luke's theological agenda to pretend to harmonize him with Matthew by intercalating Matthew 28 in between Luke 24 and Acts 1.

My point in all this is that the differences between the evangelists are not mere rough edges in reporting, inconsistencies between irrelevant details, as apologists would have it. No, there is a manifest *logic of redaction and retelling*, as later gospel writers modify the work of their predecessors. And the most damning consideration for Craig's pre-critical approach must surely be the fact that Matthew, Luke, and John's continuations of their common source, Mark's Easter narrative, are all predicated on their *discarding his ending and completely changing direction*. I submit it is no "minor detail" when Mark says—no emphasizes—that the women disobeyed the order to give the tidings of the resurrection to the forlorn disciples, and the other gospels have them obey!

Shall We Join the Ladies?

Craig tells us, "the unanimous testimony that the empty tomb was discovered by women argues for the authenticity of the story, because this would have been embarrassing for the disciples to admit."[378] Uh, what, pray tell, do the disciples have to do with it? Craig seems to think the disciples wrote the Easter stories. There is no reason to think that. Please refer back to my first chapter on gospel dating and authorship. Craig is resting an awful lot on the slim reed of Papias' testimony, he who with equal credibility "reported" that Judas' head swelled up bigger than an oxcart and that he was urinating live worms before finally exploding like Mr. Creosote in *Monty Python's The Meaning of Life*. If Craig had learned anything but InterVarsity apologetics during his much-vaunted graduate studies in Europe, he would know that if a tradition denigrates a particular faction, it probably stems from a rival faction. The empty tomb story may indeed make the male disciples look bad, but that only means the story was likely put about by Christians who did not like them.

Beyond this, it is highly misleading to appeal to supposedly unanimous, independent testimony that women were first to discover the tomb. As we have just seen, all the gospels are simply rewritten versions of Mark's (though John's appearance of Jesus to Mary Magdalene alone is probably based on Matthew 28:9–10), thus hardly independent, and where they differ, they are winging it. Equally important are two other related points. First, as everyone knows, the 1 Corinthians 15 list makes no reference at all to the women and any visions of Jesus they may have had. Surely the most natural explanation for this is that the framers of the list had never heard of the empty tomb discovery story.

We are used to the dodge that early Christian PR experts decided to omit this story, these names, because they would not score well among pagan and Jewish focus groups. Women were supposed to be unreliable witnesses. Well, this is another selective Christian appropriation of rabbinic tradition out of context, to make Judaism look chauvinistic by contrast to Christianity. There was no such ban, and Jewish law welcomed testimony from women on matters where they were the experts[379]—such as mourning for the dead at tombs!

Worse than this, Mark, the very evangelist who introduces the empty tomb story, is ashamed of it. He is making excuses for its unheard-of

---

378 Craig in Strobel, pp. 220–221.

379 Jeffrey Jay Lowder, "Historical Evidence and the Empty Tomb: A Reply to William Lane Craig," in Price and Lowder, eds., *Empty Tomb*, p. 283.

novelty right out of the starting gate. This, of course, is why he has the women disobey the command to spread the news. Mark is anticipating the reader's suspicion: "Wait a second! I've been a Christian for many years; how come I never heard of this until now?" Here, incidentally, we see an example of what apologists say could never have happened: the storyteller embellishing the story *despite the skepticism of contemporaries who knew better!*

Mark's Passion Source

Craig is righter than he knows when he says,

> we can tell from the language, grammar, and style that Mark got his empty tomb story – actually, his whole passion narrative – from an earlier source. In fact, there's evidence it was written before A.D. 37, which is much too early for legend to have seriously corrupted it.[380]

What is the evidence for so early a date for this hypothetical pre-Markan Passion? I believe, from his discussions elsewhere, that Craig is referring to the speculation of Rudolf Pesch that, since the name of the then-reigning high priest is not mentioned, we may assume Mark counted on the reader knowing it because he was still in office at the time of writing! You only call the chief executive "the President" if you mean the one currently in office; otherwise you would specify which one you meant. Nice try. It is just as likely that Mark omits the name because he simply had no idea who held the office at the time, just as John labored under the false impression that each high priest held the office for a single year (John 11:49).[381] Come to think of it, Mark couldn't keep straight who was high priest when David ate the showbread (1 Samuel 21:1–6) either; he thought it was Abiathar (Mark 2:26) when it was actually his father Ahimelech.

Was there an earlier version of Mark's Passion narrative? A 1976 symposium edited by Werner H. Kelber, *The Passion in Mark*,[382] marshaled thematic, stylistic, lexical and redactional studies by John R.

---

380 Craig in Strobel, p. 220.

381 Yes, yes, I know F.F. Bruce (*The New Testament Documents: Are They Reliable?* p. 50.) suggests John just meant Caiaphas was high priest "that fateful year," not that he was serving a term of a single year. But then why put it that way? Why not say, "just then" or "at that time" or "in those days"?

382 Werner H. Kelber, ed., *The Passion in Mark* (Philadelphia: Fortress Press, 1976).

Donahue, Vernon K. Robbins, Norman Perrin, Kim E. Dewey, Theodore J. Weeden, and John Dominic Crossan which concluded there is no reason to think the Passion as we read it in Mark is not his creation, redacting and rewriting earlier units of oral tradition with a liberal creative license. Especially concerning Mark 16, Kelber summarizes, "there is no strong or even convincing evidence of pre-M[ar]kan traditions concerning the tomb."[383]

I am not asking the reader simply to take the word of experts at face value, just pointing out that Craig is not to be believed at first sight either, as Strobel wants us to do.

But, in another sense, there certainly *was* a pre-Markan Passion source, and it is considerably older than the date Craig posits. For virtually every inch of Mark's crucifixion account seems to come not from eyewitness memory, even indirectly, but rather directly from early Christian exegesis of Psalm 22, with a few other texts thrown in. Most of these texts are not cited as prophecies fulfilled in the events. No, any Old Testament origin is tacitly suppressed. And remember, Psalm 22 is not intended as a prediction of Jesus' death, or of anything else. It is quite clearly what is called an Individual Lament Psalm, a song sung by or on behalf of someone in extremity who feels himself forsaken by his god. Let us survey the wondrous cross story, such as it is.

First, Jesus is affixed to the cross, presumably with nails, based on Psalms 22:16, "They have pierced my hands and feet." The intended reference is no doubt the wounds inflicted by the wild animals closing in on the sufferer/psalmist (Psalms 22:12–13, 16a, 20–21). Second, the soldiers dividing Jesus' garments (Mark 15:24) come right out of Psalms 22:18, "They divide my garments among them, and for my raiment they cast lots." Third, the irreverent hecklers "wag their heads," an odd phrase derived from Psalms 22:7: "All who see me mock at me, they make mouths at me, they wag their heads." Fourth, the jibes of the priests ("Let the Christ, the king of Israel, come down from the cross, that we may see and believe!" Mark 15:32) are based on those once aimed at the Psalmist: "'He committed his cause to Yahweh; let him deliver him, let him rescue him, for he delights in him!'" (Psalms 22:8). Matthew 27:43 amplifies the blasphemous derision: "He trusts in God; let God deliver him now, if he desires him; for he said, 'I am the son of God.'" Did Matthew get this from the fund of his own or others' memories of the event? No, he got it from Wisdom of Solomon 2:12–20 (which he perforce condensed):

---

383 Kelber, p. 138.

> But let us lie in wait for the righteous man, because he makes it hard for us, and opposes our works, and upbraids us for sins against the law, and accuses us of sins against our training. He professes to have knowledge of God, and calls himself the servant of the Lord. He became to us a living reproof of our thoughts. He is grievous for us even to behold because his life is unlike that of other men, and his ways are alien to us. He disdains us as base metal, and he avoids our ways as unclean. The final end of the righteous he calls happy, and he claims that God is his father. Let us see if his words are true, and let us see what will happen at the end of his life! For if the righteous man is God's son, he will uphold him, and he will rescue him from the grasp of his adversaries. With outrage and torture let us put him to the test, that we may see for ourselves his gentleness and prove his patience under injustice. Let us condemn him to a shameful death; for surely God shall intervene as this fellow said he would!

Fifth, there is Jesus' cry of dereliction, "My God, my God, why have you forsaken me?" Of course, this the opening line of Psalm 22, only Mark does not say so. Luke deems these words unbecoming, so he changes them—to something Luke knew Jesus had actually said on that occasion? No, he took it ("Father, into your hands I commit my spirit," Luke 23:46) from Psalms 31:5. John explicitly cites Psalms 22:18 about the garments and tacitly uses Psalms 22:14 ("I am poured out like water, and all my bones are dislocated; my heart is like wax, it is melted within my breast") as the basis for his unique detail of the soldier stabbing Jesus' side, "and at once there came out blood and water" (John 19:34). John, an exception to the general rule, does make Jesus' thirst and its rough satisfaction with vinegar (John 19:28–29) a prophetic fulfillment, unwittingly indicating Psalms 69:21 ("They gave me poison for food, and for my thirst they gave me vinegar to drink") as the likely origin of the whole motif, also in Mark 15:36; Matthew 27:34; Luke 23:36.

You tell me how it is possible, if the ostensibly earth-shaking event of the crucifixion of Jesus Christ was an historical event "not done in a corner" (Acts 26:26), that no eyewitness memory survived to serve as the basis for the earliest narrative account of it. Mark had to scrounge for out-of-context scripture quotes to patch together a sketchy narrative, and his followers proceeded by the same method to embellish it.

X Marks the Spot

Perhaps nothing so clearly betrays the fact that our apologists are looking at the evidence from inside the charmed circle of faith as their professed inability to imagine any naturalistic explanation for the empty tomb that is nearly so plausible as a miraculous resurrection of the dead. Especially when it is staring them right in the face.

As I already mentioned, John introduces the eminently plausible notion that, as Jesus' burial was only temporary, his body to be removed for permanent burial elsewhere as soon as the Sabbath was past, it was in fact quickly removed before Jesus' mourners arrived, and they never found out the permanent resting place. Thus there can have been no attempts to debunk or to verify the resurrection preaching by appeal to the notorious tomb. It may well be that none of the interested parties knew where Jesus' corpse was.

Craig protests that "the site of Jesus' tomb was known to the Jewish authorities."[384] How does Craig know this? Of course it comes from Matthew 27:62–66, part of the story of the Sanhedrin asking Pilate to post guards at the tomb, which naturally means they knew where to send them. But the guards at the tomb episode is so problematical that even Craig declines to base his case on it.[385] As an inerrantist, of course, he believes it, but he knows it is virtually indefensible while maintaining a straight face: if it were true, how on earth can other evangelists have failed to mention it? But Craig is after all basing his apologetic squarely on that story, since it contains the only hint that the Sanhedrin knew where Jesus' tomb was. And even that story does not explain how they learned of it.

Did the Christians even know? Remember, Mark thinks it is simply a local tomb, Luke a brand new tomb, while Matthew makes it Joseph's own intended resting place, which was not very likely to be near Golgotha. And John has the body stashed in a nearby tomb only temporarily. It sounds to me as if no one exactly knew.

Craig thinks that not only did the Sanhedrinists know where the tomb was, but that they even knew good and well that it was empty.[386] This is because "the earliest Jewish polemic presupposes the historicity of the empty tomb."[387] He refers to the tomb guards story again, which he claims he does not much use. He reasons this way: why would Jewish opponents have argued that the body of Jesus was stolen if they could have simply pointed to the tomb and the *Occupado* sign on the door?

Craig somehow just does not get it: Jews were only responding to the current Christian propaganda, much too late to prove or disprove, by taking the Christian version at face value and then debunking it, much

384 Craig in Strobel, p 221.
385 Craig in Strobel, pp. 211–212.
386 Craig in Strobel, p. 221.
387 Craig in Strobel, p. 221.

as the Protestant Rationalists accepted the event-claims of scripture but denied their miraculous causation. Think again of the Nativity story and Jewish arguments against it. Christians claimed Jesus was born of a virgin and thus had no human father. What was the Jewish rejoinder to the Virgin Birth claim? Not to refute it ("Joseph *was so* his father!"—something they could never prove one way or the other), but rather, "Sure! Joseph wasn't his father! Have it your way! But how do you know the Roman soldier Pandera wasn't his father?"

Does Craig imagine that the Jews knew Jesus was not Joseph's son and just suggested an alternative explanation? I hope not. I hope it is obvious to him that the Jewish polemic was a response, not to the historical facts (whatever they were), but to the Christian *preaching* (whether historical or not). It is the same with the empty tomb.

You realize, don't you, that I am here playing the eighteenth-century game of Craig and his anachronistic brethren just for the sake of argument. I am far from agreeing that Joseph of Arimathea is more than a fictional character, that he even appears in all known burial traditions, that the women ever visited the tomb and found it empty. I only mean to point out that if you play this outdated game, *Craig and company still wind up losing*. It turns out the Yellow Brick Road does lead someplace else. It becomes like the road to the Celestial City in John Bunyan's *Pilgrim's Progress*, where even on the verge of entry into heaven, the Pilgrim's path has a turnoff plunging into the abyss.

Chapter Thirteen
The Appearance of Evidence
Was Jesus Seen in Line at Burger King (of Kings)?

Can I Get a Witness?

One of the weakest aspects of the resurrection testimony of the gospels is its vulnerability to the charge of imposture: "Yes, yes, folks, Jesus appeared alive again all right, but it was only behind closed doors, and to people who already believed in him, and even then he didn't really look like the same guy. But it was him! Hallelujah—death has been conquered!"

Perhaps one may be excused for asking: Why such equivocality if God wanted to reveal himself, to vindicate the fact of his self-revelation in Christ definitively? Why make the supposed grounds for faith into such a dubious proposition that it takes more faith than before to believe it all? Oh, we have all heard the pious spin about how miracles are intended only for the edification of those who already believe. How convenient!

No one is fooled by this. Now if only there were some decent evidence, say of a public appearance of Jesus, out in the open somewhere. Or maybe if he appeared to people who did not already believe in him! That ought to count for something, right? Of course, I realize Reverend Strobel and his team have thought of this and have arguments at the ready.

I used to be an apologist, too, remember? I know the next step. Jesus *did* appear to a big crowd. Five hundred people! And he *did* appear to skeptics: Saul of Tarsus, and Jesus' brother James! I will take the liberty of addressing both issues in this chapter, even though Reverend Strobel saves the second for the next chapter, where J.P. Moreland discusses it.

Finding Five Hundred

Strobel asks a very good question, like a questioner on a call-in show, hoping an expert can show why there is nothing to worry about after all. And the one he calls on for reassurance is my old pal Gary Habermas. Reverend Strobel sets him up: "The creed in 1 Corinthians 15 is the only place in ancient literature where it is claimed that Jesus appeared to five hundred people at once. The gospels don't corroborate it... If it really happened, why doesn't anyone else talk about it? ... You'd think the apostles would cite this as evidence wherever they went."[388] Damn straight.

[388] Strobel, p. 231.

Habermas answers: "even though it's only reported in one source, it just happens to be the earliest and best-authenticated passage of all! ... when you have only one source, you can ask, 'Why aren't there more?' But you can't say, 'This one source is crummy' on the grounds that someone else didn't pick up on it."[389]

Alas, Gary, I'm afraid you *can*. I'm afraid you *have* to. Something is very wrong here. In fact, the presence of this item in the 1 Corinthians 15 list, when coupled with its absence from the gospels, *demands* the explanation that the appearance to the half-thousand be ruled out as an interpolation. There is just no other way to explain it. *It is just impossible for no gospel writer to have mentioned this if it had been known.*

Let me offer what I believe is an equivalent example from my own research. I stumbled across an astonishing reference to the *Testimonium Flavianum* of Josephus in the book *Jesus in Heaven on Earth* by Ahmadiyya apologist Al-Haj Khwaja Nazir Ahmad. The author says that Byzantine patriarch Photius, in his *Bibliotheca* (*ca*. 860), "referring to these passages, says: 'However, I have found in some papers that this discourse was not written by Josephus, but by one Caius, a presbyter.'" For this he offers a reference to Photius XLVIII.[390]

I was amazed! I have been interested in the problem of the genuineness of Josephus' mention of Jesus for decades, but I had never run across such an item of evidence: we actually have Photius in 860 CE discounting our Josephus passage as an interpolation, and he *names* the interpolator? The more I thought about it, there was just no way to account for the seeming universal ignorance or neglect of this vital piece of evidence—unless there were something wrong with it! And it turned out there was.

I ordered a copy of Photius, at some cost, I might add, to examine the original discussion for myself. It turned out that Ahmad was not reading his Photius very carefully. Photius was referring, not to the *Testimonium Flavianum* at all, but rather to a treatise called *On the Universe*, which scholars nowadays ascribe to Hippolytus.[391] Well, well: no wonder I had never seen anyone else mention this hot piece of evidence!

And so it is with the appearance to the five hundred in 1 Corinthians 15:6. It turns out to be an interpolation based on an expansion of Matthew's

---

389 Habermas in Strobel, pp. 231, 232.

390 Al-Haj Khwaja Nazir Ahmad, *Jesus in Heaven on Earth* (Bombay: Dar-ul-Isha'at-Kutub-E-Islamia, 1988), p. 32.

391 Photius, *The Bibliotheca:* A Selection. Trans. N.G. Wilson (London: Duckworth, 1994), p. 37.

tomb guards story as attested in the *Gospel of Nicodemus/Acts of Pilate*. There the 500 turn out to be the Roman soldiers guarding the tomb of Jesus. According to the Second Greek form:

> Thus, therefore, when the Preparation was ended, early on the Sabbath the Jews went away to Pilate, and said to him: My lord, that deceiver said, that after three days he should rise again. Lest, therefore, his disciples should steal him by night, and lead the people astray by such deceit, order his tomb to be guarded. Pilate therefore, upon this, gave them five hundred soldiers, who also sat round the sepulcher so as to guard it, after having put seals upon the stone of the tomb.
>
> And a few days after there came from Galilee to Jerusalem three men. One of them was a priest, by name Phinees; the second a Levite, by name Aggai; and the third a soldier, by name Adas. These came to the chief priests, and said to them and to the people: Jesus, whom you crucified, we have seen in Galilee with his eleven disciples upon the Mount of Olives, teaching them, and saying, Go into all the world, and proclaim the good news; and whosoever will believe and be baptized shall be saved; but whosoever will not believe shall be condemned. And having thus spoken, he went up into heaven. And both we and many others of the five hundred besides were looking on. (Roberts-Donaldson translation, chapters 12, 14)

It is, then, a very late apocryphal expansion of the Matthean tomb guards story. Someone thought this appearance just too good to be left out of the official list in 1 Corinthians. Why did the same scribe not also add it to a copy of Matthew, Mark, Luke, or John? Simply because he held the Gospel of Nicodemus as equally inspired and authoritative. So, as far as he was concerned, the vital episode was already 'in the gospels.'

Gary draws attention to another feature of the 1 Corinthians 15 text which he thinks makes it even more compelling evidence.

> Paul apparently had some proximity to these people. He says, "Most of whom are still living, though some have fallen asleep." Paul either knew some of these people or was told by someone who knew them that they were still walking around and willing to be interviewed. Now, stop and think about it: you would never include this phrase unless you were absolutely confident that these folks would confirm that they really did see Jesus alive, I mean, Paul was virtually inviting people to check it out for themselves. He wouldn't have said this if he didn't know they'd back him up.[392]

[392] Habermas in Strobel, pp. 231–232.

The hollowness of such assurance does not occur to Gary: how many of the Corinthian readers would have had the leisure or money to take off work and sail to Palestine to look up any of these witnesses? The writer does not even name any of them! All we have here is a parallel to the second-hand apologetic of John 20:29. John supposes his readers' faith in the resurrection can be built up because someone *else*, of whom they are reading (in this case, Doubting Thomas), was able to see it proven.

The reader of 1 Corinthians 15:6, like the reader of John 20:26–29, remains at second hand to the lucky characters in the text. Again, the rhetorical challenge to the reader to go ask the surviving witnesses is just like the overconfident boasts of Justin Martyr and Tertullian that any doubters may look up the facts about Jesus in the court archives of Pontius Pilate. None such existed to check; Justin and Tertullian simply supposed they *must*!

Making Jacob into James?

Everyone assumes that James was initially skeptical toward his brother's ministry but was converted to faith in it by a resurrection appearance. Indeed, one would think, that ought to do it! This idea obviously serves the agenda of apologists, but it is frequently encountered in the writings of critical scholars as well.[393] To bad it is an exegetical phantom. Nowhere is this connection made in the texts. True, we do have an unbelieving James, and elsewhere a believing James, as well as an assertion that the Risen Christ appeared to James, but the relationship between these textual phenomena is other than usually surmised.

The gospel evidence actually differs rather dramatically over whether James the Just was a disciple of his brother *before the resurrection*. John 7:5 and Mark 3:21, 31–35, echoed by Matthew 12:46–50, have it that James was unsympathetic to the ministry of Jesus. Luke, by contrast (Luke 8:19–21; Acts 1:14), rejects this earlier tradition, implying instead that all the Holy Family embraced Jesus' word from the start. Luke shares this portrayal of James with certain other late pro-James traditions such as we find in the *Gospel of Thomas*, logion 12:

---

[393] George Eldon Ladd, *I Believe in the Resurrection of Jesus*, p. 105; Clark H. Pinnock, *Set Forth your Case* (Chicago: Moody Press, 1978), p. 98; Frank Morison, *Who Moved the Stone?* (London: Faber & Faber, 1930), Chapter XI, "The Evidence of the Prisoner's Brother," pp. 196–205; Raymond E. Brown, *The Virginal Conception and Bodily Resurrection of Jesus* (NJ: Paulist Press, 1973), p. 95; Gerd Lüdemann, *The Resurrection of Jesus: History, Experience, Theology*. Trans. John Bowden (Minneapolis: Fortress Press, 1994), p. 109.

> The disciples say to Jesus, "We know that you will depart from us. Who is it who will be great over us?" Jesus says to them, "Wherever you have come from [*i.e., on your missionary journeys*] you will go report to James the Just, for whom heaven and earth were prepared."

And the *Gospel According to the Hebrews* has James present at the Last Supper, taking a vow of fasting till Jesus should rise from the dead:

> Now the Lord, when he had given the linen cloth to the servant of the priest, went to James and appeared to him, for James had sworn that he would not eat bread from that hour wherein he had drunk the Lord's cup until he should see him risen again from among those who sleep. And he said to him, "Hail!" And he called to the servants, who were greatly amazed. "Bring," said the Lord, "a table and bread." He took bread and blessed and broke and gave it to James the Just and said to him, "My brother, eat your bread, for the son of man has risen from those who sleep."

For this version of the tradition there is no conversion of James from unbeliever to believer. The resurrection appearance he received would have been just like the others: an appearance granted to a disciple. Nowhere does the early Christian tradition liken the appearance to James to that of Paul: the catching up short of an enemy of Christ to turn him into a friend. The mention of the appearance to James in 1 Corinthians 15:7 does not say James had been an unbeliever previously; it may assume, like Luke, Thomas, and the Gospel of the Hebrews, that he was already a Christian, we just don't know.

Those writers who make James skeptical of Jesus mention no appearance to him and do not mention him as an eventual believer. Maybe he actually was, or maybe he had been from the first, as per Luke, Thomas, and the Gospel according to the Hebrews, but perhaps Mark, Matthew and John are opposed to his faction and will not grant his discipleship. John 19:26–27 surely excludes (whether accurately or not) any conversion of James, since in it Jesus turns his mother over to the care of his Beloved Disciple, conspicuously *not* to his brother. Positing a "conversion" of James is just one more wishful-thinking harmonization of two very different traditions.

Making Saul into Paul?

Is the Christian conversion of Paul so unlikely an event that we must invoke a miracle to explain it? If we had to, I cannot see how that miracle would be the resurrection of Jesus. All we would need to say is that God apprehended Paul with an unexpected vision which changed the course of his life. And even that need not be literally miraculous. But in any case, what is the basis for the familiar story of Paul's conversion on the way to Damascus, as told in Acts chapters 9, 22, and 26?

Perhaps surprisingly, the writings ascribed to Paul offer no real parallel to the Acts account. To be sure, in 1 Corinthians 9:1 Paul claims to "have seen the Lord" and in 1 Corinthians 15:8 that "he appeared also unto me," but he reports nothing at all about the circumstances; nor does he even connect it to a religious conversion.

By contrast, the Acts account combines the rather different issues of Paul's conversion to Christ and his appointment to be the Apostle to the Gentiles; one cannot assume that any Pauline reference to either must imply both. All Galatians 1:15–16 says on the matter is "he who had set me apart before I was born, and had called me through his grace, was pleased to reveal his son in me, in order that I might preach him among the Gentiles." Unless we are determined to find the Damascus Road business in it, the passage will naturally be read as speaking of no conversion at all, but of a life-long (hence the reference to "before birth") religious commitment. At some point, presumably early, he was "called by the grace" of God to some form of ministry, which would eventuate in the manifestation of Christ's life within his bedraggled mortal frame, as per 2 Corinthians 4:10; Galatians 3:1; 4:14.

But doesn't the famous soliloquy in Romans chapter 7 mark a spiritual transformation in the Apostle? That passage is susceptible to too many viable interpretations, some of which will rule out the use of the passage as Pauline autobiography. Paul may rather be using 'I' like the rhetorical 'one,' implying he is picturing the frustrations of all conscientious people ruing their failures and seeking deliverance, which he seems to postpone to the future in any case ("Who *will* deliver me…?"). And that makes it unlikely he is referring to a decisive break in his own past.

We have the same problem when we consider two other passages often cited in this connection: Romans 6:3 and 1 Corinthians 12:13. They, too, may be taken as Paul rhetorically identifying with his audience. That wouldn't necessarily mean they weren't also genuine autobiographical recollections, but in that case, he would seem to be presupposing anything but a unique mode of entrance into the Christian community, *e.g.*, by a Damascus Road vision. Instead, he can speak of sharing his readers' baptismal experience just as he identifies by experience with the tongue-talking of the Corinthians (1 Corinthians 14:18). One other bit of evidence pointing in this direction is spotlighted by Anthony J. Blasi:

> The conversion account in the Acts of the Apostles presents a dramatic scene in which the risen Jesus knocks Paul off his horse on the road to Damascus and talks to Paul. None of this appears in the Pauline letters, however. Rather, we learn that "kinsmen" of Paul's were also apostles. In a letter of recommendation for the deaconess [*sic*; actually *deacon*], Phoebe, which is attached to the end of Romans, Paul notes that his kinsmen, Andronicus and Junias [*sic: Junia*], "are... of note among the apostles, and they were in Christ before me" (Rom. 16.7).[394]

Does this not sound as if, like many present-day ministers, Paul is proud to hale from a family of previous ministers? This hardly fits our accustomed picture of Paul radically turned about in his tracks, rescued like a brand from the burning by the miraculous intervention of Christ.

The utter lack of any reference to the Damascus Road vision in the Pauline epistles implies that it was not a story Paul told, and that Luke did not get it from him. Where then *did* Luke derive his inspiration? It sure looks like Luke has borrowed ideas from two well-known literary sources, Euripides' *Bacchae* and 2 Maccabees' story in chapter 3 of the conversion of Heliodorus.

> 1 While the holy city lived in perfect peace and the laws were strictly observed because of the piety of the high priest Onias and his hatred of evil, 2 the kings themselves honored the Place and glorified the temple with the most magnificent gifts. 3 Thus Seleucus, king of Asia, defrayed from his own revenues all the expenses necessary for the sacrificial services. 4 But a certain Simon, of the priestly course of Bilgah, who had been appointed superintendent of the temple, had a quarrel with the high priest about the supervision of the city market. 5 Since he could not prevail against Onias, he went to Apollonius of ***Tarsus***,[395] who at that time was governor of Coelesyria and Phoenicia, 6 and reported to him that the treasury in Jerusalem was so full of untold riches that the total sum of money was incalculable and out of all proportion to the cost of the sacrifices, and that it would be possible to bring it all under

394 Anthony J. Blasi, *Making Charisma: The Social Construction of Paul's Public Image* (New Brunswick: Transaction Books, 1991), p. 26. One can always argue that 'kinsmen' here merely means 'fellow Jews,' but other Jews are mentioned in the same passage without such terminology. To distance his 'kinsmen' from Paul in such a manner is a leaf taken from the book of Roman Catholic apologists for whom the brothers and sisters of Jesus must be his cousins, or whatever.

395 Since Tarsus never appears in the Pauline epistles, it is not inconceivable that Luke derived it from here in 2 Maccabees, too.

the control of the king. 7 When Apollonius had an audience with the king, he informed him about the riches that had been reported to him. The king chose his minister Heliodorus and sent him with instructions to expropriate the aforesaid wealth. 8 So Heliodorus immediately set out on his journey, ostensibly to visit the cities of Coelesyria and Phoenicia, but in reality to carry out the king's purpose. 9 When he arrived in Jerusalem and had been graciously received by the high priest of the city, he told him about the information that had been given, and explained the reason for his presence, and he asked if these things were really true. 10 The high priest explained that part of the money was a care fund for widows and orphans, 11 and a part was the property of Hyrcanus, son of Tobias, a man who occupied a very high position. Contrary to the calumnies of the impious Simon, the total amounted to four hundred talents of silver and two hundred of gold. 12 He added that it was utterly unthinkable to defraud those who had placed their trust in the sanctity of the Place and in the sacred inviolability of a temple venerated all over the world. 13 But because of the orders he had from the king, Heliodorus said that in any case the money must be confiscated for the royal treasury. 14 So on the day he had set he went in to take an inventory of the funds ***there was great distress*** throughout the city. 15 Priests prostrated themselves in their priestly robes before the altar, and loudly begged him in heaven who had given the law about deposits to keep the deposits safe for those who had made them. 16 Whoever saw the appearance of the high priest was pierced to the heart, for the changed color of his face manifested the anguish of his soul. 17 The terror and bodily trembling that had come over the man clearly showed those who saw him the pain that lodged in his heart. 18 People rushed out of their houses in crowds to make public supplication, because the Place was in danger of being profaned. 19 Women, girded with sackcloth below their breasts, filled the streets; maidens secluded indoors ran together, some to the gates, some to the walls, others peered through the windows, 20 all of them with hands raised toward heaven, making supplication. 21 It was pitiful to see the populace variously prostrated in prayer and the high priest full of dread and anguish. 22 While they were imploring the almighty Lord to keep the deposits safe and secure for those who had placed them in trust, 23 Heliodorus went on with his plan.

24 ***But just as he was approaching the treasury with his bodyguards, the Lord of spirits who holds all power manifested himself in so striking a way that those who had been bold enough to follow Heliodorus were panic-stricken at God's power and fainted away in terror***. 25 ***There appeared to them a richly caparisoned horse, mounted by a dreadful rider. Charging furiously, the horse attacked Heliodorus with its***

> ***front hoofs. The rider was seen to be wearing golden armor.*** 26 ***Then two other young men, remarkably strong, strikingly beautiful, and splendidly attired, appeared before him. Standing on each side of him, they flogged him unceasingly until they had given him innumerable blows.*** 27 ***Suddenly he fell to the ground, enveloped in great darkness. Men picked him up and laid him on a stretcher.***
>
> 28 The man who a moment before had entered that treasury with a great retinue and his whole bodyguard was carried away helpless, having clearly experienced the sovereign power of God. 29 While he lay speechless and deprived of all hope of aid, due to an act of God's power, 30 the Jews praised the Lord who had marvelously glorified his holy Place; and the temple, charged so shortly before with fear and commotion, was filled with joy and gladness, now that the almighty Lord had manifested himself 31 Soon some of the companions of Heliodorus begged Onias to invoke the Most High, praying that the life of the man who was about to expire might be spared.
>
> 32 Fearing that the king might think that Heliodorus had suffered some foul play at the hands of the Jews, ***the high priest offered a sacrifice for the man's recovery.*** 33 While the high priest was offering the sacrifice of atonement, the same young men in the same clothing again appeared and stood before Heliodorus. "Be very grateful to the high priest Onias," they told him. "It is for his sake that ***the Lord has spared your life.*** 34 ***Since you have been scourged by Heaven, proclaim to all men the majesty of God's power.***" When they had said this, they disappeared. 35 After ***Heliodorus had offered a sacrifice to the Lord and made most solemn vows to him*** who had spared his life, he bade Onias farewell, and returned with his soldiers to the king. 36 ***Before all men he gave witness to the deeds of the most high God that he had seen with his own eyes.***
>
> 37 When the king asked Heliodorus who would be a suitable man to be sent to Jerusalem next, he answered: 38 "If you have an enemy or a plotter against the government, send him there, and you will receive him back well-flogged, if indeed he survives at all; for there is certainly some special divine power about the Place. 39 He who has his dwelling in heaven watches over that Place and protects it, and he strikes down and destroys those who come to harm it." 40 This was how the matter concerning Heliodorus and the preservation of the treasury turned out.[396]

From 2 Maccabees Luke has borrowed the basic story of a persecutor of the people of God being stopped in his mission by a vision of heavenly

---

[396] New American Bible, 1986 revision.

beings (3:24–26), thrown to the ground in a faint, blinded (3:27), and cared for by righteous Jews who pray for his recovery (3:31–33), whereupon the villain converts to the faith he once persecuted (3:35) and begins witnessing to its truth (3:36) among Gentiles. Given Luke's propensity to rewrite the Septuagint,[397] it seems special pleading to deny that he has done the same in the present case, the most blatant of them all.

Luke found in the *Bacchae*[398] a similar story of a persecutor being converted against his will by the direct act of the god whose followers he has been abusing. King Pentheus has done his best to expel Dionysus' enthusiastic female followers (Maenads or Bacchae) from Thebes, and this against the better judgment of Cadmus, Teiresias, and others. They warn him not to be found fighting against a god (Teiresias: "Reckless fool, you do not know the consequences of your words. You talked madness before, but this is raving lunacy!" 357–360. Dionysus: "I warn you once again: do not take arms against a god." 788–789. "A man, a man, and nothing more, yet he presumed to wage war with a god." 636–637; *cf,* Acts 5:33–39).

He ought to mark how the Maenads, though they may seem to be filled with wine, are really filled with divine ecstasy ("not, as you think, drunk with wine," 686–687; *cf,* Acts 2:15), as witnessed by the old and young among them prophesying ("all as one, the old women and the young and the unmarried girls," 693–694; *cf,* Acts 2:17–18) and the harmless resting of tongues of fire upon their heads ("flames flickered in their curls and did not burn them," 757–758; "tongues of fire," 623–624; *cf,* Acts 2:3).

Pentheus, stubborn in his opposition, arrests the newly-arrived apostle of the cult (Dionysus himself incognito). An earthquake frees Dionysus from Pentheus' prison (585–603; *cf,* Acts 16:25–34), whereupon he strolls into Pentheus' throne room and mocks him ("If I were you, I would... not rage and kick against necessity, a man defying god." 793–796; *cf,* Acts

---

[397] The Septuagint, or LXX, is the Greek translation of the Hebrew Scriptures, or Old Testament, widely read by Hellenistic Jews and early Christians in New Testament times. Recent scholars have demonstrated how Luke seems to have gotten many of his own stories by adapting LXX prototypes. See Randel Helms, *Gospel Fictions* (Buffalo: Prometheus Books, 1988); Brodie, "Luke the Literary Interpreter;" Brodie, "Reopening the Quest for Proto-Luke: The Systematic Use of Judges 6–12 in Luke 16:1–18:8," *Journal of Higher Criticism*. Vol. 2, no. 1, Spring 1995, 68–101.

[398] I am using William Arrowsmith's translation in David Grene and Richard Lattimore (eds.), *Greek Tragedies*, Volume 3 (Chicago: University of Chicago Press, Phoenix paperbound edition, 1972), pp. 189–260.

26:14), then offers Pentheus the chance to track down the outlaw cultists in their secret hideaway. He may see them at their sport if he is willing to disguise his manly form in women's clothing, a distinctive doeskin costume (912–916; *cf,* Acts 9:26–30).

He mesmerizes Pentheus into agreeing to the plan (922–924; *cf,* Acts 9:17–18), and no sooner does Pentheus undergo the required make-over than he finds himself a true believer despite himself (929–930). But the joke's on him, since Dionysus sends him to his doom: he knows Pentheus will be detected and killed by the Maenads. Such poetic justice! It seems Pentheus could dish it out but not take it. He wanted to persecute the Maenads? Let him! He'll see how it feels from the standpoint of the persecuted! He becomes a true believer, only to suffer the fate of one. And so does Paul.

In light of the parallels with the *Bacchae* (Dionysus to Pentheus: "You and you alone shall suffer for your city. A great ordeal awaits you. But you are worthy of your fate." 963–964), we can catch the terrible irony of Acts 9:16, "I will show him how much *he* must suffer for the sake of my name!" Paul, too, will find his punishment fitting his crime: he will suffer as a member of the same community he had persecuted.

Giving 'em Hell, then Heaven

But doesn't the simple fact that Paul had first persecuted Christians, then became one, *by itself* attest a pretty dramatic conversion? If Paul recalls his days as a persecutor, does he even need to make his conversion explicit? I believe that every single one of the supposed Pauline references to former persecution is secondary. Each can be shown to be an interpolation or to occur in a pseudepigraphon, all such references presupposing the same Pauline legend we read in Acts.

Parenthetically, I know I am getting in deep here, because evangelicals just refuse to consider interpolation hypotheses. They cling to the text as we know it from the turn of the third century and insist that it cannot have changed prior to that date. Their stubbornness here, like that of their brethren who are sworn to defend the *Textus Receptus* of Erasmus, is itself a piece of apologetics, as I suggested back in Chapter 3: if they admitted the earliest texts might not have contained this or that passage, something we could never know for sure since there are no manuscripts for that period, all theological proof-texting would be rendered suspect, and the game would be impossible to play. So a dogmatic religion such as evangelical Christianity simply will not take interpolation hypotheses seriously. It is not that they are methodologically untenable; *they are just theologically distasteful*. Maybe my readers will try to be more open-minded. I hope so. Anyway, here goes.

John C. O'Neill amassed a pile of arguments that Galatians 1:13–14, 22–24 did not originally belong to the text of that epistle. "These verses have been interpolated into Paul's argument by a later writer who wished to glorify the apostle. The argument is irrelevant and anachronistic, the concepts differ from Paul's concepts, and the vocabulary and style are not his." "The astounding reversal of roles he underwent, from a fierce persecutor of the Church to an evangelist of the faith, and from a precociously zealous Jew to an opponent of Jewish customs, is no argument in favour of Paul's position,"[399] which seems to be the thread of the passage otherwise.

The reference to 'Judaism' is anachronistic, implying that Christianity and Judaism are separate religions, like 'Judaism and paganism.' And πιστις as a reference to "the faith," the Christian religion, characteristic in Acts 6:7 and the Pastorals, does not occur in Paul. And Paul elsewhere uses the word εκκλησια for local congregations, not for the Universal Church. The way it is used in Galatians 1:13 (*cf.* 23) sounds more like the later Church Aion doctrine of Ephesians. The word αναστροφη is elsewhere to be found over Paul's name only in Ephesians and 1 Timothy, while Ιουδαισμος, πορθοω, συνηλικιωτας, and πατρικος are absent even there. The frequency of the enclitic ποτε (three times) in these few verses is closer to that in Ephesians and the Pastorals (seven) than the other Paulines (once more in Galatians 2:6, nine times elsewhere in the Corpus). Stylistically these verses are not like Paul, the sentences being even and regular, with 20, 19, 12, and 20 words respectively. And that's not all.[400]

I have argued at some length elsewhere[401] that Winsome Munro, J.C. O'Neill, Arthur Drews, R. Joseph Hoffmann, and others are quite correct in seeing 1 Corinthians 15:3–11, containing another reference to Paul's pre-conversion persecutions, as an interpolation.

1 Timothy 1:13 refers to the havoc raised by the pre-Christian Paul, but it is no more genuinely Pauline than the epistle which contains it. The same is true of Philippians 3:6, "as to zeal, a persecutor of the church." As

[399] O'Neill, *Recovery of Paul's Letter to the Galatians*, p. 24.

[400] *Ibid.*, pp. 24–26.

[401] Robert M. Price, "Apocryphal Apparitions: 1 Corinthians 15:3–11 as a Post-Pauline Interpolation." In Price and Jeffery J. Lowder, eds., *The Empty Tomb: Jesus beyond the Grave* (Amherst: Prometheus Books, 2005), pp. 69–104

F.C. Baur pointed out long ago, Philippians, too, must be secondary, with its anachronistic references to bishops and deacons,[402] the Gnosticizing kabbalism of the Kenosis hymn in 2:6–11, its unusual vocabulary, and most of all, its heavy martyrological irony.

Its Paul assures his readers that, though he would naturally prefer to ascend to glory and there receive his crown of perfection, he will continue ministering to them, which 'he' does by means of this very pseudepigraph. The poignancy depends on the implied reader already being aware that Paul was in fact executed immediately after 'he' wrote these sweet sentiments. Here we have another Acts 19, another 2 Timothy. So naturally, it, too, presupposes the legend of Paul the persecutor.

Whence the Pauline persecution legend shared by Luke and his fellow Paulinists? The historical Paul never instigated violent attacks on any group of rival religionists. "The legend of Paul's persecution of Christians… may have been invented by the Petrine party, as the Paulinists invented the legend of Peter's denial of his Lord."[403] But was it cut from whole cloth? Not exactly. His reputation as one who, *as a non-Torah Christian*, opposed the 'true,' Ebionite faith and 'fought' against it would have eventually crystallized into stories of his actually taking up "worldly weapons of warfare" (2 Corinthians 10:4).

The original point was simply that Paul *as a Christian apostle* strove, polemicized, against the Nazorean Christianity of James and Peter. "They have heard concerning you that you teach all the Jews who are among the Gentiles to forsake Moses, telling them not to circumcise their children or observe the customs" (Acts 21:21). The Gentile, Pauline Christians could never have interpreted his promulgation of the Law-free gospel as opposing the true faith, so when eventually they heard the charge that Paul had been an enemy of the faith they took it to mean he had once persecuted what *they* considered the true faith: their own Hellenized Christianity. And this in turn seemed to imply he had previously been a non-Christian and then had undergone a major about-face.

---

402 I realize Yamauchi, *Stones and the Scriptures*, p.138–139) and others argue that the Qumran office of the *mebaqqer* ('overseer') secures the possibility of such an officer in the Pauline congregations. What such apologists fail to see, however, is: the point is not that no one had yet invented bishops, but that such an ecclesiastical structure evolves again and again when new religious movements evolve from sect to church, and that this development is too late for Paul.

403 L. Gordon Rylands, *A Critical Analysis of the Four chief Pauline Epistles: Romans, First and Second Corinthians, and Galatians* (London: Watts, 1929), p. 353; Loisy, *Birth of the Christian Religion*, pp. 119, 129.

Apparent Appearances

Reverend Strobel reproduces Gary Habermas's list of resurrection appearances from the gospels. Let's take our turn at reviewing them. It becomes clear that Gary, like all apologists, does not give enough weight to each of these episodes in its own right. He is like the mythical Noah, who packed all manner of species into his ark, heedless of the fact that some must prey on others.

The first appearance, he reckons, was that to Mary Magdalene in John 20:10–18. This pericope is ultimately a rewrite of the Matthew-manufactured appearance in Matthew 28:9–10. It must be. Mark and Luke knew nothing of any appearance to the women. Only angels (or men) met them at the tomb. Matthew speculated Mark's young man might have been the resurrected Christ, so he split the scene into two, splitting Mark's 'young man' into an angel on the one hand and Jesus on the other, each sharing the original message. Is there really any other reasonable way to read this one? Jesus Christ reappearing from the dead only to say, "Copy *that*!"

John then uses someone's rewriting of Matthew's version, supplying a bit of genuine dialogue, probably based on Tobit 12:16–20: "They were both alarmed; and they fell on their faces, for they were afraid. But he [*the angel Raphael*] said to them, 'Do not be afraid; you will be safe. But praise God for ever… All those days I merely appeared to you and did not eat or drink, but you were seeing a vision. And now give thanks to God, for I am ascending to him who sent me.'"

As Randel Helms[404] argues, the derivation from Tobit makes new sense of the odd reluctance of the Risen Jesus to let Mary touch him. It is an intentional (redactional) reversal of the women's gesture in Matthew 28:9, reflecting the angelic docetism of Raphael, who, despite appearances, *could* not be touched. And, like Raphael, Jesus says he is about to ascend back to God who sent him, *etc.*

There is a big problem with this pericope: it is incompatible with any other resurrection appearance story, whether in the Synoptics or the rest of them in John, since it clearly implies that Jesus is planning on *appearing to no one else*! Notice, please, that he does *not* tell Mary to tell Peter and the others to meet him in Galilee. No, he says to *tell them goodbye*, for he is about to return to God (John 20:17).

This scene belongs to the same trajectory we will meet in the *Pistis Sophia*, the *Gospel of Philip*, the *Dialogue of the Savior*, the *Gospel of*

---

404 Helms, *Gospel Fictions*, pp. 146–147.

Mary, etc., in which Mary Magdalene is the recipient of unique revelations from the Risen Christ. If you take the wording seriously, if you read it closely, instead of just tossing it into the bag with the other Easter stories as Exhibits A, B, *etc.*, you realize the choice is between this one and any/all of the others. I know the harmonizing instincts of the apologists will not allow them even to consider this seriously. Take off the blinders, will you guys?

Gary's second appearance of the Risen One is to the other women, in Matthew 28:8–10, but, as we have seen, this is no real appearance story, just a transformation of Mark's "young man." And here let me register my utter rejection of the line parroted by Blomberg, Craig, Boyd, Habermas and the rest: namely that the disagreements among the resurrection narratives concern mere matters of detail. Is it mere detail whether the women *saw Jesus* on this occasion or *didn't* see him? "Jesus Christ, an angel, *eh!* Six of one, a half dozen of the other!" Does it really matter so little? Put it this way: is it a mere trifle *whether it is the story of a resurrection appearance or not*?

Third comes the appearance to Cleophas and another disciple on the road to Emmaus, in Luke 24:13–32. This story is of a well-known literary type: that of the pious host who "entertains angels unaware." Two famous examples are Abraham and Lot, entertaining Yahweh and/or angels on the eve of Sodom's destruction. Also think of Zeus and Hermes visiting Baucus and Philemon and various others, but the closest is a story, recorded four centuries before Luke, from the healing shrine of Asclepius at Epidauros.

A woman named Sostrata journeys to the holy site to be delivered of a dangerously long pregnancy. There she expects to have a dream of the savior who will tell her what to do. But nothing happens. Disappointed, she and her companions head for home again. Along the way they are joined by a mysterious stranger who asks the cause of their grief. Hearing her story, he bids them lay her stretcher down, and he cures her of what turns out to be a false pregnancy. Then he reveals his identity as Asclepius himself and is gone.[405] It is not impossible that Luke borrowed the story, but that is not my point. The Emmaus story is recognizable as another tale of the same type. Why should we insist that the one is a legend but the other is historical?[406]

---

405 Francis Martin, ed., *Narrative Parallels to the New Testament* SBL Resources for Biblical Study 22 (Atlanta: Scholars Press, 1988), p. 229.

406 Right about now, I can just hear some reader shouting, "Parallelomania!" This invocation of the shade of Samuel Sandmel recalls a warning he issued

Fourth is the Christophany to the eleven disciples in Luke 24:33–49, which Gary should see is a doublet of the next one, which Gary describes as "to ten apostles and others, with Thomas absent, in John 20:19–23." He misdescribes it because the latter does *not* eliminate Thomas. That is a retroactive retooling of the story by the writer of the next one after this ("to Thomas and the other apostles," in John 20:26–30), who wants Thomas to have been absent at the time so as to use him as an example of faith without sight.

It is clear that the writer of John 20:19–23 must have assumed the presence of all but Judas Iscariot, because this is the "Johannine Pentecost" to which the apostles trace their appointment and equipping to share the charisma of Jesus to absolve or retain sin. Thomas *has* to be there, nor does this story say he is not. It is only the next episode, John 20:26–30, trying to piggyback on this one, which it did not originally do, that absents Thomas.

I have already suggested that the Luke 24:33–49 appearance originally meant to depict Jesus as having escaped dying, not having returned from the dead. It is at least certainly a natural way to read it. Thus it is doubtful whether one may properly even claim it as "evidence for the resurrection."

When Jesus appears "to seven apostles in John 21:1–14," we have a problem apologists never seem to notice: this is supposed to be the *first* resurrection appearance. All signs point to that. The disciples have dropped their delusions and have wearily returned to their mundane pursuits. If you knew the Son of God had returned from Hades and was about to set up the new Christian dispensation of gospel preaching and world evangelization,

---

to history-of-religions scholars not to assume that one ancient text is derivative from the other on the basis of scanty evidence, too few dots to connect. He also deemed it parallelomania whenever scholars suggested that, if a fragmentary source showed parallels with a more complete source, then the lost portion must have paralleled the longer section even where such parallels are unattested. Sandmel's caution, in other words, was quite specific. Parallelomania is "that extravagance among scholars which first overdoes the supposed similarity in passages and then proceeds to describe source and derivation as if implying literary connection flowing in an inevitable or predetermined direction" (Samuel Sandmel, "Parallelomania," *Journal of Biblical Literature* 81 (1962): p. 1) He never meant to condemn the appeal to extensive and detailed parallels between sources and consequent inferences about dependence, much less about genre categories. Apologists love to quote Sandmel as if he had condemned all inference based on striking parallels. Is there were anything wrong with this? They never say why there is, merely quoting Sandmel the same way they like to proof-text the Bible, out of context.

would you really waste time fly fishing up in Galilee? No, the whole point is that they have given Jesus up for dead but now see, to their shock, that they were wrong. When the disciple whispers to Peter, "It is the Lord!" let us not deflate the marvelous drama of the scene by saying that they already knew he was alive. "Him again!" But if this is supposed to be the initial appearance, we have to write off the appearance to the disciples behind closed doors in Jerusalem. That one cannot be the first appearance, and this one, too.

As for the one "to the disciples, in Matthew 28:16–20," that, too, has the disbelief element, something put to rest in each of the other 'first-appearance' stories. To have the disciples equally flabbergasted several times, one for each appearance, claiming that they all happened in series, is even more absurd than pretending Jesus multiplied the loaves and fish twice before the disciples, with them responding just as incredulously to Jesus' suggestion that *they* feed the crowd the second time (Mark 8:4) as the first (Mark 6:37)! Both are cases of a clumsy placing side by side of disparate stories, or versions of stories, that were originally competing with each other.

Finally, Gary counts the time Jesus "was with the apostles at the Mount of Olives before his ascension, in Luke 24:50–52 and Acts 1:4–9."[407] There's a problem, since Luke 24 places the ascension on Easter evening, while Acts 1 explicitly makes it 40 days later! The two are incompatible even if they come from the same author. No one can read the departure scene in Luke 24 and come away with the impression that the disciples will shortly be seeing Jesus again, for lunch and another training session, which must be the case if we try to keep both Luke 24 and Acts 1.

Besides, the Acts version, in which Jesus is training the disciples in the mysteries of the kingdom of God, is a pure fiction, as is plain from the fact that, minutes before the ascension, the disciples are just as dense as they have been from the beginning: "Lord, is now the time you will restore the kingdom to Israel?" This is more of the same nonsense as when they have been shown bickering over who is to be greatest in the kingdom, who will have the seats to the right and left of Jesus, and so on. What can he have been teaching them during the forty days? Nothing: it is a Lukan fiction.

You just cannot have all these appearances at the same time. Too many of them exclude the rest. Is the best explanation for this mess that Jesus really did rise from the dead? No, just the opposite: that the resurrection

[407] Habermas in Strobel, p. 234.

was a matter of rumor, fiction-mongering, myth-borrowing, and rewriting of Jewish scripture. The apologists seem to feel obliged to look at a photo collage from disparate sources and pretend they are a series of successive stills from the same movie. Anyone can see they are not.

Chapter Fourteen
The Circumcision Evidence
Is a Supernatural Resurrection the Best Explanation for Folks no Longer Trimming their Sons' Foreskins?

Reverend Strobel's final interview, the one with J.P. Moreland, is so embarrassing, so pathetically weak, that for the sake of his book's impact, he really should have cut it. Strobel asks him for "five pieces of circumstantial evidence that convince you that Jesus rose from the dead."[408]

The first is the old saw that the disciples wouldn't have died for their belief in the resurrection if they knew it was false. I dealt with that argument in Chapter 2, when Craig Blomberg offered it. It is a stupid argument. First, it presupposes that the twelve died as martyrs, something not even claimed in any early source, nor anywhere in the New Testament, except of course for James son of Zebedee in Acts 12. Second, even if we knew they died as martyrs, this would only mean they had not invented the resurrection as a witting hoax, as if that were the only alternative to it having happened. Third, martyrs were typically not nabbed and killed off for their belief in a particular tenet of faith or historical claim. Their executioners were not like the thought policeman O'Brien in Orwell's *1984* trying to get Winston Smith to believe two plus two equals five. The martyrs, courageous souls as they were, would just be picked up for being Christians and killed. They would be killed for refusing to sacrifice incense to the Emperor's divine spirit, but this had nothing to do with the resurrection of Jesus as far as we know.

The second 'exhibit' is that Paul and James, initially skeptics, were converted. I've just dealt with that in the preceding chapter.

The third bit of circumstantial evidence is that immediately, as of Pentecost, many Jews, those who became Christians, dropped the practices of animal sacrifice, observance of the Mosaic Torah in general, Saturday worship, circumcision, strict monotheism, and the belief in a warrior Messiah who would destroy Rome.[409] Moreland adds the gross improbability that Christians would have invented the sacrament of communion if Jesus had only died and not risen.[410]

---

408 Strobel, p. 246.

409 Moreland in Strobel, pp. 250–251.

410 Moreland in Strobel, p. 253.

This poor man is a philosopher? Strobel says he is, but he can never have made the acquaintance of logic. The arguments are absurd, completely confused.

First, there is no evidence, not even any New Testament claim, that these innovations happened that rapidly, as if the very first Christians made all these changes. Matthew preserves the saying "So if you find yourself bringing your offering forward to the altar and you suddenly remember that your brother has a complaint against you, leave your sacrificial animal standing there at the altar. First, go be reconciled to your brother, and only then return and offer your sacrifice if you want God to accept it" (Matthew 5:23–24). Doesn't this mean he expected his readers would still be offering sacrifices? Acts has the disciples meeting at the temple at assigned service hours, and nothing says they had stopped sacrificing and just went there to heckle.

Moreland seems unclear as to whether he thinks Christians dropped the Law or merely supplemented it with faith in Christ, but in either case these issues were slowly hammered out over many years as Gentiles sought admission to the Christian community, something the original Jewish Christians had not anticipated (remember the Cornelius story in Acts 10–11). There were many views on whether Jews, Gentiles, neither, or both were obliged to keep the Torah, as Galatians makes crystal clear.

As for switching to Sunday worship, something Moreland imagines could not have happened had not Jesus risen that day, he is confusing various questions. First, even if Sunday worship was based on the notion of a Sunday resurrection, why must this be the result of an *actual* resurrection and not just of subsequent *belief* in the resurrection? And even if one wanted to celebrate the resurrection every Sunday, why on earth would that necessitate dropping Sabbath worship with other Jews?

Most early Jewish Christians no doubt attended both until Christian Jews were expelled from the synagogues near the end of the first century. But outside Palestine, Christians went to the synagogues on the Sabbath even into the sixth century when John Chrysostom complains about it. And was resurrection belief even the origin of Sunday worship? I think not.

As all recognize, the early Christians had some sort of relation to the John the Baptist movement. The Mandaeans, who claim quite plausibly to be descendants of John's sect, worshipped on Sunday. My guess is that Jewish Christians got Sunday, as they did water baptism, from John's sect. At least that's a reasonable enough possibility that we hardly have to invoke a real resurrection to answer the question: that would be like shooting a mouse with an elephant gun.

Jewish Christians never abandoned circumcision. Some Gentile Christians embraced the practice. That occasioned the Epistle to the Galatians. It is not as if Christians dropped the practice as soon as Jesus emerged from the tomb, as Moreland seems to imagine. What is he thinking?

Moreland comes perilously close to admitting that Christians rejected monotheism when they embraced Trinitarianism, but he doesn't want to deny Christianity is monotheistic, and he seems to stumble over his own argument. He wants to argue, at any rate, that it must have taken one heck of a stimulus to get Jews to modify monotheism, and that must have been the resurrection. Er, don't you mean '*faith* in the resurrection'?

Did the eyewitness apostles already teach Trinitarianism? If so, why do we see it taking shape gradually through the later writings of Athanasius, Tertullian, and the Three Cappadocians? Moreland is plainly a biblicist who doesn't feel he has the right to believe anything that doesn't spring full-blown from the Bible's pages like a genie from Aladdin's lamp. So he has to try to find everything he wants to believe in the Bible, even if it takes some fancy ventriloquism to do it.

Did Christians instantly—or ever—drop the Jewish notion of a warrior Messiah who will come in the last days to destroy Rome? That seems to me a pretty good picture of the Second Coming of Jesus Christ according to the Book of Revelation.

Finally, is it impossible that a slain teacher's followers might meet regularly to celebrate their leader's martyrdom, even if they did not believe he had been resurrected? I am not advancing any particular theory as to the origin of Holy Communion here, but Moreland's claim is ludicrous. Has he never heard of the veneration of the saints and martyrs? In the early church, on scheduled holy days, the faithful would gather at the tombs of the martyrs and read accounts of their courageous deaths. They might even ask them to intercede with their heavenly Father, since they were closer to him and fully sanctified. These saints hadn't already been resurrected; they didn't need to be (though it was believed they would be one day). They were with their god in heaven already. The Eucharistic meal "in memory of me" may, for all we know, have arisen the same way.

Please understand me: I do not for one minute mean to suggest that the utter failure of Moreland's arguments threaten the truth of Christianity. They are pointless and irrelevant to the larger debate over the resurrection.

That is why I cannot understand their inclusion here. But they do tell us one important thing: Reverend Strobel has apparently never met an apologetical argument he didn't like. It reminds me of what a *TV Guide* reviewer once said about the astonishingly stupid *Benny Hill Show*: "There is no joke so old, so worn-out, so down on its luck, that Benny will not pick it up, dust it off, and use it again." That's Strobel, and that's his apologetic. Anything including the kitchen sink. If it might convince some idiot out there, then by all means use it. He wouldn't know a convincing argument if it bit him. It is all after-the-fact rationalization.

CONCLUSION

CONCLUSION
The Failure of Apologetics

I dare to render this verdict, that apologetics for the resurrection are one and all arrows that fall short of their target. How dare I? I know that they failed me. Bill Craig would say this means only that *I* failed *them*, that I was insufficiently open to the Spirit's urgings through cogent arguments, perhaps because I cherished some private sin and did not want to repent of it, which I should have to do if I admitted the cogency of apologetical arguments.

But that is insulting, invidious, and false. In fact, that may be the worst of all apologetics arguments: character assassination. "If you were morally earnest, you'd agree with me!" Unbelievable. That is a gross evasion. Motivation does not mean a thing. I have tried to evaluate arguments individually, on their merits and demerits. You see the results. Judge them for yourselves. I stand by them.

Here at the end, let me just reiterate one important point that does have to do with my personal stance and my life experience, mainly because I have (understandably) been misrepresented on the point. I am usually referred to, on the rare occasions apologists see fit to mention my work, as one of the phalanx of "skeptics." I am indeed skeptical of their arguments, and now you know why. But you need to remember something, so to spare yourself the temptation of writing me off as an apologist for Atheism.

I am what should not exist according to apologists: an apologist who found himself bitterly disappointed by the defenses offered for his faith. I found that did not necessarily mean what the apologists said it would mean: that unless one could prove the truth of evangelical Christianity, there would be no alternative. One would face an endless night of moral and intellectual despair. I realized that, too, was a poor apologetic. It was pretty much the same scare tactic used by cults to terrify members into staying with the cult at all costs.

I went on to study the broader spectrum of Christianity and of other religions. This search was very enriching. It might be worth knowing that it was only subsequent to this process that I served as the pastor of a Baptist congregation, albeit a liberal one. I pastored First Baptist Church of Montclair for nearly six years and an independent Universalist house church for another six. I have found more spiritual growth to be available from questions that must remain open than from answers that can never be established with certainty anyway.

But do you get it? I once believed and used the arguments I attack root and branch in this book. I most certainly did not mount an attack from without. No, I was a soldier on the front lines who was horrified to discover I was only firing blanks. And these blanks proved ironically fatal once they backfired. That was the end of my faith. That does not prove my arguments in this book are cogent. You must decide that on the basis of the arguments themselves—if you are willing to do that. In my experience, most evangelicals will listen only to look for loop holes and armor chinks. They are never open to learning from what first scares them. Some are; they are the ones who eventually pack up their bags of New Testament research and go elsewhere—to some graduate program in biblical criticism. Just ask some of these 'liberal professors' how they got interested in the Bible. You will be surprised to find how many of them come from the ranks of ex-apologists. There may be a reason for that.

BIBLIOGRAPHY

A

Ahmad, Al-Haj Khwaja Nazir. *Jesus in Heaven on Earth.* Bombay: Dar-ul-Isha'at-Kutub-E-Islamia, 1988.

Alexander, Charles. *Alexander the Great.* NY: E.P. Dutton and Company, 1947.

Allen, Woody. "Manhattan," in *Four Films of Woody Allen: Annie Hall, Interiors, Manhattan, Stardust Memories.* NY: Random House, 1982, pp. 181–276.

Anderson, J.N.D. *Christianity: The Witness of History. A Lawyer's Approach.* London: Tyndale Press, 1969.

__________. *The Evidence for the Resurrection.* Downers Grove: InterVarsity Press, 1966.

__________. *A Lawyer among the Theologians.* Grand Rapids: Eerdmans, 1974.

Argyle, A.W. "The Greek of Luke and Acts." *New Testament Studies* 20 (1973–1974), pp. 441–445.

B

Babinski, Edward T. ed. *Leaving the Fold: Testimonies of Former Fundamentalists.* Amherst: Prometheus Books, 1995.

Barker, Margaret. *The Great Angel: A Study of Israel's Second God.* Louisville: Westminster / John Knox, 1992.

Barr, James. *Fundamentalism.* Philadelphia: Westminster Press, 1977.

Barth, Gerhard. "Matthew's Understanding of the Law." In Günther Bornkamm, Gerhard Barth, and Hans Joachim Held, *Tradition and Interpretation in Matthew.* Trans. Percy Scott. New Testament Library. Philadelphia: Westminster Press, 1976, pp. 58–164.

Barthes, Roland. "The Writer on Holiday," in Barthes, *Mythologies.* Trans. Annette Lavers. NY: Hill and Wang. 1972, pp. 29–31.

Baur, Ferdinand Christian. *Paul, the Apostle of Jesus Christ: His Life and Work, His Epistles and Doctrine.* Trans. A. Menzies. London: Williams and Norgate, 1876.

Be Duhn, Jason David. *Truth in Translation: Accuracy and Bias in English Translations of the New Testament.* NY: University Press of America, 2003.

Berger, David. *The Rebbe, the Messiah and the Scandal of Orthodox Indifference.* Portland, OR: Littman Library of Jewish Civilization, 2001.

Berger, Peter L. *The Sacred Canopy: Elements of a Sociological Theory of Religion.* Garden City: Doubleday Anchor Books, 1969.

__________ and Thomas Luckmann, *The Social Construction of Reality: An Introduction to the Sociology of Knowledge.* Garden City: Doubleday Anchor Books, 1967.

Blasi, Anthony J. *Making Charisma: The Social Construction of Paul's Public Image.* New Brunswick: Transaction Books, 1991.

Blomberg, Craig L. *Contagious Holiness: Jesus' Meals with Sinners.* New Studies in Biblical Theology 19 Downers Grove: InterVarsity Press, 2005.

__________. *The Historical Reliability of the Gospels*. Downers Grove: InterVarsity Press, 1987.

Brettler, Marc Zvi. *The Creation of History in Ancient Israel*. NY: Routledge, 1995.

Brandon, S.G.F. *The Fall of Jerusalem and the Christian Church: A Study of the Effects of the Jewish Overthrow of A.D. 70 on Christianity*. London: SPCK, 1951.

Brodie, Thomas L. "Luke the Literary Interpreter: Luke-Acts as a Systematic Rewriting and Updating of the Elijah-Elisha Narrative in 1 and 2 Kings." Ph.D. dissertation presented to Pontifical University of St. Thomas Aquinas, Rome. 1988.

__________. "Reopening the Quest for Proto-Luke: The Systematic Use of Judges 6–12 in Luke 16:1–18:8," *Journal of Higher Criticism*. Vol. 2, no. 1, Spring 1995, 68–101.

Brown, Raymond E. "The Pater Noster as an Eschatological Prayer," in Brown, *New Testament Essays*. Garden City: Doubleday Image Books, 1968, pp. 275–320.

__________. *The Virginal Conception and Bodily Resurrection of Jesus*. NJ: Paulist Press, 1973.

Bruce, F.F. *The New Testament Documents: Are They Reliable?* Grand Rapids: Eerdmans, 5th ed., 1960.

__________. *Tradition: Old and New*. Contemporary Evangelical Perspectives. Grand Rapids: Zondervan, 1970.

Bultmann, Rudolf. *The Gospel of John: A Commentary* Trans. G.R. Beasley-Murray, R.W.N. Hare, J.K. Riches. Philadelphia: Westminster Press, 1971.

Burton, John. *The Collection of the Qur'an*. NY: Cambridge University Press, 1977.

Butterfield, Herbert. *Christianity and History*. London: Fontana, 1958.

C

Cadbury, Henry J. "The Alleged Medical Language of Luke." In Cadbury, *The Style and Literary Method of Luke*. Cambridge: Harvard University Press, 1920, pp. 39–64.

Carrier, Richard C. "Pseudohistory in Jerry Vardaman's magic coins: the nonsense of micrographic letters," in *Skeptical Inquirer, March, 2002*. (http://findarticles.com/p/articles/mi_m2843/is_2_26/ai_83585959/pg_3)

__________. "The Spiritual Body of Christ and the Legend of the Empty Tomb," in Robert M. Price and Jeffrey Jay Lowder, eds., *The Empty Tomb: Jesus beyond the Grave*. Amherst: Prometheus Books, 2005, pp. 105–232.

Casey, Maurice. *Is John's Gospel True?* NY: Routledge, 1996.

__________. *The Son of Man: The Interpretation and Influence of Daniel 7*. London: SPCK, 1979.

Chapman, Graham. John Cleese, Terry Gilliam, Eric Idle, Terry Jones, Michael Palin, *Monty Python's The Life of Bryan (of Nazareth)*. NY: Ace Books, 1979.

Charles, R.H., ed. trans. *The Apocrypha and Pseudepigrapha of the Old Testament*. Oxford at the Clarendon Press, 1913.

Clark, Albert C. *The Acts of the Apostles: A Critical Edition with Introduction and Notes on Selected Passages*. Oxford at the Clarendon Press, 1933.

Cohn, Norman. *Cosmos, Chaos and the World to Come: The Ancient Roots of Apocalyptic*. New Haven: Yale University Press, 1993.

Colani, Timothee. "The Little Apocalypse of Mark 13." Trans. Nancy Wilson. *Journal of Higher Criticism* (10/1) Spring 2003, pp. 41–47. Excerpted from Colani, *Jesus-Christ et les croyances messianiques de son temps*, 1864, pp. 201–214.

Collingwood, R.G. *The Idea of History.* NY: Oxford University Press Galaxy Books, 1956.

Conzelmann, Hans. *The Theology of St. Luke*. Trans. Geoffrey Buswell. NY: Harper & Row, 1961.

Craig, William Lane. *The Son Rises: Historical Evidence for the Resurrection of Jesus*. Chicago: Moody Press, 1981.

Cullmann, Oscar. "Dissensions within the Early Church," in Richard Batey, ed., *New Testament Issues*. NY: Harper & Row / Harper Forum Books, 1970, pp. 119–129.

D

Davies, Philip R. *In Search of 'Ancient Israel.'* Journal for the Study of the Old Testament Supplement Series 148. Sheffield: Sheffield Academic Press, 1992.

Derrett, J. Duncan M. "Financial Aspects of the Resurrection," in Robert M. Price and Jeffrey Jay Lowder, eds., *The Empty Tomb: Jesus beyond the Grave*. Amherst: Prometheus Books, 2005, pp. 393–410..

Derrida, Jacques. *Of Grammatology*. Trans. Gayatri Chakravorty Spivak. Baltimore: Johns Hopkins University Press, 1976.

Dibelius, Martin. "The Speeches in Acts and Ancient Historiography." In Dibelius, *Studies in the Acts of the Apostles*. London: SCM Press, 1956, pp. 138–191.

Dobson, C.C. *Did Our Lord Visit Britain as They Say in Cornwall and Somerset?* Merrimac, MA: Destiny Publishers, 1944.

Dodd, C.H. "The Fall of Jerusalem and the 'Abomination of Desolation." In Dodd, *More New Testament Studies*. Grand Rapids: Eerdmans, 1968, pp. 69–83.

Dowden, Ken. "Introduction" to *The Alexander Romance*. In B.P. Reardon, ed., *Collected Ancient Greek Novels*. Berkeley: University of California Press, 1989, p. 651.

Drews, Arthur. *The Christ Myth.* Westminster College-Oxford: Classics in the Study of Religion. Amherst: Prometheus Books, 1998.

Dungan, David L., and **David R. Cartlidge,** eds. *Sourcebook of Texts for the Comparative Study of the Gospels*. Society for Biblical Literature Sources for Biblical Study 1. Missoula: Scholars Press, 4th ed., 1974.

E

Eddy, Paul Rhodes, and **Greg Boyd,** *The Jesus Legend: A Case for the Historical Reliability of the Synoptic Jesus Tradition.* Grand Rapids: Baker Academic, 2007.

Ehrman, Bart D. *Misquoting Jesus: The Story behind Who Changed the Bible and Why.* San Francisco: Harper One, 2005.

__________. *The Orthodox Corruption of Scripture: The Effect of Early Christological Controversies on the Text of the New Testament.* NY: Oxford University Press, 1993.

Eisler, Robert. *The Enigma of the Fourth Gospel: Its Author and Its Writer.* London: Methuen, 1938.

Erb, Peter C. (ed.). *Pietists: Selected Writings.* Classics of Western Spirituality. Ramsey, NJ: Paulist Press, 1981.

F

Finegan, Jack. *The Archeology of the New Testament: The Life of Jesus and the Beginning of the Early Church.* Revised edition. Princeton, NJ: Princeton University Press, 1992.

Fiorenza, Elisabeth Schüssler. *In Memory of Her: A Feminist Theological Reconstruction of Christian Origins.* NY: Crossroad, 1984.

Franklin, Eric. *Christ the Lord: A Study in the Purpose and Theology of Luke-Acts.* Philadelphia: Westminster Press, 1975.

G

Gasque, W. Ward. *A History of the Criticism of the Acts of the Apostles.* Grand Rapids: Eerdmans, 1975.

Geisler, Norman L., and **William E. Nix.** *A General Introduction to the Bible.* Chicago: Moody Press, 1980.

Gibran, Kahlil. *Jesus the Son of Man: His Words and Deeds as Told and Recorded by Those Who Knew Him.* NY: Knopf, 1976.

Goldziher, Ignaz. *Introduction to Islamic Theology and Law.* Modern Classics in Near Eastern Studies. Trans. Andras and Ruth Hamori. Princeton: Princeton University Press, 1981.

Goodspeed, Edgar J. *Famous Biblical Hoaxes, or Modern Apocrypha.* Grand Rapids: Baker Book House, 1956.

Grant, Robert M. *Irenaeus of Lyons.* The Early Church Fathers. NY: Routledge, 1997.

__________. (ed. and trans.). *Second Century Christianity: A Collection of Fragments.* Translations of Christian Literature. Series VI. Select Passages. London: SPCK, 1957.

Green, Michael. *Man Alive!* Downers Grove: Inter-Varsity Press, 1971.

Guillaume, Alfred. *The Traditions of Islam: An Introduction to the Study of the Hadith Literature.* London: Oxford University Press, 1924.

Gunkel, Hermann. *An Introduction to the Psalms: The Genres of the Religious Lyrics of Israel.* Ed. Joachim Begrich. Trans. James D. Nogalski. Mercer Library of

Biblical Studies. Macon: Mercer University Press, 1998.

Gurdjieff, G.I. *Meetings with Remarkable Men*. Trans. A.R. Orage. All and Everything, Second Series. NY: E.P. Dutton, 1969.

H

Haenchen, Ernst. *The Acts of the Apostles: A Commentary*. Trans. Bernard Noble and Gerald Shinn. Philadelphia: Westminster Press, 1971.

Harnack, Adolf von. *The Date of the Synoptic Gospels and the Acts*. Trans. J.R. Wilkinson. Crown Theological Library. New Testament Studies IV. NY: Putnam's. 1911.

Harvey, Van A. *The Historian and the Believer: The Morality of Historical Knowledge*. NY: Macmillan, 1966.

Held, Heinz Joachim. "Matthew as Interpreter of the Miracle Stories," in Günther Bornkamm, Gerhard Barth, and Hans Joachim Held, *Tradition and Interpretation in Matthew*. Trans. Percy Scott. New Testament Library. Philadelphia: Westminster Press, 1976, pp. 165–299.

Helfaer, Philip M. *The Psychology of Religious Doubt*. Boston: Beacon Press, 1972.

Helms, Randel. *Gospel Fictions*. Buffalo: Prometheus Books, 1988.

Hooker, Morna D. *Jesus and the Servant: The Influence of the Servant Concept of Deutero-Isaiah in the New Testament*. London: SPCK, 1959.

Horsley, Richard A. *Galilee: History, Politics, People*. Valley Forge: Trinity Press International, 1995.

Howkins, Kenneth G. *The Challenge of Religious Studies*. Downers Grove: InterVarsity Press, 1973.

Hunter, Archibald M. *According to John: The New Look at the Fourth Gospel*. Philadelphia: Westminster Press, 1968.

J

Jeremias, Joachim. "Abba." In Jeremias, *The Central Message of the New Testament*. NY: Scribner's, 1965, pp. 9–30.

__________. *New Testament Theology, Part One: The Proclamation of Jesus*. Trans. John Bowden New Testament Library. London: SCM Press, 1971.

__________. *The Parables of Jesus*. Trans. S.H. Hooke. NY: Scribner's, rev. ed., 1972.

Joseph, Isya. *Devil Worship: The Sacred Books and Traditions of the Yezidis*. Boston: Gorham Press, 1919.

Juynboll, G.H.A. *Muslim Tradition: Studies in Chronology, Provenance and Authorship of Early Hadith*. Cambridge Studies in Islamic Civilization. NY: Cambridge University Press, 1983.

K

Kähler, Martin. *The So-called Historical Jesus and the Historic Biblical Christ*. Trans. Carl E. Braaten. Seminar Editions. Philadelphia: Fortress Press, 1964.

Kannaday, Wayne C. *Apologetic Discourse and the Scribal Tradition: Evidence of the Influence of Apologetic Interests on the Text of the Canonical Gospels*. Society of Biblical Text-Critical Studies, Volume 5. Atlanta: Society of Biblical Literature, 2004.

Kant, Immanuel. *Religion within the Limits of Reason Alone*. Trans. Theodore M. Greene and Hoyt H. Hudson. NY: Harper & Row Torchbooks, 1960.

Kelber, Werner H., ed. *The Passion in Mark*. Philadelphia: Fortress Press, 1976.

Klein, Günter. *Die Zwölf Apostel: Ursprung und Gehalt eine Idee*. Göttingen: Vandenhoeck & Ruprecht, 1961.

Kloppenborg , John S. *The Formation of Q: Trajectories in Ancient Wisdom Collections*. Studies in Antiquity & Christianity. Philadelphia: Fortress Press, 1987.

Knox, John. *Chapters in a Life of Paul*. NY: Abingdon Press, 1950

__________. *Marcion and the New Testament: A Chapter in the Early History of the Canon*. Chicago: University of Chicago Press, 1942.

Koester, Helmut. *Ancient Christian Gospels: Their History and Development*. Trinity Press International, 1990.

L

LaBarre, Weston. *They Shall Take up Serpents: Psychology of the Southern Snake-Handling Cult*. NY: Schocken Books, 1969.

Ladd, George Eldon. *I Believe in the Resurrection of Jesus*. I Believe Series # 2 .Grand Rapids: Eerdmans, 1975.

Lanternari, Vittorio. *The Religions of the Oppressed: A Study of Modern Messianic Cults*. NY: New American Library / Mentor Books, 1965.

Lemche, Niels Peter. *The Israelites in History and Tradition*. Library of Ancient Israel. London: SPCK / Louisville: Westminster John Knox Press, 1998.

Lewis, C.S. *Mere Christianity*. NY: Macmillan, 1960.

Loisy, Alfred. *The Birth of the Christian Religion*. Trans. L.P. Jacks. London: George Allen & Unwin, 1948.

__________. *The Origins of the New Testament*. Trans. L.P. Jacks. London: George Allen and Unwin, 1950.

Lord, Albert. *The Singer of Tales*. Cambridge: Harvard University Press, 1960.

Lowder, Jeffrey Jay. "Historical Evidence and the Empty Tomb: A Reply to William Lane Craig," in Price and Lowder, eds., *The Empty Tomb: Jesus beyond the Grave*. Amherst: Prometheus Books, 2005, pp. 261–306.

Luckmann, Thomas V. *The Invisible Religion: The Problem of Religion in Modern Society*. NY: Macmillan, 1970.

Lüdemann, Gerd. *Paul, Apostle to the Gentiles: Studies in Chronology*. London: SCM Press, 1984.

__________. *The Resurrection of Jesus: History, Experience,*

Theology. Trans. John Bowden. Minneapolis: Fortress Press, 1994.

M

MacDonald, Dennis Ronald. *The Homeric Epics and the Gospel of Mark.* New Haven: Yale University Press, 2000.

Mack, Burton L. *The Lost Gospel: The Book of Q and Christian Origins*. San Francisco: HarperSanFrancisco, 1993.

Maier, Paul. *Pontius Pilate*. Wheaton: Tyndale House, 1968.

Manson, T.W. *The Servant Messiah: A Study of the Public Ministry of Jesus*. Cambridge at the University Press, 1961.

Marshall, I. Howard. *Eschatology and the Parables*. Leicester: Theological Students Fellowship, n.d.

__________. *I Believe in the Historical Jesus*. I Believe Series # 5. Grand Rapids: Eerdmans, 1977.

__________. *Luke: Historian and Theologian*. Contemporary Evangelical Perspectives. Grand Rapids: Zondervan, 1974.

Martin, Francis, ed. *Narrative Parallels to the New Testament*. SBL Resources for Biblical Study 22. Atlanta: Scholars Press, 1988.

Martin, Marie-Louise. *Kimbangu: An African Prophet and his Church*. Grand Rapids: Eerdmans, 1976.

Martin, Ralph P. *Mark: Evangelist and Theologian*. Contemporary Evangelical Perspectives. Grand Rapids: Zondervan, 1973.

Mason, Steve. *Josephus and the New Testament*. Peabody: Hendrickson, 1992.

McDowell, Josh., ed., *More Evidence that Demands a Verdict: Historical Evidences for the Christian Scriptures*. Arrowhead Springs: Campus Crusade for Christ, 1975.

Michaels, J. Ramsey. *John*. A Good News Commentary. San Francisco: Harper & Row, 1984.

Merrill P. Miller. "'Beginning from Jerusalem…' Re-examining Canon and Consensus," *The Journal of Higher Criticism* 2/1 (Spring 1995): pp. 3–30.

Miller, Robert J. *The Complete Gospels: Scholars Annotated Version*. Santa Rosa: Polebridge Press, 1995.

Montgomery, John Warwick. *History & Christianity*. Downers Grove: InterVarsity Press, 1974.

Moosa, Matti. *Extremist Shi'ites: The Ghulat Sects*. Syracuse: Syracuse University, 1988.

Morison, Frank. *Who Moved the Stone?* London: Faber & Faber, 1930.

Mowinckel, Sigmund. *The Psalms in Israel's Worship*. Trans. D.R. Ap-Thomas. NY: Abingdon Press, 1962.

Munro, Winsome. *Authority in Paul and Peter: The Identification of a Pastoral Stratum in the Pauline Corpus and I Peter*. Society for New Testament Studies Monograph Series 45. NY: Cambridge University Press, 1983.

N

Nau, Arlo J. *Peter in Matthew: Discipleship, Diplomacy, and Dispraise*. Good News Studies Vol. 36. A Michael Glazier Book. Collegeville: Liturgical Press, 1992.

Nongbri, Brent. "The Use and Abuse of P52: Papyrological Pitfalls in the Dating of the Fourth Gospel." *Harvard Theological Review* 98 (2005), pp. 23–52.

O

J.C. O'Neill. *Paul's Letter to the Romans*. Pelican Commentaries. Baltimore: Penguin Books, 1973.

__________. *The Recovery of Paul's Letter to the Galatians*. London: SPCK, 1972.

__________. *The Theology of Acts in its Historical Setting*. London: SPCK, 1961.

Oosthuizen, G.C. *Post-Christianity in Africa*. Grand Rapids: Eerdmans, 1968.

Overman, J. Andrew. *Matthew's Gospel and Formative Judaism: The Social World of the Matthean Community*. Minneapolis: Fortress Press, 1990.

P

Parry, Milman. *The Making of Homeric Verse: The Collected Papers of Milman Parry*. NY: Oxford University Press, 1987.

Pelton, Robert W. and **Karen W. Carden.** *Snake Handlers: God-Fearers? Or Fanatics?* NY: Thomas Nelson, 1974.

Perrin, Norman. "Mark 14:62: The End Product of a Christian Pesher Tradition?" in Perrin, *A Modern Pilgrimage in New Testament Christology*. Philadelphia: Fortress Press, 1974, pp. 10–22.

Pervo, Richard I. *Dating Acts: Between the Evangelists and the Apologists*. Santa Rosa: Polebridge Press, 2006.

__________. *Profit with Delight: The Literary Genre of the Acts of the Apostles*. Philadelphia: Fortress, 1987.

Photius. *The Bibliotheca: A Selection*. Trans. N.G. Wilson. London: Duckworth, 1994.

Pinnock, Clark H. *Set Forth your Case*. Chicago: Moody Press, 1978.

Price, Robert M. "Apocryphal Apparitions: 1 Corinthians 15:3–11 as a Post-Pauline Interpolation." In Price and Jeffery J. Lowder, eds., *The Empty Tomb: Jesus beyond the Grave*. Amherst: Prometheus Books, 2005, pp. 69–104.

__________. *Beyond Born Again: Toward Evangelical Maturity*. Eugene: Hypatia Press, 1993.

__________. *Deconstructing Jesus*. Amherst: Prometheus Books, 2000

__________. *The Incredible Shrinking Son of Man: How Reliable Is the Gospel Tradition?* Amherst: Prometheus Books, 2003.

__________. *The Paperback Apocalypse: How the Christian Church Was Left Behind*. Amherst: Prometheus Books, 2007.

R

Reardon, B.P. ed. *Collected Ancient Greek Novels*. Berkeley: University of California Press, 1989.

Reimarus, Hermann Samuel. "Concerning the Intention of Jesus and His Teaching." In Charles H. Talbert, ed., *Reimarus: Fragments* Trans. Ralph S. Fraser. Lives of Jesus Series. Philadelphia: Fortress Press, 1970, pp. 59–269.

Reitzenstein, Richard. *The Hellenistic Mystery-Religions: Their Basic Ideas and Significance*. Trans. John E. Steely. Pittsburgh Theological Monograph Series Number 15. Pittsburgh: Pickwick Press, 1978.

Richard, Earl. *Acts 6:1–8:4: The Author's Method of Composition*. SBL Dissertation Series 41. Missoula: Scholars Press, 1978.

Robbins, Vernon K. "By Land and by Sea: The We-Passages and Ancient Sea Voyages," in Charles H. Talbert, ed., *Perspectives on Luke-Acts*. Perspectives in Religious Studies, Special Studies Series No. 5 Edinburgh: T&T Clark, 1978, pp. 215–242.

Robinson, John A.T. "The New Look on the Fourth Gospel," in Robinson, *Twelve New Testament Studies*. Studies in Biblical Theology No. 34. London: SCM Press, 1962, pp. 94–106.

Rudolph, Kurt. *Gnosis: The Nature and History of Gnosticism*. Trans. R. McL. Wilson, P.W. Coxon, and K.H. Kuhn. San Francisco: Harper & Row, 1983.

Rylands, L. Gordon. *A Critical Analysis if the Four chief Pauline Epistles: Romans, First and Second Corinthians, and Galatians*. London: Watts, 1929.

S

Salm, René. *The Myth of Nazareth: The Invented Town of Jesus*. Cranford: American Atheist Press, 2008.

Sanders. Jack T. *The Jews in Luke-Acts*. Philadelphia: Fortress Press, 1987.

Sandmel, Samuel. "Parallelomania," *Journal of Biblical Literature* 81 (1962), pp. 1–13.

Schechter, Solomon. *Some Aspects of Rabbinic Theology*. NY: Macmillan, 1910.

Schierling, Stephen P. and **Marla J. Schierling.** "The Influence of the Ancient Romances on Acts of the Apostles" *The Classical Bulletin* 54 (April 1978).

Schleiermacher, Friedrich Daniel Ernst. *The Christian Faith*. Paragraphs 126–172, trans. Hugh Ross Mackintosh. Edinburgh: T&T Clark, 1928.

Scholem, Gershom G. "Redemption through Sin." In Scholem, *The Messianic Idea in Judaism and other Essays on Jewish Spirituality*. Trans. Hillel Halkin. NY: Schocken Books, 1971, pp. 78–141.

__________. *Sabbatai Sevi, the Mystical Messiah 1626–1676*. Trans. R.J. Zwi Werblowsky. Bollingen Series XCIII. Princeton: Princeton University Press, 1973.

Schürer, Emil. *A History of the Jewish People in the Time of Jesus Christ*. Peabody: Hendrickson, 1989.

Schmithals, Walter. *The Apocalyptic Movement: Introduction and Interpretation.* Trans. John E. Steely. NY: Abingdon Press, 1975.

_________. *The Office of Apostle in the Early Church.* Trans. John E. Steely. Philadelphia: Westminster Press, 1969.

_________. *The Theology of the First Christians.* Trans. O.C. Dean. Louisville: Westminster John Knox Press, 1997

Schweitzer, Albert. *Out of my Life and Thought.* Trans. C.T. Campion. NY: New American Library / Mentor Books, 1953.

_________. *The Psychiatric Study of Jesus: Exposition and Criticism.* Trans, Charles R. Joy. Boston: Beacon Press, 1948.

_________. *The Quest of the Historical Jesus: From Reimarus to Wrede.* Trans. W. Montgomery. 1906; rpt. NY: Macmillan, 1962.

Segal, Alan F. *Life after Death: A History of the Afterlife in Western Religion.* NY: Doubleday, 2004.

Sell, Edward *The Faith of Islam.* London: SPCK, rev. ed., 1907.

Sherwin-White, A.N. *Roman Society and Roman Law in the New Testament.* Twin Brooks Series. Grand Rapids: Baker Book House, 1992.

Soards, Marion L. *The Speeches in Acts: Their Content, Context, and Concerns.* Louisville: Westminster / John Knox Press, 1994.

Strauss, David Friedrich. *Life of Jesus for the People.* London: Williams and Norgate, 2nd ed., 1879.

Strobel, Lee. *The Case for Christ: A Journalist's Personal Investigation of the Evidence for Jesus.* Billy Graham Evangelistic Association special edition. Grand Rapids: Zondervan, 1998.

T

Talbert, Charles H. *Luke and the Gnostics: An Examination of the Lucan Purpose.* NY: Abingdon Press, 1966.

Theissen, Gerd. "The Wandering Radicals: Light Shed by the Sociology of Literature on the Early Transmission of Jesus Sayings," in Theissen, *Social Reality and the Early Christians: Theology, Ethics, and the World of the New Testament.* Trans. Margaret Kohl. Minneapolis: Fortress Press, 1992.

Thompson, Thomas L. *The Mythic Past: Biblical Archaeology and the Myth of Israel.* NY: Basic Books, 1999.

Tillich, Paul. *Dynamics of Faith.* World Perspectives Series Volume X. NY: Harper Torchbooks / Cloister Library, 1958.

Trobisch, David. *The First Edition of the New Testament.* NY: Oxford University Press, 2000.

_________. "Who Published the New Testament?" *Free Inquiry* 28/1 (December 2007/January 2008), pp. 31–33.

Tyson, Joseph B. *Marcion and Luke-Acts: A Defining Struggle.* Columbia: University of South Carolina Press, 2006.

V

Van Voorst, Robert E. *Jesus outside the New Testament: An Introduction to the Ancient Evidence.* Grand

Rapids: Eerdmans, 2000.

Vermes, Geza. *Jesus the Jew: A Historian's Reading of the* Gospels. London: Fontana / Collins, 1976.

Vielhauer, Philipp. "On the 'Paulinism' of Acts," in Leander E. Keck and J. Louis Martyn, eds., *Studies in Luke-Acts: Essays presented in honor of Paul Schubert Buckingham Professor of New Testament Criticism and Interpretation at Yale University*. NY: Abingdon Press, 1966, pp. 33–50.

W

Wainwright, Arthur W. *The Trinity in the New Testament*. London: SPCK: 1975..

Walker, William O., Jr. *Interpolations in the Pauline Letters*. Journal for the Study of the New Testament Supplement Series 213. London: Sheffield Academic Press, 2001.

Weeden, Theodore J. *Mark: Traditions in Conflict*. Philadelphia: Fortress Press, 1971.

__________. *The Two Jesuses. Foundations and Facets Forum* New Series 6/2 (Fall 2003).

Whiston, William (trans.). *The Works of Josephus*. London: Ward, Lock & Co., nd.

Whitelam, Keith W. *The Invention of Ancient Israel: The Silencing of Palestinian History*. NY: Routledge, 1996.

Wisse, Frederik W. "Textual Limits to Redactional Theory in the Pauline Corpus," in James E. Goehring, Charles W. Hedrick, Jack T. Sanders, and Hans Dieter Betz, eds., *Gospel Origins &Christian Beginnings: In Honor of James M. Robinson* Forum Fascicles 1. Sonoma: Polebridge Press, 1990, p. 167–178.

Y

Yamauchi, Edwin M. "Easter: Myth, Hallucination, or History?" *Christianity Today* Vol. XVIII, No. 12 (March 15, 1974): pp. 660–663.

__________. *Jesus, Zoroaster, Buddha, Socrates, Muhammad.* Downers Grove: InterVarsity Press, rev. ed., 1972.

__________. *Pre-Christian Gnosticism: A Survey of the Proposed Evidences*. Grand Rapids: Eerdmans, 1973.

__________. *The Stones and the Scriptures*. Evangelical Perspectives. NY: J.B. Lippincott / Holman, 1972.

__________. "Tammuz and the Bible," *Journal of Biblical Literature* 84 (1965): pp. 283–290.

Z

Zeller, Edward. *The Contents and Origins of the Acts of the Apostles Critically Investigated.* Trans. Joseph Dare. 1875; rpt. Eugene: Wipf & Stock, 2007.

Zimmerli, Walter, and **Joachim Jeremias.** *The Servant of God.* Studies in Biblical Theology, No. 20. Trans. Harold Knight. Naperville: Alec R. Allenson, 1957; rev. 1965.

Zindler, Frank R. "Where Jesus Never Walked," *American Atheist*, Winter 1996–97, pp. 33–42.

Scripture Index

Scripture Index

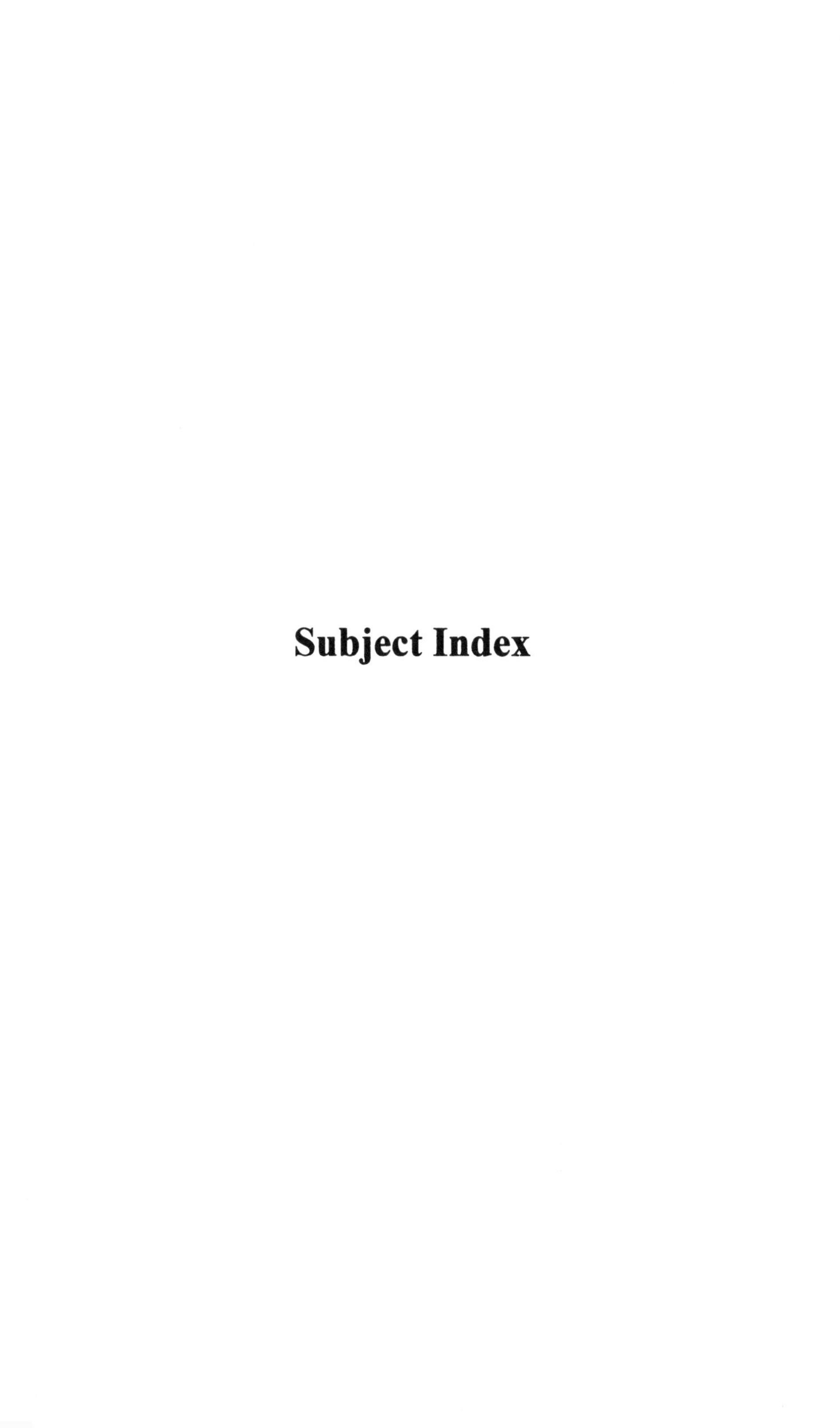

Subject Index

Subject Index

A

B

C

F

G

H

K

L

M

N

Q

R

S

T

Robert M. Price

Jesus is Dead

Published By **$18.00**
AMERICAN ATHEIST PRESS **ISBN-10: 1-57884-0007**
Cranford, New Jersey **ISBN-13: 978-1-57884-000-7**

JESUS IS DEAD

By Robert M. Price

The postal clerk asked the routine "Is there anything flammable, explosive, breakable…?"

"Well," said the editor of this book, "This is a manuscript of a book that is going to be quite explosive—but I don't think it violates the postal code."

The clerk smiled, and then a rather prim woman at an adjacent counter somewhat sneeringly asked, "What's the title of the book?"

"Jesus is dead," the editor replied in a matter-of-fact tone of voice.

The woman appeared to have been struck dumb. She tried to talk, but the muscular contractions in her face allowed no sound to emerge. She swallowed and looked as though she would try to speak once again. Still no sound. As the editor turned to leave, she was stuck in a pose of obvious distress, still mute as a mime. She may yet be permuting and combining all the possible meanings of those three words.

Those who read this book almost certainly will agree that it is explosive in its argument that (1) not only is there no good reason to think that Jesus ever rose from the dead, (2) there is no good reason to suppose he ever lived or died at all. Unlike the lady in the post office, readers will *not* be struck dumb. Rather, they will have material for hundreds of stimulating conversations and discussions. Better yet, they will have 'ammunition' with which to counter the arguments of muscular apologists such as Gary Habermas, N. T. Wright, and William Lane Craig. Best of all, readers will be entertained by Professor Price's deconstruction of the *Da Vinci Code*-type books that have flooded the religious book market in recent years—and provided the raw material for many a mirthful moment.